# Crook Frightfulness

BY A VICTIM

# Crook Frightfulness

## By a Victim

*They are the most powerful, terrible and pitiless killers, cunning, amazingly and enormously treacherous.*

The serpent...more subtle than any.
Genesis iii. 1.

**Renfield's Garden**

FROM THE J.G. HAMMOND EDITION OF 1936

Crook Frightfulness
Based upon the J.G. Hammond Edition of 1936
First Edition by Cornish, 1932



www.renfieldsgarden.com

ISBN 978-0-9864035-0-7

First Edition

Test Ramp: 99 98 97 96 95 94 93 92 91 90 85

# Contents

# Preface

I SINCERELY HOPE THAT THIS TRUE NARRATIVE WILL BE BELIEVED and its menace appreciated. Though it lacks variety of theme (ceaseless and unremitting persecution) it is important that all of it should be read, as its foul purpose is undoubtedly robbery and murder. I have portrayed the incidents as well as my powers of description allow, but it only gives a shadowy idea of the real awfulness which I endured for nearly eleven years from this seeking to prevent my mind having any rest, this attempt to keep my brain and mind held in perpetual turmoil and bewilderment.

These harrowing experiences cost me some thousands of pounds in one way or another, so, perhaps, you are getting valuable information at a low price.

They rely on their persistence to accomplish their aim, which is to get the victim in the trap by which they mean to rob.

Should the information be fresh to the police of this country, attention to it should be immediate, as at present the freedom of all is at the mercy of the underworld. This mind torture holds you continually in real torture, in horror of dread and in agitation and anxiety and tends to make you lose all balance of mind.

I should state it must be recognized by law that crimes against the mind are no less criminal and grave than attacks on body or possessions. The law must be vindicated against all lawless forces. Torturing one's brain is physical outrage and worse, it's maiming.

A very clever crook, Adam Worth, said that in the long run crime does not pay. But in my case the crooks determined to make it pay in the long run. If ever crooks worked hard and continually and audaciously, they have in my case been hellishly so. Their object would whack the wits of the most astute. It is only because I did not soon succumb to their machinations, by which they sought to encompass me, that time showed me their probable aim. They take a long view and never tire, never stop and never let molesting flag, trusting eventually to get a big "bag," by keeping your brain and mind in their "hands." Probably they have had some successful and large and astounding coups by this ceaseless scientific assault and torture of the intended victim's brain.

Their indefatigable set purpose (in such cases as mine) is to keep your mind worried in a perpetual turmoil by a constant din to fill you with anxiety, and also the molesting is done in such tone and words as to cause your resentment and anger. This is to deprive you of your mental serenity and balance, and to make you always befogged; to make you feel your futility and helplessness and to thoroughly distress you. They ambush you with their hidden fiendish scoundrelism. Eleven years of perpetual molesting and mental agony with no rest and without any protection under the British flag!!

There was no one to whom I (or any one so molested) could go for help against the forces of the gangsters and the underworld, and their devilry was unchecked.

They are so clever they give no clue, so that any you approach scorn its reality. The victim alone has the actual knowledge of it. At present it appears there is no protection for anyone so molested and all are at the mercy of the crooks.

Of course when I say *all* I really mean those men or women who are lone, either for robbery or other reason, are persecuted in this manner freely by the underworld, unchecked in any way.

It makes one wonder how many have been victims of this insidious felony of bewildering one's mind and very life for a prepared trap or traps to rob and murder.

I hope this book will secure that at least some such poor souls may be rescued from these devilish fiends.

# Prologue

I WAS THE VICTIM OF A PERSECUTION WHICH HAS DRIVEN ME around the circuit of the globe in my efforts to escape. I fled from England to the Antipodes to save my soul alive.

I found the number of my enemies was as great there as at home.

After three years in New Zealand I looked at the map of the world for a place belonging to the mother-country where I might avoid these pests of society and find peace.

I thought whither can I turn now? I settled on B.W.I.[1] as likely to afford me safety.

The old Saxon legends of our forefathers made the descendants of Cain, the first murderer, walk the earth in misery, the friend of no man. They became the progenitors of dragons and monsters who revenged themselves on mankind by ravage and by slaughter. They were at the same time the terror and the hatred of man. Their life was utter loneliness.

Like a modern Cain, I had been sentenced to solitude, more than solitude, to that state in which the victim is followed everywhere and persecuted by scoundrels. The hands of many men were lifted against me.

I have done no wrong. I have no murder on my conscience, no mark of God on my brow. My worst enemy could not call me criminal. My best friend could not say that my life has been any better than a convict's.

To what tribunal can I appeal? Only to those whose humanity

---

1 The British West Indies

can vindicate me, and turn the verdict of common justice against the murderous fiends.

The story of my misfortunes begins in London. I was in business there, and my ventures there were not entirely unsuccessful. I often think it would have been a far, far better thing if prosperity had not smiled so graciously on me in my initial undertaking. It is strange that poverty in the metropolis would have been better than material prosperity, both in London and what I got to Britain's daughter States.

But my prosperity was the beginning of my troubles. It attracted to me the attentions of some of the most villainous desperadoes in London and some of the leading international crooks of the world too.

It is for the benefit of the public that I have recounted my experiences. I want it to be known to the world that these pages are a true and accurate survey of the actual horror of unremitting and ceaseless molesting, and permanently and incredibly grim and potent torture with which crooks make one's life a real tragedy.

My object is to seek to describe and explain as plainly as possible the strangle-hold, the continual "besieging," the "dead set," with not a day's relaxing, that I endured for ten and a half years from those "beasts of prey," the murderous crooks.

If I had not written this book I would have failed to do my duty and it would have been a tragic omission. It is my direct concern that I should write it. I want each and all to realise that all I have described did happen despite the law and police. It may be dreary reading, but unless these facts are known it offers a great and terrible menace to everyone.

This increasing and relentless devilry was inflicted upon me by the crooks for some trap or plot they had hatched against me for robbery. The object of it was an enigma to me for years; it was quite obscure to me until 1932, when I realised that most probably they had abstracted some of my old wills (that I should have burnt), or they meant to produce a forged will, or intended forcing me to sign one. I feel certain their plan was to "get" me when they had driven me to my London haunts. They do nothing without an object – robbery.

Doubtless the master-mind or minds behind all this looked upon me as a very likely and very easy "case" to "scoop" up. I was lone and had a one-man business. I had a lock-up office which, unknown to me, they entered of a night whenever they liked. This I did not realise till 1931. I had often found books unaccountably moved from one place to another, and also papers had been missing and stolen out of my office.

I had had some crooks as workmen (at one time or another), though I had not been aware of their being "wrong 'uns" at the time of my employing them. In 1922, when this continuous molesting commenced, I had three "doubtful" workmen in my employ, two of whom were heavy drinkers, and if "boozed" would tell anyone all about me and my business, and also one other man who was not an honest man, and was friendly with some very dubious characters.

Perhaps, in order to carry out the devilish scheme and design that they had plotted, the crooks gave me unusual or special or quite exceptional treatment. Or is it a common occurrence, this awful infliction?

In London and New Zealand I could see by the actions of the ever-vigilant foxers and watchers that if they once got me alone or got hold of me, their design was to injure me. Possibly they meant to make a murderous assault on me. The watchers were always endeavouring to catch me alone. I felt the need for an escort for safeguard and protection, and also to be a witness to any attack on me. The need of a continual escort was very obvious to me.

For instance, on my companion going into a shop to make a purchase, I stood upon the kerb of the pavement. An evil-looking man (who was foxing us) was following from a little distance in the rear, and he at once made a hurried dart towards me with violent intent written on his face. I at once walked to the shop door, and this villain at once stood still, hesitating for a few seconds, when my friend came out of the shop and we proceeded along.

Another instance. I got out of a vehicle after my companion had alighted. I then walked along by some costers' roadside barrows to the next opening to the pavement. Directly I was noticed to be apart from my companion, a crook of very vile appearance made a quick dart off the pavement towards me, but I noticed him in time to quicken my pace and I rejoined my companion on the pavement.

Numberless similar instances were always occurring.

On some occasions it appeared that my abduction was sought, and I presume this would have been followed by murder.

A few months before leaving for New Zealand I had left the draft of an important document on my office table one night. When I arrived at the office on the following morning this draft had disappeared. I searched for it for a long time and was at a loss to think how it could possibly have gone.

At B.W.I. No. 2. In 1931 a molester called out the details of this very document.

Also, some while before I left for New Zealand in 1924, I tried to find all my private papers that I had stored in a particular place in my office. Some of these were papers and books that I had kept from childhood, and school certificates and things of all kinds. Also papers relating to lectures and classes that I had attended.

All these had unaccountably disappeared *in toto* absolutely.

During the molestings in 1931, all of these were alluded to, and the molester said "We've got all your old junk."

I had an idea that this persecution was somewhat from the Communists, for though so much of it was obviously by the worst criminals, men of robbery, violence and murder, yet molesting also came from the unemployed and down and outs, from some hawkers and public house loafers, and even some road workers. Many of these men gave me looks of evil design and hatred whenever they were near me.

Wherever an intended victim goes the crooks follow and send word amongst all the underworld that he is a marked man, and the gangsters and all the underworld promptly dog his trail and begin to make his life unbearably miserable, that, in desperation, he looks about for another refuge, doing this until eventually they can get him at some place in their power and at their mercy.

## Your Thoughts are Heard

I must now give particulars of perhaps the most important part of my narrative.

I must ask the reader to peruse page 235, where I describe the apparatus that is being freely used by the underworld for the perpetration of crime. It is vitally important that its use should be stayed at once. The significant thing about it is that our police appear to be totally unaware of its existence.

As soon as I came to know of its existence I "wrote up" all I knew about it and visited Scotland Yard, where I was summarily sent away each time I visited these authorities about it. (See pages 240 and 244.)

The existence of this apparatus was unknown to be until 1932, though it had actually been brought to my notice at various times previously. I should have "tumbled" to it before, as I first experienced it early in 1929, and several subsequent experiences of its use had "befallen" me too.

The following are the instances that I recall vividly: See page 173. It was in February, 1929, when I was in B.W.I. No. 1 that the hotel factotum *spoke* loudly the words that I had *read* only quietly to myself. At the time I "explained" it by thinking that this had been done by means of a periscope. I could not think of any other explanation. (I believe in this case a white crook was usually on duty "listening-in" to me – to my thoughts). See page 186. About six months after the above incident and at B.W.I. No. 2, when I visited the merchant's office to take a book, I found a "select" crowd outside his office, who were there to royally "receive" me. This made me feel sorely puzzled. Someone must have known my intention. How did they know of it?

See page 189. At B.W.I. No. 2, after each time that I visited the gentleman, the whole of my conversation was repeated to me verbatim that night by a molester. At the time I put this down to eavesdropping by the gentleman's servants. There is not the least doubt the negroes in the motor car had the listening apparatus and were "listening-in" each time.

See page 191. It was in 1930, at B.W.I. No. 2, when sitting in an office waiting room, that I was "marvelously" molested. I could not account for how this was done. It might be one of the uses that the "listening" apparatus is available for, or was something similar to a stethoscope used? It is rather a conundrum!

See page 194. In the early part of 1931, at B.W.I. No. 2, as I laid under a palm tree in the back garden, an awfully vile "crook" neighbor almost simultaneously repeated my *quiet reading, speaking* what I was quietly reading to myself. At the time I worried about it, and then forgot it.

I have found in this terrible excruciating molesting that they could only hear your thoughts by means of the fact that when you think (in 95 cases out of a hundred) you actually shape your words in your throat and mouth. When we breathe through our mouth or nose it is possible for these fiends to hear your thoughts and reading with their listening apparatus.

If you hold your breath when thinking, they are unable to hear you, but doing this is not only painful, but might be the cause of a broken blood vessel.

In mining and countermining operations during the Great War, "listeners" were brought to a fine art. Possibly these instruments were used then, and the crooks have been probably using them ever since!!

No doubt in the breathing and snoring incidents related in pp. 94-95 and 104, this crook was using the listening apparatus. When my mouth was shut he could not hear my thoughts, or he could not hear them so distinctly.

Doubtless ear 'phones are used with this instrument, both for the crooks' protection, and so as to get the least sound.

At present it appears there is no protection for any lone person (man or woman), molested and persecuted day and night everywhere, as described in "Crook Frightfulness." The victim alone has knowledge of its reality. They are completely at the mercy of the underworld's fiendish tactics. Those using the listening apparatus and also those who so persecute and molest, should be liable to be hung.

It is a tremendous public menace in that all the evil forces of the criminal element are in these cases united in the services of the gangsters.

I expect their pay is in a share when the victim has succumbed.

I have had some experiences which suggest crooks sometimes use a stethoscope apparatus which enables them to hear your thoughts, the sound travelling through the floor you are standing on, or through the chair or bed you are on, and so through the floor to perhaps the next room or adjoining house to the crook listener. (*See incidents, pp.* 191 *and* 202-203.)

See page 198. At B.W.I. No. 2, in the middle of 1931, when I was in my room, I heard the young woman speak to her mother. Probably generally a neighbour "crook" used it to listen to me, as one of them from the same house used it in the following instance.

See pages 202-203. It was towards the end of 1931, at B.W.I. No. 2, that a neighbour heard my eyelid move on the pillow, showing that this wonderful hearing apparatus enables the user to hear the most "minute" sound.

With the use of this instrument the crooks to some extent rule you; they are masters with no hindrance, holding the upper hand over anyone they choose. An unknown, unseen listener, ever present (from somewhere near), all night and all day listening, and in my case molesting also. No one is free from these fiendish monsters.

It is vitally important that the diabolical use of this apparatus should be known, so I trust anyone aware of it will report it to Scotland Yard, London, England. I was surprised at the way Scotland Yard rejected my information. It depressed me because none would believe me or examine into my reports. Six months previously the Commander at B.W.I. No. 2 had treated me as though I was a fool, and now Scotland Yard had done the same. That the crooks should be masters with no hindrance, simply through official foolery or slackness riled me, and made me feel overwhelmed with a feeling of uselessness and incapability of doing anything in the matter of such tremendous importance.

I should mention that a doctor informed me that my lungs are as though I had pneumonia. I do not know whether that state makes one's thinking any more hearable (by the breathing).

Anyhow, they can hear the slightest whisper from quite a distance.

---

When travelling in unoccupied or deserted country you are often coming across the works of man, some place where he resided perhaps many years ago, but he has left a trace in a piece of shaped wood or stone, or in some design worked upon it, or in an avenue of trees or bushes in a straight line, or a piece of a machine. Now because of the order, the design and exactness, we know that man has made it. So we know God's work by its wonderful design, from the whole of Creation to animals and human beings. The length of the days does not vary by a second!

If we learn about Creation we learn of God's greatness and power. The very existence and order and design are the greatest miracle and show God's supreme wisdom. It holds us in awe and wonder. We learn that owing to the world's rotation the surface about the equator moves at the rate of about one thousands miles per hour; we also learn that every twenty-four hours the world travels over a million miles on its yearly journey round the sun; also, that owing to the angle of the earth's axis, the seasons come yearly to all parts of the earth, thereby enabling the vegetation, etc., to grow, which enables man to exist. We learn also that the moon causes the tides all over the waters of the earth, and that this continual motion of the water aerates the waters, owing to which all sea life is able to exist.

All this shows God's design and handiwork.

Showing how truly God provides, the births in every country in the world are practically equal in the numbers of boys and girls, which also shows God does not intend polygamy. God did now make us for animals or brutes.

When we are born we are simply animals, but quite helpless for a long time. If, as we grow, we are unguided and untaught, we grow very much like ordinary brutes. Many of us would become much worse than brutes. We would become more like devils.

Many of those that the crooks seek after as intended victims are those that have some moral weakness, some moral failure (or even the semblance of one). Some of these failures must have been due to the want of guidance, to the want of instruction. We must remember that a careless or unchristian childhood answers for a lot.

God knows that we are sinful and He has not left us alone in our weakness. If we obey God we cease to be slaves of sin. God sent Jesus Christ to teach and to show us God's love and truth. God gives us forgiveness for all our past sins if we will but accept His Son Jesus Christ in faith and love, seeking to obey Jesus from now and hence until death. Jesus is our testimony that God loves us and that He has a loving purpose for each one, that is, to serve Jesus and be a saved soul alive. Make the Gospel your guide and truly serve Jesus. Human life is a puzzling enigma without Jesus; Jesus is the core of all its meaning. It is at the peril of our soul to reject Jesus as our Saviour and Friend. Growing in obedience to His teaching we soon know that we are walking with God in Truth. Sin is falsity to ourselves. Jesus tells us, "I am the resurrection and the life; he that believeth in Me, though he were dead (in sin) yet shall he live: and whosoever liveth (obeys) and believeth in Me shall never die."

Physiology teaches that continence is quite natural, it going to the use of the body; it has no evil effects, neither does continence cause any atrophy, though practiced for any number of years. The most eminent physicians confirm all these facts.

We cannot make real headway against sin until we believe in Jesus and seek Him daily in the Gospel and in prayer.

---

When you read of the molesting by staring looks, of the persecution of these people always staring at you, you will perhaps think it a trivial thing to endure. Let me remark that the crooks do nothing without a felonious object.

With infinite trouble and care to see that it was unfailingly done, incessantly and unceasingly, the crooks practiced this infliction upon me when this and other molesting started in July, 1922, and they kept it up unremittingly until January, 1933, that is to say, for every day unfailingly for ten and a half years, and half way around the globe!

It is undoubtedly a well-practised and used old method of organised molesting. It is certainly done systematically under the orders and special instructions of the international leaders of the underworld, with some criminal intent. It is one of their weapons, a weapon of the underworld, used to a purpose. This haunting horror of incessant, everyday molesting for over ten years caused a life of fixed, permanent torture. It started in London in 1922, when I was in business, just after the attempted raid.

When I was walking anywhere in the locality of my occupation these men would intentionally seek to meet me to give me these evil stares. They always placed themselves on the paths of my customary walks and journeys. Anywhere and everywhere that I went they haunted me, tracking me so as to meet me on any road or path that I took. Generally their cast of countenance and their villainous stares belied, as told you, whom they were.

There were certain spots where I was always unfailingly molested; at certain road corners and public houses and certain hotels, railway stations, garages and public libraries in London and Auckland.

They foxed me to anywhere I went, even on occasions of short journeys or excursions, and on long journeys. On all these trips the crooks have, in a remarkably brief time, got many of the "lower" orders and "scum" of each place that I visited to inflict this "staring" persecution. They get all their "crowd," all of their associates, all who make a practice of crime, that is, all the worst types, many of them the lowest of mankind, to "catch your eye" and give you telling looks, so that you have all the tricksters, confidence men, burglars, footpads, pickpockets and ruffians, bullies and prostitutes "at" you. With all this lot of the underworld you get an awful infliction wherever you go. On occasions I have had as many as nine men in a group altogether doing this molest of staring intimidation.

The staring is done in such style that is a really telling and shocking infliction. As I approached their direction they fixed a steady gaze upon me, a set gaze, and they endeavoured to catch my eye, one of them nods or points towards me when I am a little way off, or he turns round several times always "returning" to look fixedly at me. Perhaps accidentally, cursorily or casually, I looked at them and I saw them giving me a disconcerting, rigid, murderous stare, and trying to hold my eye by their evil, startling gaze.

You have then an undoubting impression of the evil nature of the molester, and sometimes you get to fear that harm and violence is intended there and then. Their looks often create a haunted feeling, a lasting impression of dread, giving you an idea that they mean to wreak violence or murder on you.

Whoever they were, all these molesters made their looks as evil and "cruel" as possible; they put all the evil they could into it to express hatred, violence and contempt, so as to make it as disconcerting as possible. Many of them make their gaze so offensive, so severe a molesting, that it makes the persecution really amount to an outrage and assault. It is exceedingly distressing and disconcerting, and a well-calculated, trying torture: you are continually wondering what is going to befall you, what is "in the wind;" it causes you continual anxiety. It makes you always nervy and put out, and the effect of this is to inculcate a continual real dread and fright. You are in an everlasting horror and fear of the unknown going to befall you, in dread of some dire calamity overtaking you. You see in them evil desperation, brutishness and violence writ large on their cast of countenance. You see in many evil intent in their gestures when you are a little way off; and when you approach nearer you see much vileness from these men of crime and violence, some of them the worst criminals and felons, and no doubt some murderers, too. Their looks are hardly human in their shocking evil awfulness.

What terrible telling looks some of them can give you!

Some of these molesters endeavour to puzzle and mystify you by looking in such a manner as to give a meaning to it that you cannot make out, some sort of suggestion that you cannot fathom. Others fix their eyes upon you with great intensity, following the direction of your eyes in their every look and your every movement.

If they have companions with them, as you get towards them you will sometimes hear one of them hurl some few remarks around to his gang, and they all gaze together as you get nearer. Some awful looking down and out, or ruffian of the lowest type imaginable, or a footpad, will come along, and as he approaches you, will give a broad smile of recognition or a knowing familiar grin.

I am convinced that some of those who have tried to catch my eye have had commanding or subtle eye-power. In some cases their looks were so suggestive that there is little doubt they were skilled in hypnotism. While they stare at you they try to make sub-conscious suggestions, which is done to affect the mind of the other party and reduce him to nonentity.

Many times in all places wherever I have been I have overheard my molesters talking amongst themselves, urging one another to molest me unflaggingly, by saying to each other: "We must do it to keep him out of his head." It is done to disable, to make the victim always nervous, frightened, and so weak-minded and brainless – a nonentity. Its constancy is so unflagging that you cannot even "recover" yourself, it makes you and keeps you irrational; partly deranged.

It makes you appear mad, and always in such a state that any accusation you might make against your molester would be put down as imagination. Even though you were attacked, your report of the assault would be perhaps disbelieved because of your very irrational state.

They generally inflict stares when you are with company, but they see to it that only you "get it," and not your company.

It was apparent when I was in London in 1922 and 1924, and also in New Zealand, that these watching, staring and other molesters were seeking to catch me alone. This caused me continual anxiety. I was in danger and would have been attacked. The style of the watching man in Auckland, who was standing about on "my" road corner, was always that of a "bruiser" and scoundrel. I saw many indications that they meant to dart upon me and inflict violence, their looks and movements indicated this if I were alone for only a minute or two.

Very probably General MacDonald and Barney Barnato were subject to like infliction, and had some similar persecutions to endure.

## Ventriloquial Terrorism in 1932

To illustrate the crooks' use of ventriloquism, I will describe an experience. It's one of their chief torturing and molestings to "hold" you with.

Going to a small town about twenty miles from Aberystwyth, I went into a main road cafe. I had only been seated a short time when the B.W.I. Nos. 1 and 2 molesting sentences started "flowing." As I was taking a meal, I was wondering as to where the voice was coming from in its distinct quiet tones, when looking out of the window up the road which is right opposite the cafe, I observed two men standing on the kerb, one of them very occasionally turning facing towards me.

Apparently they were quite harmlessly loitering. There was no one else about. *They* were the ventriloquists who were shouting these sentences ventriloquially so the people near them could not suspect them. They stayed until I left the cafe. They were standing about 110 feet from the cafe, and their motor-bikes were just by them. They molested so for about half an hour. They use ventriloquism as it confounds everyone, the victim included.

The crooks study lip-reading and ventriloquism to great perfection: they are masters of both arts. By watching they are quite aware of what any intended "quarry" is conversing. I have even had ventriloquial replies (when I have been conversing with my friends) from lip-reading crooks standing 50 feet away.

It is only now when I have finished this book that I realise the important and vital part that ventriloquism takes in their awful molesting persecution. The listening apparatus seemed (and is) so all important. I had failed to notice that ventriloquism contributed so largely to the frightfulness. They study the mimicking of the voices of people speaking to such faultlessness that it is impossible to detect that it is the "chiming in" you are hearing: the crooks' ventriloquial molesting. You are easily deceived and think that innocent people are saying awful things about you or to you.

When I returned to Great Britain ventriloquism was practically always used in 1932, both at Aberystwyth and elsewhere. Everywhere I went I was always molested and this was by ventriloquism, whether I was indoors or out, or walking or riding on 'buses or railways, when I was in friends houses (!), at churches, in concert halls and cafes. When I visited London to pay visits to Scotland Yard, I went to the United Services Museum in Whitehall, also the Natural History Museum, the National Gallery, and also Kew Gardens. Whilst at each of these, I was molested by ventriloquial voices all the several hours that I stayed, even when partaking tea in Kew Gardens. The usual B.W.I. Nos. 1 and 2 sentences were used. The voices were alternatively of male and female. In the Gardens I was watched by a well-dressed tall and thin clean shaven Chinaman of about 50. He gave me a continuous foxy ingratiating smile of recognition. He wore a black jacket.

Ventriloquism is their chief means of warfare when they are endeavouring to trap you. They do this to not only deceive the victim, for they lay low in ambush so as to remain unknown to anyone. They never leave you and the usual molesting sentences (interspersed with intimidating threats, etc.), are heard wherever you go. Of all the crooks' devilry, ventriloquism is in the highest degree the worst thing that you suffer from. They seek to make you and keep you enfeebled in your mind, or maddened, so your mind is attacked incessantly day and night without any rest being permitted. This cripples you mentally. They "hold you down" from one year's end to the other in awful "shackles" to your mind.

Ventriloquism enables them to hold you unhindered and undetected. Wherever you are they inflict it on you generally even when you are in company or in the houses of your friend (!). When there is a listener using the listening apparatus and this crook repeats your thoughts, it inflicts terrible mind torture, especially when you are fagged or in bed or have just awoke.

A molester using ventriloquism may be in a house or building or walking along or in a train or 'bus or in a car, yet he can throw his voice to anywhere undetected by those who are near him. He can cast it into either the front or rear of adjoining or other premises, to the other side of a hall, or to the other side of the street, or to a distance in his front or in his rear, yet he cannot be detected: even if he is continually "at it" in a house yet those in the house are not aware of his being so occupied.

A "detector" is wanted that will give the direction and distance that the ventriloquial voice derives from.

I now relate another experience to illustrate the use crooks put it to: –

During a concert I had been molested during the performance of each item, since it had commenced (by the usual so well-known sentences). Towards the end of the programme I involuntarily turned round at a specially hair raising intimidating threat by this molesting voice (there had been several shockingly foul sentences). I was seated almost at the very back of the hall. On this turning I was quite surprised to notice that practically everyone who had been sitting in the rear seats had left. There was only a man of about 28, and he was about 30 feet from me. I had turned quickly and as I did so he had very suddenly turned his head from my direction so as to hide his face from me. I got no more molesting during the next two concert items and at their conclusion I went out by the nearest door into the vestibule, and as I did so I caught the full face and light blue eyes of this man. Our eyes met and he gave a "caught red hand" look of guilt which immediately turned into a glaring expression of contempt and intimidation, but he could not quite eliminate the look of chagrin, the "caught" expression. He ran to the outer door and out into the street and disappeared amongst the passing throng. He was fair, and had light blue eyes and looked quite a smart hatless gentleman in his sports jacket and faultlessly seamed grey trousers. He had good features and a high forehead. His hair was inclined to be red and was cut short.

I had just bidden adieu to a friend on the Aberystwyth Marine Parade and had just turned away from him when I heard the words –

"The old sod"

said in my voice tones too! There was no one else near us two and my friend probably thought that I had said these insulting terms. Of course, a ventriloquial crook had done this trick as a trying to molest me. Mind you, the nearest person to us was about 100 feet away. Possibly done to estrange one's acquaintances too! so there you are, if possible, bereft of all decent friends and are simply prey of the crooks.

As I walked down towards the sea-front, there were two gentlemen on the opposite side of the road walking in the same direction. They were almost level with me. As they walked along all the usual molesting sentences and some others, such as "He's no good," "He's a scoundrel," appeared to come from these gentlemen, whom I recognised as two business gentlemen on their fortnight's holiday. These molesting sentences came from a car which was about 130 feet in the rear of us.

All these persecutions are done with the object of keeping the intended victim in a weak mental state.

Their plan is to achieve their aims without any "come back:" that is, to get the victim in a resistless state both mentally and physically, probably also to get him without friends or decent acquaintances, to have no one that's concerned with his welfare and to rob and murder him, both being done by some tricky plan unknown except to the leading gangsters.

In 1932 these stunts were inflicted on me practically every day.

Alluding to the Scotland Yard Officials' remark to me

"Who is to pay them?"

I recall a visit to Criccieth where I fortunately saw one whom all Britishers owe thanks to: Lloyd George. As we returned from the golf links we turned down a fresh path. Not far along this I could hear men's voices, and I heard my name mentioned! As we proceeded, the talking still went on, and then I heard one of these men say "We must not mind spending a little on her as we will get it back 100 times."

Now this conversation came back to my mind lately, as I feel sure this *her* meant *him* and this meant me, because on the train journey I was molested in the quiet usual tones both going from and back to Aberystwyth. These men were on the other side of the hedge.

CHAPTER I

# How it Began

WAS I EVER HAPPIER THAN ONE MORNING WHEN MY EMployer, a prosperous builder, called me into his office and gave me the glad news that I was promoted to the post of rent collector to his properties in the East End of London? I left the office stool – which I had found tedious – for what I thought was to be a happy and interesting life out of doors. How was I to know that I had of my own volition opened the doors of Hell – to turn me from a cheery, care-free youth of 18 to a prematurely aged man, terrified by horrible men, threatening my sanity and my life?

The East End of London was tougher in those days than it is to-day. Sordid, loathsome slums to-day are giving way to factory buildings and council houses, but forty years ago, the East End was a place of horror, wherein were to be found all the hideous vices one usually associates with some foul Eastern seaport, rather than with the capital of one of the world's greatest and richest Empires. Yet I was happy on my few shillings a week, even in this sink, and went cheerfully on my appointed rounds.

I expect that my employer had an eye to my simple and abstemious life when he promoted me. Two of his previous collectors had been permanently incapacitated as a result of injuries received in some dark alley and – what my employer regarded as important – both victims had been robbed of the takings of a score or so of houses. He mentioned these facts to me, but being young and confident, I paid little attention to his warnings.

My first round was a lesson to me as to how low humanity

can sink – yes, even the humanity of England, the ruling race. Women had always been objects of reverence to me, and I vividly recall the shock of horror I received on entering one house in an East End street. A plump, weary-eyed girl – she could not have been twenty – came to the door stark naked. In the dirty hall I saw a man, he was very dark, and I observed to my disgust that he was a coloured person – probably a seaman from some ship.

A few hours later, while still in the same district, I visited another house which was clearly a den of thieves. Even now I shudder to recall the reeking ill-lighted house. In answer to my knock the front door opened and a coarse-featured, dirty, unshaven brute glowered at me from within the ill-lit hall. Beyond him I could hear the rumble of many voices, men's and women's, shrill and brutal to listen to. When I made known my mission, the ill-favoured householder burst out laughing.

"Hey Jen – Jen," he bawled, and in answer to his summons, a lean, toothless harridan darted from one of the dark doorways, eyeing me with that hostile curiosity with which a person bearing any of the outward signs of decency is commonly regarded by women of her class.

"Blime, Jen," raved the man, laying a large and uncleanly paw on my shoulder. "'E wants the – rent. Cripes, son," – the latter to me – "you must be new to this game. Don'cher know 'oo I am?"

I pleaded ignorance of this important knowledge, and told him that as his name was on my list I must have his money. His eyes narrowed, while my information seemed to strike the woman almost speechless. Suddenly the man leaned forward, until his foul breath was hot on my face, and began to talk rapidly and in terribly menacing tones.

"Listen, lad," I heard him growl. "You nor your boss don't get no rent out on us – get me? You're new to this job, I reckon, else you'd know better nor to worry Joe T. about rent. Nah then, lad, get – and get pretty quick."

I saw that he meant every word he said. Rightly or wrongly Joe T. did not pay rent, and nothing short of a Court Order would make him do so. Somehow or other this brute had managed to bully the previous collectors into actually paying his rent for him from their own meagre earnings. They could, of course, have returned to their employers and told the facts, when legal measures would have been taken to make Joe T. pay. However, swift and sure vengeance would have fallen on the unhappy collector. One night on his way through some dismal side street, half-a-dozen men would have fallen on him, and his battered body would have lain in the muck and slime until salvaged by the police for the hospital or the mortuary.

But I was to learn all this much later. In the meantime, I accepted Joe T. merely as a man who refused to pay his legal debts. To me the whole affair seemed simple. I returned to my employer, and reported the facts. A curt letter was promptly sent to the house ordering Joe T. to pay up or take the legal consequences that must follow. Personally, I forgot the matter then, and did not remember it until the next collecting day when I called at T.'s foul den. The man himself opened the door, and drew his lips back from his jagged teeth in a beast-like snarl as he saw me.

"You ——," he hurled an unprintable oath at me. "Get out o' here – and mind you don't come round 'ere ever no more. I'll get yer – d'yer 'ear me – and kill yer if yer do."

Behind him I saw other ominous, menacing figures. The street was a quiet one, and no welcome blue uniform was in sight. Suddenly I realised how utterly alone I was, and how powerful were the forces of terror in London's underworld. T.'s blood-shot, cruel, murderous eyes mirrored – had I but known it – the horror and misery that was born to me that day.

CHAPTER II

# The Coming of the Terror

DECENT PEOPLE, UNFORTUNATELY FAMILIAR WITH THE LEGAL processes of eviction, may think that the law moves swiftly and harshly in that direction. That this is frequently so in cases of hard-working, honest people, I do not doubt, but the rogue provides a very different proposition and not only knows how to take full advantage of every weakness in the law, but is ever ready to go well outside legal limits.

Consider these points carefully while reading of the case of Joe T., which serves as a fair criterion of many others which came my way early in my business career. The owner of the property had never seen Joe T., and knew of him only as an entry in his books. In the space for recording payments outside T.'s name, were a number of blanks, and because of this the due processes of the law must be invoked against this undesirable tenant. The actual minion of the hated capitalist landlord with whom T. came into touch, and who knew the desperado not as a written cypher, but as a potent – and perhaps fatal – force, was the collector, myself.

Immediately the first warning letters were dispatched to T., I was threatened. On the first occasion two men, toughs of that despicable type which gets its living from foolish women, approached me in the street. In my bag at the time was close on £30 of my employer's money, and my grip automatically tightened on the handle. They made to get on either side of me, but I moved quickly, got my back against a wall, slipped my bag to the ground between my feet, and turned to face my molestors, showing them that I meant business. Greatly to my surprise, however, they made no attempt to attack me, but stood a few yards away and made clumsy attempts to pacify me.

"Listen, cock," growled the bigger of the two men. "We don't want your bloomin' bag. Take it easy enough if we did, but we got other orders about you. Now just lay off Joe T. He ain't gonna pay no rent. Never 'as and never will. Now just get that into your 'ead, mate, an' everything'll be all right."

I saw the man meant what he said. There was something deadly earnest about him as he spoke, but not unnaturally I felt that he was waiting for a chance at my bag, and so decided to keep him talking in the hope that assistance might arrive.

"Well," I temporised. "You see there's not much I can do about it. I'm only the collector. What good will it do if you molest me?"

The pair of them laughed, and the bigger man drew closer to me, but stepped back hastily as I raised a clenched fist. I still retained the impression, however, that the men were not after my bag. There was something far-reaching in their intentions, I felt, and the feeling of menace thus engendered was greater than if I feared immediate physical attack. These men were clearly acting on instructions, but how was I to know that important people in the underworld regarded it as vital that on principle Joe T.'s rent must not be paid? In the next chapter, I shall show clearly how this seeming anomaly occurred, and explain the importance to the underworld of an implicit obedience to its leaders' orders. However – to return to that side-street, and the menacing pair facing me.

"Collector, eh!" grinned the leader. "Don't matter down 'ere what you are. You're the man wot's to catch it if they don't let Joe T. alone. You settle this job somehow – or ——." The unfinished threat was more eloquent than any words from the foul mouth of this powerful brute. Scarcely had he finished, then both men disappeared round the corner of the road, as might the very beasts of the pit.

Youth is ever impetuous, and a thousand times I have wished that I had given more thought to the dark forbodings which beset me as I ploughed my way quickly through the street. True, I felt as I looked about me that in those quarters I was at the mercy of the most merciless and desperate men. A swift, flashing descent and a dozen fierce blows could have maimed me for life, and no man have been the wiser as to whose hand struck me down. Yet such was my youthful ardour that I disregarded these warnings, pinning my faith to that Law which every Briton prides himself on, and believes will stand by him in time of need.

At the nearest police station I found an old sergeant, sympathetic but not very helpful. Had I any particular person in mind from whom I had anything to fear? Why, yes, Joe T. Was I prepared to make specific charges against him? Had I witnesses of any threatening words from him or other persons? Of course, I had nothing definite to put before the police, so that I was given clearly to understand that they could not help me.

The old sergeant put a friendly hand on my shoulder.

"We know what you're up against, lad," he said kindly, "and personally I should advise you to find another job. If you're beaten up, of course, we may pin the attack on to T.; but would that help you at all? We'll help you all we can, but I warn you that you're up against a pretty bad bunch of so-called men. Now then, sonny, I know the world better than you do – think it over."

I walked from the station hot with resentment. Damn T., and all the filthy gangsters under him and behind him. I would do my duty without fear from the drunken ruffian or any of his murderous kind.

## CHAPTER III

# Why Joe T. was Important

LARGELY THROUGH MY INSTRUMENTALITY, THE LAW EVICTED Joe T. in record time. The evil house was put up for fresh tenants, but for some mysterious reason no one, even in that crowded region appeared anxious to occupy T.'s former residence. Meantime, I continued my work in the district, and for some weeks was left severely alone.

Then suddenly word went round of a big police raid in the East End. The raided premises were not far from the city limits, and the raid had been carried out as a result of repeated complaints from occupants of a big block of business offices not far from the house in question. Appalling things had been revealed when the raiding police broke in the doors, and fought their way through a gang of armed ruffians in the hall. In one large room were found six women, all of them young and pretty. These woman were under the influence of drink and drugs, and the police soon learned that they were undoubtedly being kept in this condition, prior to being shipped abroad to Continental and South American houses of ill-fame. Evidence of every other known form of vice was to hand, and the police decided that the man in charge of the establishment was a prominent underworld character, although it was equally clear that he was only a "front" for men higher up who reaped the benefits of his nefarious doings.

The man in charge of the place was Joe T., who, until I served his eviction, had been doing the same things in the house of my employer. Small wonder that he had been so anxious to stop his eviction.

Naturally the outside reader will ask why it is that T., with his powerful connections, did not pay his rent. Even if the money had been paid to him by his superiors, and he had used it for other purposes, why did he not pay up and stop the eviction process? To illustrate my answer, let me explain that in those days there were houses in the East End which were as immune from both landlords and the law as Buckingham Palace is immune from the entry of the curious who throng its railings at different times. Long ago these premises ceased to pay rent, and as a result of numerous assaults and murders, the owners gave up trying to collect their dues. So long as the occupants gave no trouble to the police, these gentry were content to leave them to themselves. This was ideal for the purpose of the rogues who filled these houses. It meant that they could carry on the most nefarious activities without the slightest chance of a visit from a landlord's representative or a rent collector. The men concerned could have paid the miserable rentals a hundred times over, but they preferred to do otherwise, and keep their premises free by sheer terror. Any one doubting my statement can ask police officers of the period, who will readily tell them that such places have existed, and probably exist to-day.

The object of T.'s gang in intimidating the rent collectors was based on this principle. Had my fellow collectors and myself seemed trustworthy they would undoubtedly have tried to get us into the gang. Then, of course, we would have been paid money, from which we would have paid T.'s rent, and kept the balance for ourselves. As it was, terrorism had suited them better and in the long run they might have achieved their objective. My quick action, however, had completely shattered their plans, and the fact that they had to move quickly undoubtedly forced them to take the new premises in so perilous a situation.

The gang could, of course, have stopped eviction by paying the rent and costs, but this could only have been done with the consent of the owner, and it happened that I had reported T. as a very bad tenant. In the circumstances, the eviction proceeded, and the ultimate loss to the gang was terrific. Immediately word went out that a campaign of systematic terrorisation was to begin against me, and no man can ever have devised a more terrible and lasting revenge against another. Of course, all this information I have pieced together on reflections over a period of years, and I give it here only in order that the reader may take a more understanding grasp of what is to follow.

My first indication of the gang's intentions occurred shortly after the raid while I was working late at my office. Pondering over some accounts, I did not notice a dark figure take up a position in front of the plate-glass window and stand looking in – looking, nothing more. Suddenly I glanced up, with that nervous start one gives when awakened to the fact that one is under observation. Clearly I saw the man's face, and recognised it as that of the bigger of the two men who had waylaid me some weeks previously. On his lips was a cruel snarl, while his bleary, bloodshot eyes leered at me with indescribable menace. As I started, he raised one arm, and something shot through the window as the glass shattered beneath a heavy blow. Instinctively I ducked, and felt something hiss over my head, and heard it land with a thud against the far wall of the room. My fears dispersed by furious indignation, I leaped to my feet, but reached the door just in time to see the figure of my nocturnal visitor disappear round a corner. I would have given chase, but I could hardly leave the office unguarded. Blowing a police whistle which we always kept handy, I re-entered the office and took a glance round. My eye caught the heavy stone lying against the wall, and I noticed that it was wrapped in paper.

CHAPTER IV

# Some Facts about East End Dwellers

In these humane days, I do not doubt that many of my readers will have considerable sympathy with that class of East End dweller which it was formerly my lot to handle. While sympathy with our less fortunate, but honest brethren is a good and Christian thing, it is grossly misplaced when accorded to the men and women of the kind which caused me so much trouble and suffering.

The rent control of houses during the Great War led to revelations of gross profiteering among many house tenants. Rooms were rented for a great deal of, and in some cases the whole of the amount paid for the entire house, and frequently such properties were used for highly questionable purposes. The latter is nothing new, and was rife amongst some of the tenants of my district in my early days – and to this class of person I showed no mercy.

Following the stone throwing episode in my office, I informed the police and hinted that further molestation was likely if I was to continue my campaign against this class of person. At that time, it should be remembered, I was not sufficiently experienced to understand the strength of the underworld forces as typified by Joe T. and his supporters. I knew nothing of the strange freemasonry existing between keepers of questionable and openly undesirable houses, and could not realise the magnitude of my self-appointed task.

Within a few weeks I had formed definite conclusions regarding a dozen houses, and was convinced that not only did they shelter every conceivable form of vice, but that they were a genuine criminal menace. People familiar with the East End of those days must recall the frequent murders and violent assaults so common amongst seafaring men. The British mercantile sailor, afloat and ashore, is a fine type of man, but unfortunately when he sets foot in a home port after a long and arduous voyage, he invariably begins a wild carouse. There were plenty of heartless women ready to take advantage of these poor fellows, whom they lured to houses of vice and there robbed and beat them.

I found indisputable evidence of this sort of thing, and as the class of person concerned was a bad payer – even when the vile trade was at its best – it was not hard for me to press eviction proceedings against them. Honest tenants were to be had, and I found them, thus gratifying my employers, and savagely embittering the dispossessed.

Three times within a week I was attacked by men from the enraged keeper of one house of ill-repute, against whom my employers were pressing proceedings. First they sent two men, then three, and finally four. On the first two occasions I escaped from my attackers – knowing their tactics – but on the third occasion I found the odds too heavy and was forced to run. My body for a long time afterwards bore scars from these encounters, but I became only the more resolute in my determination to oust the vile scoundrels of whom my cowardly attackers were fair samples.

Soon after these attacks it became clear that my enemies – with the inherent cowardice of their kind – had adopted a policy of nerve-shattering intimidation rather than violence. In later years I decided that this was obviously indicative of some highly educated mind controlling the gangsters, who themselves would never have conceived a scheme of such clever mental cruelty, and would either have attacked by sheer brute force, or have left me alone.

For a time I did not notice the men who followed me wherever I went. Then I became aware of familiar figures always close to me. When I entered buildings they were waiting outside when I emerged. Should I pause to eat lunch, or drink a glass of beer, they stood just outside the windows and looked in at me. At last this form of persecution became so intolerable that I complained to the police. They could, of course, do nothing as the men had committed no breach of the peace.

I had just congratulated myself that I was out of danger, when one morning as I was leaving on my rounds, a hard-faced man with the traditional broken-nose and "cauliflower" ears of the professional pugilist walked across the street towards me. It was obvious that he had been waiting for me to appear, and instantly he seized my coat lapel in a grip of iron.

"Nah, cockey," he grunted in a brutal voice, lifting a huge fist to within a few inches of my face. "You gonna give any more trouble to B——." He mentioned the name of a particularly foul rascal – a modern Fagin, in fact – whom I had persuaded my employers to take action against. This scoundrel ran a regular school for young criminals, and had blighted hundreds of young human lives. Immune from the police by virtue of his animal-like cunning, he was a power in the underworld, as I was to learn at my cost.

I looked into the merciless eyes of "Fagin's" emissary, and decided that for once it would be better to temper my natural impulsiveness with a little discretion. There was not a policeman in sight, and I knew that I would not stand a dog's chance against an experienced rough of this type. Accordingly, I smiled.

"I'm afraid I can't do anything else, can I?" I suggested. "What do you want me to do?"

The ruffian sneered. "Thought I'd make you see sense, cockey," he growled. "You just tell that guv'nor of yours to leave B—— where 'e is, an' to stop the court talk, see." Again the gnarled fist rose, and I nodded discreetly. This seemed to suit him, for he pushed me roughly aside, and walked quickly down the street.

I smiled after him. He had won for the moment by virtue of his superior strength, but I had decided – even while I fenced verbally with his ambassador – that "Fagin" was going out quicker than he thought. Which might happen to me in consequence, did not enter my head.

## CHAPTER V

# The Underworld Wants Me

THE EVICTION OF "FAGIN" WAS PROMPTLY CARRIED OUT, AND I have every reason to believe that the police should have been grateful for my action in securing the man's enforced removal. True, they never showed it, but they hung so closely to "Fagin's" trail from the day he was bundled, cursing, into the street, that he never had the chance to re-establish himself on his old scale. I saw some of his pitiful little victims that morning, and the memory of their tragic faces is with me to this day. When I walk through fragrant parks on a summer's day, and see the happy, smiling children, whom Fate consigned to good and fortunate parents, I think of those dismal creatures that memorable morning. Who am I to judge? Yet I cannot but feel that human justice is a figment of man's imagination; a sop to the mutterings of his conscience, when I think of poor, helpless children, born to a life of suffering, debasement and crime, which all too frequently ends in a prison or a workhouse grave. How do we let this go on these days?

Such were my feelings when I saw Fagin lean towards me with a horrible leer disfiguring his Satanic features. His thin lips were drawn back over jagged teeth, giving his normally horrible face the appearance of something one sees only in a nightmare.

"Throw me out, would yer, eh?" he raged, punctuating his sentences with vile oaths. "You'll regret this day my lad. I'll make you wish you'd never been born."

A policeman pushed him aside, and a little later I left the sorry scene, pursued and jeered at by the very children for whom my heart bled. Yes, poor, warped, miserable children, brought up to love evil and never to know goodness, love or kindness. Small wonder that they hated me as much as they did their loathsome master. Little though I knew it, some of these very youngsters – the gangsters of the future – were to be used against me in the years to come.

But let me again stress the astonishing affinity which one underworld gang bears to another. "Fagin," although he lived far away from Joe T., was quite aware of the fact that I was primarily responsible for the downfall of that ruffian. Can it be doubted, therefore, that a further item was added to the underworld's score against me when I had "Fagin" evicted? Swiftly the word passed round that I was "for it," and I knew this myself from the evil glances directed at me by street loungers when I went my rounds.

On three occasions within a month after "Fagin's" eviction, my pocket was picked in broad daylight, and I knew that first-class men had been sent to do the work. The little money gained would not normally have interested these princes of their profession, so that it was easy to infer that the men were sent out after me in furtherance of a campaign to break my spirit. The loss of the money, and a number of private and business papers was very embarrassing, but at that particular time I received some compensation in the form of a promotion in my work.

I was given sole charge of the outdoor section of our estate office, a job carrying better remuneration and much greater responsibility. In order to familiarise myself with the new duties, I spent most of my nights at the office, and the pressure of work took my mind off my troubles. Then one night, the enemy changed their tactics. They had decided that I was more useful as an ally than as an enemy, and acted accordingly. A woman, beautiful and smartly dressed, stopped me outside the office door and enquired the way to the main road. When I pointed it out to her, she hesitated, and then asked me whether I would mind escorting her there, as the night was dark, and the streets were uninviting to a lonely woman.

I agreed, and as we walked, I would not have been human had I failed to notice that in this strikingly beautiful woman, I had made a decided conquest. However, I had no desire to mix women and work, so I gave her no encouragement. We had reached the main road which I had pointed out to her, and I was about to walk off when she stopped me with a gesture.

"Don't be a fool," she hissed in my ear, "I know who you are – and I'm not paid to hurt you. Listen, my friend, you're making yourself too much of a nuisance. Now, why not listen to reason? We can give you all the money you want. Don't you like the idea? You can have money – and women like me – just for doing what you are told.

I stared at her, and saw that she meant every word she said. For a brief moment I hesitated, then a vision of Fagin, of T., and his ruined, tortured women swept before my eyes. No, by Heaven, I would never join with such men as they. Young, foolish, inexperienced, I might be all of those things, but I knew the underworld, and knew that none but a fool, or a criminal would willingly fling himself into that foul vortex, from which none of its victims is ever free. Roughly, I flung off the soft, clinging arms about me, and with a muttered curse strode swiftly on my way. For a second she stood staring at me in astonishment, then she hurled a savage oath – it sounded odd, I remember, from one so lovely – at my retreating back.

---

Of course when I got rid of known bad tenants, I replaced them with as good tenants as I could find. Notwithstanding all my endeavours in this direction, it was quite unavoidable that by false references I still got some bad tenants and, of course, experienced trouble with them.

The average of good tenants was now much greater, and so my work and anxiety were much lessened. Indeed, a good tenant is a great acquisition, and it is a pleasure to deal with him.

Some tenants were "bad" tenants because they could not pay

their rent through bad health, bad employment, and various other causes; and it was often very trying to eject tenants through one of the heads of the family failing to pay because of using intoxicating liquors too freely. Drink is certainly the working man's great curse, and makes him a miserable wretch instead of a happy man; and betting is another great curse to the home of the Briton. Fancy a full-grown person betting money which he can ill spare on the running of a horse or a dog, or even on a football game! If he doesn't want the use of the money, why not put it in the Post Office Savings Bank, where it is always at his call, and where it increases while he is asleep. A bird in the hand is worth two in the bush.

A "smart" man (the blockhead) thinks that he is going to win. Chasing a bubble is smart indeed, especially when you are giving something real for it.

---

Thinking of when the indications of any general watching of my movements started, I can recall the following incidents.

One Sunday during 1914, I journeyed to Woolwich, from there I took a tram to Eltham, and then walked to Avery Hill Park, Sidcup. As I wandered round the flower gardens I observed a dark-eyed and dark-eyebrowed, clean-shaven, thick-set man, about five feet eight inches in height, of about 43, and wearing a dark-blue suit and a light grey felt hat. He appeared to be watching me narrowly, and kept an even distance between us. He had the look of a bad character. Presently, as I entered the refreshment rooms, he came out, staring hard at me as he passed.

While I was partaking of a light lunch I overheard two waitresses discussing matters in audible tones, apparently for my benefit. I gathered that the foxy-looking fellow I had seen in the gardens had been making overtures to the blonde female, while the buxom brunette seemed very desirous of attracting my attention. Their further conversations led me to judge that the artful fellow had deliberately followed me from Woolwich, and that he had promised a bribe to the waitresses to take note of my movements and, if possible, to get friendly and inveigle me to obtain personal acquaintance with one of them. His schemes in this direction, however, were completely frustrated, for I paid my bill, checked my change, and left the refreshment rooms without even commenting upon the weather or enquiring the correct time.

A few weeks after my visit to Sidcup I went to the White City, where a band was playing in the very picturesque sunk bandstand, where the audience has a clear view of the players. I had been sitting in a back seat for some time when I noticed a man in the front row stand up and look over the sea of faces as though in search of someone. His eye at last caught mine, and instantly I recognised the foxy-looking fellow who had dogged my footsteps at Sidcup. I sat for a time, musing upon the incident, and noticed how from time to time certain flashily-dressed women would stand up and gaze around at me. They were all apparently "single" women, and never more than one stood up at the same time. As the last strains of Handel's "Largo" were lost amid the applause I took my departure. Although I glanced in passing at the front row of seats I could not see any signs of my watcher.

I cannot recall any further incidents of interest until the summer of 1919. While listening to the orchestra on Southend Pier, a girl of about fifteen commenced dancing to the strains of a popular tune. I noticed that she only danced when I chanced to glance pointedly in her direction and seemed desirous of attracting my attention. Presently she strolled past me accompanied by a black-bearded fellow who may have been her father. Once more she tried to attract my attention with an engaging smile, while the man stared hard at me. As the couple moved away I at once recollected the dark man's features, and realised that he was often in my district in London, accompanied by some men of very suspicious character.

---

Some two years later, in 1921, I was again on Southend Pier, this time with several friends (of mine). It was a cool autumn day, and there were not many people about. We walked to the far end of the Pier and sat down facing the sea. Soon we noticed one or two couples who walked to and fro past our seats, staring hard at *me* as they passed. Presently one couple sat down beside us. In a few minutes the man walked away, and the woman immediately moved closer to me and raised her feet to the railings in front of her, boldly displaying her legs. From time to time she would glance at me, and appeared to be very interested in our conversation, which of course was on general topics. About an hour later we left (she still there) and went into the Pier Hotel for tea. Very soon several foxy-looking individuals came in and occupied the table next to us. I quickly recognised the man who had accompanied the woman at the end of the pier. From this time I am now convinced I was being persistently followed and shadowed almost everywhere; and, as further incidents will prove, it was not any trick of the imagination, but a deftly planned espionage which developed into a positive menace and molesting, and unique actual terrorising.

As I strolled to the station with my friends after tea I chanced to drop my umbrella. When I recovered it I was for a moment behind my companions. Instantly a gang of six black-suited, shortish, clean-shaven young men attempted to surround me, but my companions halting at that moment the attempted molest was frustrated.

## I am a Marked Man

I must mention that while walking in Barking Park near the lake one sunny Sunday in 1919, I noticed several clean-shaven, blue-suited, well-dressed men, all wearing light grey felt hats, staring hard at me. Presently I realised they were trying to surround me as I was viewing the flower beds. The Park was deserted, for it was just lunch time, and I wondered what I should do. As the leader of the gang (all of them were from 40 to 50 years old) accosted me in a very forward manner, a voice hailed me from the far side of the lake. On seeing my friend this lot of mobsmen withdrew.

---

On another occasion in 1919, as I descended from a tram at the corner of Green Street, Barking Road, I passed a gang of clean-shaven, blue-suited, well-dressed big men (all about 50 years of age), wearing light grey felt hats, and some fat young women, also nicely dressed. They all stared fixedly at me as I passed, making low remarks, then one woman giggled, and one of these men called out, "Well, Sarah, how would you like to have him?" as they pointed at me.

---

When leaving the railway station at Brentwood one Sunday in 1921, I noticed a young, well-dressed woman staring hard at me as she walked on ahead. All the way across the bridge and down the steps she turned round repeatedly to stare at me, and finally dropped her bag a few yards away from me. I also noticed a very ruffianly looking fellow of about 58 on the far side of the bridge give a sign to this young woman. He had been staring hard at me, but turned his head when I glanced in his direction, and appeared to be studying the railway line stretching far in the distance. Meanwhile, the woman had vanished down the steps. I was aware of the ruffian, having seen him before, dogging my footsteps on several occasions at Southend.

---

In May, 1922, another incident occurred which shows that my idea and suspicions have not been ill-founded. I was out collecting rents as usual when I became aware of the presence of a tall, well-made, brown-faced, desperate looking, shabby individual of about 42, and of rather Italian appearance, with a small brown moustache. As I waited upon the steps of one house he leaned on the railings opposite and scowled at me. For some time now I had been in the habit of sometimes taking a companion with me on certain occasions, partly to help me with the collecting, but chiefly for companionship in the byways of East London. As I descended the steps the lounger came directly towards me, and I was very thankful to see my friend come whistling round the corner.

The following Sunday I chanced to be travelling by train to Southend. The first step was Wickford Junction, where several passengers left the train. Just before the guard blew the whistle, an evil-looking, blue-suited man of about 43 came down the platform and glared at me menacingly through the carriage window. As the train drew out of the station I recognized the owner of the malicious glare – it was the man who had recently dogged my footsteps in London several times.

---

As I was walking across the fields from Shenfield Church to Brentwood (which was my usual Sunday stroll) one Sunday about two o'clock in the afternoon, I noticed a powerful, big man approaching. In the distance I could see that he had his gaze intently on me, and as he drew nearer I saw that he was "dressed up" after the style of a cattleman. He had a darkish brown moustache and was about 45 years of age, with a swarthy face and about six feet two inches in height. As he drew nearer he put on a contemptuous, evil, aggressive smile as he stared familiarly at me. He looked as though about to molest me; all was quiet and there was no one in sight. But just then boys' voices came from some bushes 150 feet away. Immediately this man's intent look of desperateness left his ruffianly face and he passed by me looking quite disconcerted. I had seen this man watching me from a distance once or twice in the East End of London.

No one who has not experienced being perpetually followed and spied upon can imagine the persistence with which scoundrels carry out their work. The following sketch of my movements for several consecutive days illustrate this point.

During the Whitsuntide of the year 1922, I journeyed with a friend to Southend on the Saturday afternoon. As we were applying at Southend for lodgings for the night I noticed a man at the corner of the road staring fixedly at me. He was about 45 and had dark eyes and eyebrows, was strongly built, clean-shaven and respectably dressed in a dark blue suit and light coloured felt hat. We were successful in finding rooms in this particular street, and when we came out for our evening stroll the man had disappeared.

The next morning, Sunday, we took the boat to Margate and decided to seek rooms directly we arrived. The moment we commenced our enquiries at Margate a man appeared in the road and kept us in sight as we went from house to house. He was dressed in just the same style (and might have been the same man) as the one who had watched us in Southend. After fixing up our rooms for the night we walked to Broadstairs. As we stood on the slipway admiring the cliffs of Calais gleaming white in the evening sunlight, an evil-looking man of about 30 came up to me and attempted to push me into the water. My friend, who had been standing some distance away from me, turned at this moment and came up to me. Immediately the ruffian apologised and pretended he had accidentally jostled me. I knew better, for I caught the malicious gleam in his ruthless eyes as he moved away.

We returned to Margate by tram, and I was fully aware of the watchful glances of several rough-looking individuals on the top of the tram. We went into a cafe in Margate for a light supper, and soon after we entered I saw one of my "followers" standing by the counter chatting to a waitress. He gave me a stare of recognition as I passed, then as we strolled towards our lodgings this individual preceded us to the corner of the road and then vanished down a side street, after giving me a malicious stare.

The next morning we sat on the bench at Cliftonville for about two hours. A smartly-dressed young woman came and sat quite near to us, and kept staring at me. Evidently she was one of the accomplices of those who were endeavouring no doubt to rob or molest me. For that robbery or violence was their objective has been easily apparent. As we walked back to Margate this young woman kept ahead of us and kept staring round at me.

Once again we entered a cafe in Margate and several young fellows lounged around chatting to the waitresses, but keeping me under strict surveillance. In the afternoon of the same day, Monday, we returned to Southend by boat and re-engaged the rooms we had occupied on the Saturday. As we entered the house I glanced down the street, and there at the corner of the road was the same individual who had watched our movements on the Saturday afternoon. As usual we went out to a cafe for supper. A ruffian standing by the cafe door at once attempted to follow us inside. But very fortunately the proprietor refused him admittance, and his language to the proprietor was shockingly obscene, with his eyes gleaming and evil steadily on me.

---

About six weeks before the ejectment of the tenant a man told me that at the local meetings of the unemployed, speakers were strongly denouncing me and arousing men against me for seeking to eject a poor man from his house. The man had been under notice for a year.

Two weeks before the attempted raid a very powerful, heavy-jawed "convict-face" man, stoutly built, came right near me as I stood on the pavement at the same tram stop that the raiders gathered at. This man was clean-shaven and had the look of a jail bird on his big face, which had a most reckless and intimidating brutish expression. He looked as though he intended making an attack "right away." He was about 5 feet 9 inches in height and about 50 years of age. He looked equal in strength to two ordinary men. A mighty awful man to look upon.

---

No further incidents of moment occurred until the Monday previous to the ejectment in July, 1922. I must say that I almost always ventured abroad collecting rents in the streets of London without an escort. I had just finished collecting rents from one area, and was on my way to the bank with a friend, when a young fellow with the appearance of a mechanic came to the corner of the street and commenced beating time with his feet. This was evidently a pre-arranged signal, for as we turned the corner and neared the tram stop we saw quite a number of men there standing about separately (most of them looking covertly at me). About five of them had the appearance of labourers dressed in their Sunday suits and some of these men had moustaches, and one of two had beards also; the six others were well-dressed, tall men in blue suits, all clean-shaven and between 30 and 40 years of age, and all of them looking alert. All of these well-dressed men wore light coloured felt hats.

In a few minutes a tram came up, and several of the men moved a bit. I felt suspicious, as generally at this stop there were very few waiting on the pavement, so I did not move to board the tram; the tram just started off again when the whole lot of these men immediately jumped on to the tram. Just as this happened an empty motor car came along, and my friend said:

"I expect that car belongs to those gent's and they meant to rob you and get off in that motor car."

I boarded the next tram and lost sight of the mobsmen. The mobsmen had got on to the tram with wonderful agility, which without practice could not be attained, so that I presume all were crooks. I refer to this as the "attempted raid" as from shortly after this incident the all time and everywhere foxing and molesting commenced that lasted for ten and a half years. A real continuous besieging. Seems they had a grudge and were working it off. Their design was something big, but it was hid.

To make the next incident quite clear I must revert to a little matter which occurred some six days before Easter. I had occasion then to warn the family mentioned that if they did not pay their arrears for a certain date I should be obligated to eject them. Some days before the attempted raid a respectably dressed man of about 38, of slightly Jewish cast of countenance, made enquiries for a house. I asked for his name and address and to my surprise he gave the address of the house of the defaulting tenant. I felt suspicious and then looked carefully at the man. I had never seen him before; he returned my look with a sarcastic and enigmatical smile on his reckless face, and walked briskly away from the office. This incident was recalled to my mind the Wednesday that the tenant was ejected by the County Court Bailiff.

The tenant did not appear on the scene at all, only his wife remained to see the furniture carried out to the pavement. She had several women friends in the house, and pleaded with me to dismiss the policemen whom I had asked to wait outside. In all probability the tenant relied on help from the Communist leader of the unemployed. I knew that this leader was said to be in Russian pay, and that his followers numbered thousands. After the ejectment the women loudly abused me as I walked down the street, but fortunately I had an escort. I was sorry to have found it necessary to exercise extreme orders upon this family, but they had been under notice to quit for many long months, and had never once asked for any consideration or made any efforts to pay.

The following day the Communist leader of the unemployed called at my office, accompanied by the ejected tenant and two other men. He demanded the tenancy of an empty house adjoining my office. I explained that the above-mentioned building was not under my management, and that he must pursue his enquiries elsewhere. He then spoke threateningly and abusively about the rights of the working man, and what he would do to me. However, I moved away without talking to him any more.

Practically for ever after the ejectment episode I was obliged to take an escort with me when I collected rents, for I always found groups of the unemployed at the street corners who glared maliciously at me and appeared very threatening. For example, on the Saturday as I made my usual calls for some overdue rents I noticed a group of men outside a public house. These men shouted abuse at me as I passed, and would certainly have molested me had I not had an escort. When I stepped off a tram on my return to the office I noticed the ejected tenant standing outside a public house with a group of the unemployed. He recognised me at once and turned upon me with a shower of abuse and oaths.

The following Monday a young, short fellow of Jewish appearance in a black suit walked deliberately almost into me as I was on my way to the office. He assumed a threatening attitude and very fierce and vicious look, as though he meant to attack me, but he passed on. There was a group of unemployed near the corner of a road, and as we passed they shouted abusively at me. One of them demonstrated a kick upon one of his companion's ankle, calling out "This is what we ought to do to him!"

Have you ever had that feeling, vague and at the same time intense, of being the centre of men's eyes? If you have, you have doubtless also dismissed it.

The incidents that followed only served to convince me of the reality of my original feeling. If there had only been one incident I could have dismissed it as a coincidence, but there were many.

For instance, on the following Tuesday morning as I proceeded on my rent-collecting round, unaccompanied, a young man came into the road riding a bicycle. He slowed down, backpedalled, and kept his eyes glued on me when he had come more or less level with me. He suddenly stopped, turned his bicycle and rode away, only however to re-appear a few minutes later. This he did half a dozen times, until I had completed the collection of my rents. I thought his behaviour most extraordinary, and doubtless you would have come to the same conclusion as myself: that he was either mad as a hatter or deliberately trying to irritate me. That the latter explanation is more than likely the true one is shown by the fact that during this bicycling "act," a man, hefty, tall, clean-shaven, came along and stood on the kerb as I went into a house. He was ostensibly reading a newspaper but, as I discovered later, for at the end of the street he threw it away, the newspaper was over a week old and was opened at a page covered with food-stains. The printed matter on the page was the typical "housewife's corner," and this ruffianly man, who had followed me down the street, was not the kind to be so engrossed in such domesticities! In addition to this man there was another clean-shaven man of the same huge, bull-dog variety, who stared at me fixedly, following me and my every movement with unflagging interest. They were both about 50. The cyclist had brought these men to watch me, for they appeared separately and from opposite ends of the street on occasions when my cyclist watcher disappeared at these respective ends before returning to repeat his little performances. In the light of further consideration I came to the only possible conclusion: that these men were of a gang of crooks who were planning some concerted attack upon me with the object of robbing me.

Seeing a policeman I hailed him and asked his protection. He walked with me up a narrow alley, where we almost ran into a gang of "toughs," who, when they saw us, hurriedly made off. As we neared the top of the alley I happened to look back. Peering at me was a very rough, malicious looking individual. His face was a study: a look of unbelievable surprise slowly enlarged into a vacant stare, only to be followed by a stare of full understanding, as if his mind were completely focused upon one object. All this occurred with extreme rapidity, and in a few seconds the rough-looking individual had disappeared from sight like smoke. I quite believe this ruffianly footpad had been deputed to make a murderous attack upon me and was tracking me with that intent, but the policeman baulked him.

I was of course considerably shaken by this experiment, which perhaps had one effect more important than any other, namely, to make me more sensitive to my surroundings, more suspicious of those I met, and more aware of the crudity, vulgarity and viciousness to which so many men give expression.

Commonplace surroundings took on sinister aspects, and

one morning even the Railway Station at Brentwood became the breeding ground of suspicion. Here, one morning, as I went over the bridge to catch the train to London – for I was at this time residing at Brentwood – I passed about twelve rather short young men who were standing together. They were nicely dressed, and clean shaven, and all wore black suits and felt hats. As I approached them I felt their evil influence, though the other pedestrians who passed over the bridge seemed not to be affected as I was. But I noticed that all these men did not gaze at anyone except me with that malevolent "I know you" kind of expression. As I passed them they made little gestures – almost imperceptibly and very rapidly – gestures of offence, such as the throat-slitting gesture where a forefinger is drawn suddenly across a throat and the breath drawn in rapidly with a slight hiss. A similarly dressed tall man of about 40 stood quite near to these men. Now there were trackers trailing me everywhere I went and watching me like hawks.

Naturally this kind of thing happening in the ordinary surroundings known to me all my life began to have its effect, making me fearsome – and this, doubtless, was the intention of those so evilly disposed toward me. There was a hidden threat of something sinister lurking in the atmosphere.

Another day I set out as usual to collect rents from some houses in Wanstead. As I ascended to a 'bus top with my escort I noticed a villainous looking ruffian standing by the kerb. He must have mounted the 'bus just as it was moving off, for by the time I had secured a seat on the top of the 'bus he was beside me. It just happened that we were the only passengers on the top of the 'bus, and the individual assumed a very threatening manner. Fortunately I had arranged to make an unusual call that morning and therefore got off many stages before my office. I have no doubt now that I had just escaped some dreadful assault or interference from the ruffian who had followed me.

A few days later I was out collecting rents at East Ham with an escort, when I noticed groups of men at each corner at both ends of the street. As I journeyed from this street the men both followed and preceded me. I had occasion to pass one of these groups of men on my way to the tram, and I noticed that every other man seemed to be carrying a small brown paper parcel tucked under his arm. The similitude in size of all these parcels convinced me that they were sandbags they carried. I boarded the tram and kept downstairs and sat inside. I usually went on top. Several of these men jumped on with me, they sat directly opposite me and stared maliciously at me all the time. This continual shadowing and dogging of my footsteps got on my nerves, and the evil looks of these men gave me many uncomfortable feelings, although I was with an escort, so I thought that it would be safe to get out. I murmured some excuse to my companion and we left the tram several stages sooner than our usual custom. Otherwise I feel sure I would have been raided and perhaps injured.

On another occasion I had collected several rents from a district in Forest Gate. Being desirous of banking the money as soon as possible I waited in a lane while my companion took the money to a bank just round the corner. When we returned we strolled to the main road to take a tram. Immediately we were surrounded by a large gang of ruffians (poorly dressed) at the tram stop. But suddenly they all drew away; as the tram came up I boarded it in peace. I said to my companion afterwards that in all probability they had dispersed when they somehow discovered that I had banked the takings.

For some time I had a notice posted up in the window of my office, "No Houses to Let," and for a considerable period there were no enquiries.

## Terrorism

Quite suddenly (just after the eviction), however, a horde of people descended on my office. They were from all parts of the globe, and a lot of them were foreign and English Jews. Few of them – if indeed any – could be described as anything else but criminal in appearance. Desperate-looking countenances would peer at me maliciously and disappear only to leave their ugly visages vividly imprinted on my brain, which would sometimes automatically parade these images, giving me the most horrible idea of dire things to come to me. Some of these desperadoes would knock at the door of my office and demand from my man to see me. When I went to the door, they would simply give me a malevolent glance, or make some murderous gesture and disappear without saying a word. Some, however, made false attempts to be bona-fide enquirers, but from long experience I knew them to be false.

Now I began to feel that I was safe nowhere, not even in my own business premises. One morning, for instance, I was standing on Ilford Station, when a man of about five feet four inches, nicely dressed in a dark suit – thick-set and about fifty – came right "for me." He was the picture of aggressiveness; his face, full of what appeared to be suppressed fury; his eyes burned with an intense hate. They were fixed upon mine in a horrid, provocative manner. The train came in, however, and in the rush for seats I lost sight of him. In the railway carriage my man said to me that if anyone had treated him like that he would have wanted to know the reason why. Though I did not like the implied suggestion that I was a bit of a coward to take it lying down, yet I was pleased at his observation. These malefactors had actual existence, and, alas, I was at the focus of these malefactors.

It would seem as if the whole neighborhood in which I was living was being infested with undesirables: and those, not only of the ordinary, witless variety, whose brutalities were all the more awful because they were unintelligent, but also of the "gentleman" crook sort. About this time a policeman, whom I knew well, told me that a few days previously he had had occasion, when in private clothes, to visit the most respectable local hotel. He was impressed by a number of well-dressed, "aristocratic" looking men in the saloon-bar. After a while some of the worst jail-birds in the district entered the common bar, and to the surprise of the policemen they soon entered into conversation with the "aristocratic" looking crowd. The talk seemed to be of the friendliest nature and was carried on in a kind of confidential jargon, the meaning of which, in a large measure, was lost even on the policeman who was acquainted with many varieties of slang of East-end crooks. Now, these people were not in the neighborhood of all my business for nothing, and I was advised to be exceedingly careful in the transporting of my money and of my person. This warning was not necessary for now began a period of strange molestation.

If I were travelling on a tram, often a man looking like a footpad would jump on the rear-step, start talking to the conductor and keep on looking at me with a steady, malevolent stare. On several occasions when I appeared to take no notice of him or his antics he shouted down the entire length of the tram, "He put them in the gutter." He would ride for about ten minutes and then jump off. His entire journey was concentrated public insult, and its object was myself. All this made me very miserable indeed.

Then after the ejectment began an insidious and a most subtly organized molestation. *Every night for over a year* the same man was always within two hundred feet of my office. He positioned himself so that I had to pass him on my way to the railway station. The look he gave me is a little difficult to describe, except perhaps in the words of my man who accompanied me to the station. "It was," said my man, "a mysterious stare in which he tried to put a meaning, if you understand, sir, for you to be puzzled what he meant." His eyes were certainly the most cunning I had seen, otherwise he appeared to be a respectable old gentleman of about sixty-four years old and five feet six inches in height, neither thin nor stout. He wore respectable clothes and in the summer a straw hat. He also wore a moustache and had side-whiskers. But, despite this most genteel exterior, I knew him to be a crook, not only from his behaviour toward me but also because I had seem him very often talking to some really bad characters whom I knew by sight and whose criminal record was awful and who also molested me now.

---

It was my custom on warm sunny Sundays to journey alone, but now I went with my friend to Westcliff, and listened to the band. During the days of the attempted raids upon me I was always conscious of couples or individuals who kept me under observation. One Sunday I remember noticing several couples who stopped and scrutinised me for almost half a minute every time they passed me during their strolls in the enclosure round the Westcliff bandstand in the intervals between each item. They were all nicely dressed couples, but the evil expressions on their faces labelled them as crooks, wrong 'uns. After listening to the band for some time we walked back to a Southend cafe for tea. My chair faced the interior wall of the cafe, and I amused myself for some time by watching the reflections of the holiday makers passing by in a great mirror which practically covered the top part of the inner wall. Presently my attention became riveted to this mirror, for I was suddenly struck by the similarity of some of the faces of those who passed and re-passed. Then I realized that many of these were the crooks who had followed me about all the day, and that they were staring in the mirror as they passed and re-passed the cafe in order to molest me with an evil scowling stare, seeking to make me feel concerned for my safety.

Another day I visited Southend with my companion, and we lay luxuriantly on the sands among the happy crowd of holiday makers to enjoy the warmth of the sun in Thorpe Bay. I had been lying with my eyes closed for some time, when on looking up I became conscious of someone staring at me. I sat up and noticed several ruffians sitting quite close to me. I could hear sounds of conversation among them, and yet their lips were not moving at all. Some time after this a police friend told me that was a prison dodge for carrying on a conversation without appearing to be talking. Each of these men stared at me in turn and gave me a hard vicious look for quite a minute.

Some Sundays I would go to my office to do booking and put

various papers in order. On these occasions I was always alone, and I arranged for a boy from a neighboring house to bring in my dinner. One such Sunday I glanced through the cracks in the venetian blind to see if the boy was in sight for he was a little later than usual. As I peeped through the blind I saw a tall, extra big, clean-shaven, well-built, middle aged man with a large round face standing in the road directly opposite my office, and staring at the window. He wore a billycock hat and was dressed in clothes resembling a farmer. I recognised his burly features and ruddy face, and knew him to be one of the ringleaders of the gangs who so relentlessly followed me. No doubt he had taken stock of all my movements and knew I was alone in the office. Therefore when the boy came with my dinner I sent him to fetch my companions to keep me company.

---

Some of the innumerable watchers and foxers of August, 1922, I can describe.

About this time a fat, big mulatto with a large round, clean-shaven face, and nicely dressed, generally with some well dressed white men of crime, used to watch me narrowly. He was about 30 and was about five feet nine inches in height.

Also a very slim man of about 32 years of age with flaxen hair. He was about six feet four inches in height and was clean shaven. He was nicely dressed.

Also a young man of about 25 in a black suit, and showing a lot of white cuff; he was clean-shaven, slightly built and about five feet three inches in height and of a Jewish cast of countenance.

I have said these ruffians were relentless in their watching of my movements. They were indeed more tenacious than a bulldog in their efforts to intimidate me. They did not let me get out of their sight. It seemed as though there were spies all round and that I could do nothing without their getting to know about it. Their strategy was of a subtle order, i.e., I wrote a City firm that

I would be calling and when I arrived at this City office I found several of my usual crook molesters standing by and gazing murderously at me.

---

I had heard of young girls being hustled into waiting cars and taken completely away from their homes, but never had the idea of such methods being adopted by my persecutors entered my head until one September evening when darkness had fallen earlier than usual. I was walking down Balfour Road, Ilford, where I was then living, on my way home, when I passed a clean-shaven, dark eyed and eyebrowed man, wearing a light-coloured overcoat. I caught sight of his face in the light of a street lamp and recognised one of my foxers. I caught the malicious gleam in his eyes, and a cool feeling ran down my spine. Then I noticed another fellow watching me from right under the shadows of another street lamp. At this moment a car came slowly up the road with its door open, and slowing down beside me kept even with me as I walked quickly along. All the time I could feel the two footpads closing steadily in upon me, and in the dark and deserted street I felt quite helpless. Then suddenly a wave of relief swept over me. Round the corner of the road came a policeman, the even beat of his footsteps echoing cheerfully through the gruesome shadowy atmosphere that surrounded me. Immediately the sinister figures faded away and the car sped away up the road.

The following night, as I went home, I went as usual to a letter box with several important business letters. I noticed two well dressed, dark-suited young men, clean-shaven, and both wearing black gloves, standing by the box. One of them was tall and the other was short, and as I approached the letter box one of them put his hand just above the opening of the box and appeared to be chatting to his friend. I felt quite convinced that he held a catch for my letters, and therefore I walked along to another box some distance away.

The reason that I mention the ejectment of the tenant is

because the real "set" upon me by crooks continually molesting commenced and followed on just after I had complained to the police to inform them of the groups of men (presumably the unemployed) that were now continually watching (after the ejectment) on the corners of the road near my office.

After I had been to the police these watching men ceased standing on these particular road corners, through wherever I went I was followed about by several determined-looking, ruffianly men, and I knew by their aspect that I was not safe even with my man as escort. These men appeared to be desperately bent on doing me bodily injury. They followed me about quite openly and boldly wherever I went, though I was accompanied.

This was the first time when the crooks thought it a suitable way to fog and confound me. They thought to delude me and the police into thinking that in the event of anything untoward happening to me it would be ascribed to the unemployed.

By the middle of August, 1922, I was in constant danger from both the unemployed and from the crooks. I was living then at Brentwood, and several times on the railway journeys, smart, well dressed crooks had "accompanied" me and got into near proximity to me in the train and had had conversation with me. I could see an attack of some kind coming to me when I was alone. So as not to have such a long journey back and forth I changed my place of residence to Ilford.

I think that I made this change only just in time, as by this time the crooks had put a "seal" upon me. I now always had to be accompanied not only for escort but also as witness to any assault upon me. There was now always a crook watcher on the way from my house to the railway station every morning, though I was accompanied, and when I got out of the train there was always a watcher or two standing and glaring murderously at me as I walked to my office. When I left my office at night there was a crook who stationed himself in my way seeking to "catch" my eye; when I left the train another watching crook or two would be in my path on the way to my home.

All these men always watched me approaching with their gaze

set upon me, and in the event of my turning round and looking back after I had passed them by, I invariably found these men still staring evilly and vilely at me.

When I was collecting rents now, though I had a companion with me, yet groups of two or even three crooks would come especially by me to give me looks of intimidation as they passed by. Sometimes these men were quite well-dressed, but the majority of such molesters were respectably dressed. All of these men bore the stamp of rogues and villains ready for outrage and violence of any kind.

The staring may seem trivial. Is it?

The majority of these molesters were evidently and unmistakably felons and criminals and bad characters generally, and men of violence too. Men of terrible aspect. It was not only the staring but it was the class of men so molesting that made their contemptuous and murderous looks so telling. They could look what they were – scoundrels.

Their actions made it apparent that if they caught me alone they meant to do me physical violence.

Who arranged that these men should punctually and always be on my tracks?

It was a molesting with a felonious intent; intimidation without words; and it made me feel always anxious.

Again, who arranged the following? From about the same time, as I got out of the train, on my way to my office every morning there was always a man – this time a fairly young one – standing in practically the same place. It was a different man each morning, though they were usually of about the age of 30 to 40, and their clothes were poor. Every morning, then, for over a year a man of the "jail-bird" type – "proper desperadoes they are, sir," as my man said – would aggravate me with a vile, murderous stare, calculated to un-nerve me and weaken my resistance to their intended ultimate attack upon my person.

These men would endeavour to catch my eye. If they succeeded in doing this all kinds of evil stares and gestures were doled out to me, my days at work were indeed miserable ones.

If I turned round there to be sure was a man gazing at me with ferocity. The eyes of the beasts were far kinder than the eyes of these men.

On some occasions there would be two men performing this morning "staring stunt," and then it was most difficult to avoid seeing them and being treated with their debilitating molestations. Usually these men took up their "positions" before my train arrived, but sometimes they would be a little late and I would see them hurrying to their "places of vantage" so as to be there in front of me in time to treat me to their evil eyes and intimidating gestures as I walked by.

These men not only are not invented by me, but, on the contrary, were of flesh and blood, wanted by the police. Some of them I recognised from their likeness to the pictures of old jail-birds or wanted criminals, which appeared from time to time in the illustrated and daily papers. The method of these men, in words of my assistant, was "a *telling* insult for intimidation with a foul purpose of weakening you mentally, sir, and of causing dread or intimidating." I do not think it could have been put better. The mental effect was awful. To feel forever hunted and haunted!

After the ejectment, each Monday morning for many months there was a nicely dressed man in a dark suit and light brown overcoat, wearing a light brown cap, aged about forty years, and about five feet nine inches in height, standing in the road along which I had to walk, close to my office. He would stare at me as I proceeded to business, though I must confess in this instance that until my man pointed him out to me I had not noticed his molestations. When I emerged from my office about half-an-hour after entering it in the morning, this person was always there with another, a ruffian of the most obvious "bruiser" variety. As I left the office and proceeded to the main road to collect rents, the first man would nudge his "bruiser" companion and point directly at me with his hand. Both of them would stare fixedly at me.

"Why do they do it?" I asked my man one morning.

"That's easy, sir. It's to frighten and affect one mentally, if you understand, sir. To weaken one's nerves."

There must have been many involved in this particular crime, for there was a different "bruiser" every Monday morning, though the "leader" was always the same man.

On two occasions, as I left Ilford Station on my way home at night, the "bruiser" of the previous Monday morning was awaiting me in the road outside the station. On the first of these occasions the fellow had a large riding whip in his hand, which he cracked in the air. Then he opened his overcoat and put the whip against his body, looking at me in a most intimidating way all the time. He then closed his overcoat.

A few days after this occurred the same fellow was standing right outside my house, and as I approached he made the most menacing gestures. I felt afraid and asked my man to accompany me right to my door.

Some weeks after the ejectment I began to meet my molesters wherever I happened to go. For instance, as my Brentwood train stopped at the express-train platform at Stratford in the morning there were sometimes as many as six or seven well-dressed men between the ages of thirty and forty, all rather tall, some with moustaches, all with devil-may-care murderous looks at me. They seemed to be the worst kind of callous desperadoes I had ever seen in a group. One I recollect vividly had an awful, murderous expression in his light-blue eyes. He was of moderate build, rather tall, with a thin red moustache and red hair. They boarded this express train to get to Liverpool Street, the next stop.

On one fine Sunday my man and I went by boat to Clacton-on-Sea. It was not long after the attempted raid. When we boarded the paddle boat we found our way to the back of the vessel, and went to the lower deck and seated ourselves there. After we had been sitting there a few minutes two men of fairly respectable dress, but both with the appearance of footpads, came and stood within five feet of me, where they remained standing until my companion and self left these seats. Both of these men (who looked dangerous ruffians) were clean-shaven and of about thirty years of age and about five feet seven inches in height. There was an appearance of premeditated evil purpose in the every look and move of these two men as they watched me closely all the time. We two sat there for about two hours and neither of these men spoke to the other all the while they stood there, but they occasionally gave knowing looks to one another. My companion frequently shut his eyes and managed almost to doze on several occasions; on each occasion that he was nearly dozing these two watching men moved discernibly slightly nearer to me. These men when doing this slight move looked as about to attack me. Was their intention to throw me overboard, to injure me, or to rob me?

A few days after the attempted raid I was about to cross a road at a usual crossing that I always made; a car that had been slowly coming along behind me increased its speed and shot at me like a bullet from a gun. I jumped back just in time to miss the car's wheels. The looks of the two men in the front seat of the car were quite enough to convince me that this was a deliberate attempt to murder me.

Another experience which I had about this time was in a London suburb where my man and I occasionally went on business. When we were there we generally lunched in a coffee-house where we were well-known as customers, though not in any other way. One day we were about to start our meal when there entered two suspicious-looking men of about 40 – dark sun-browned (by some "foreign" sun) and dark eyes and brows. Both of them were about five feet eight inches and stared at me most of the time. One of them got into conversation with the waitress and talked for a long time with her. During their conversation both of them kept looking at me in a strange manner. Whenever I went to the coffee-house after this the waitress attempted to engage me in conversation as though seeking my intimate acquaintance. Previously she had been ordinarily civil and nothing more – which is as it should be. These men, who wore dark clothes, were simply using her to exploit me and, in future, I avoided this coffee shop.

Another experience in a cafe was that which happened during 1924. My man and I were in the City doing business and we took tea in a cafe near the Mansion House. We had not been seated a few moments before a bearded man of about 60, in rather shabby clothes, entered and sat quite near us. As "our" waitress approached us he called her, and during their subdued conversation, they kept looking over at me. Indeed the waitress looked hard at me until we left. The man, who might also be called a rough, partook of no refreshments, and left shortly after addressing the waitress.

The following year my man and I decided to take a holiday. I hoped to escape from the trying molestations which seemed to surround me in my business life. So we took the train to Yarmouth and I was happier than I had been for a long time. We went on the Saturday before Bank Holiday Monday by the afternoon express. My lightness of heart, however, was soon to be dissipated, to be followed by a sad, heavy feeling of utter weariness. It happened in this way. When the train stopped at Ipswich for ten minutes my man expressed a desire for stretching his legs. Directly he had left the carriage a clean-shaven, scoundrelly, villainous looking fellow of about 45, dressed in a good blue suit, came in and sat opposite me. He gave me a continuous hard, unflinching steady stare, and appeared to be settling himself for the rest of the journey. What for? When my man returned, however, the scoundrel got up and left the carriage. All I *do* know is that such men were making a hell of what had been a pleasant existence.

As we left Yarmouth Station I noticed ahead of us on the bridge over the Yare a big brute of a man, and evilly staring fixedly at me. Soon he was joined by another of the same type. As I approached them they were openly laughing at me, jeering in my face. They must certainly have known of my coming. But how? The evil jeering was continued. Even the Sabbath was not a day of rest for these loathsome creatures. This jeering seemed to be catching, for on Sunday evening, as we neared our apartments, we met about eight shortish young men, all nicely dressed in black suits and all clean-shaven. Directly they saw us they gave me a hard glare and all of them put on, as it were, a "jeery, evil smile," to quote the words of my man.

Yarmouth was to be no holiday for me, for on the following morning we went to Caister and had the following experience. We had dinner in a cafe where the waitress served us quietly and properly. We returned later, but this time the waitress was extraordinarily familiar in her attitude to me, so much so that my man remarked about it to me.

"Of course," he said, "she has been tampered with since we were here last time."

But this was not the only surprise we were to have here, for at another cafe in Caister which we visited later we were followed in by a pale, poor-looking individual. He seemed a bag of nerves. After a little while the three of us had fallen into a casual conversation. He looked rather strangely at me: as my man put it, "a very covert foxy look." His conversation made me wonder what he did for a living, for I had the sort of feeling that he was not an ordinary working man. He told us that he came from Portsmouth. Then he asked me if I knew such and such a place (naming the very district I came from). It came like a bombshell. He rose quietly, a jeer on his face, and departed. No doubt he had been and was foxing me.

Our express took us back to Liverpool Street from which station we had to take a suburban train to Ilford. At the barrier a clean-shaven, respectably dressed man of about 32 and about five feet six inches, of Jewish appearance, "spotted" me and hurried away at once. We saw him again as we were about to enter our carriage. He ushered three women into the same carriage we decided to occupy, and one of them came and stood and almost sat at times right against me all the journey.

My remembered position and occupation were to be no more. I was suddenly removed from my ordinary atmosphere of every day into an appalling tragic position. I was moving in a world now where figures terrible and obscene and foul followed and made my life a hell, a struggle against the desperate elements. They hang on like leeches once they "set" on a victim. I had endured this for over two years now.

I will not recount in detail any further incidents with regard to the continual watching of my movements. But I wish to impress upon my readers the awful, haunting persistence with which my persecutors worked against me. Every day since and for years after the incident of the ejectment I have previously mentioned, there was a man stationed in the road near my office. Whenever I entered a train or tram I was under strict observation; and frequently groups of men outside public houses or at the corners of streets would shout abuse at me, or endeavour to waylay me on my journeys from house to house when I was collecting. My office was besieged by ruffians or well dressed men, who were worse than ruffians. Altogether I could not move without knowing that spying eyes were upon me. You may wonder why I did not have the ringleaders convicted. That is just where my chief difficulty lay. So subtly and craftily were their plans made, and so vast were their numbers, that it was useless to lay hands on any one man.

I soon discovered that even the waitresses of the cafes I usually frequented had been influenced by the crooks to work on their behalf. Girls who had formerly been civil and businesslike now persistently tried to be flirtatious, and would hang about my table and try to draw me into conversation.

Sometimes my memory would recall the loss of my freedom and peace and instantly a solemn harrowing realisation of the predicament of my present position. The axis round which my whole mental outlook revolved was stupefying. They hid by strategy of a subtle order their design which with deliberation they seek to obtain.

So, for over two years, this silent molest continued. By infinite cunning and relentless pursuit some gang hoped to profit by my eventual mental collapse. I was constantly molested and watched so that every one of my actions might be known. Who had instituted this cruel and wearing persecution I could not guess. I was quite certain that some portion of the molesters were members of the unemployed. I knew too that the ejected tenant had taken part in some of the molests, and yet the first signs of trouble had been present before the final ejectment.

I have detailed many little incidents in the above account of my experiences in the East End of London in an endeavour to describe the inexorable, relentless power of evil which casts its fearful shadow and ghastly spell over some victims.

CHAPTER VI

# The Voyage Out

AFTER THIRTY-ONE YEARS OF HARD AND STRENUOUS WORK I decided to leave London and find a peaceful retreat abroad. It it a wrench for anyone to leave the land of his birth, but when forced to do it by crooks it is more than rough. Fancy the unconstrained forces of evil driving one so! It is an outrage.

It was with a feeling of boundless confidence that I stepped on board the mighty vessel that was to take me away from the sorrows that I had endured, and to enable me to start a life afresh in a new world. At last, I thought, I was away from all that nightmare of torment.

It was a wonderful ship – an oil driven vessel of the good type – which gave surprisingly little discomfort to us passengers from such things as the black sooty smoke which so many ocean-going vessels emit, and which has been in the past a constant source of annoyance, both to passengers and crew. We sailed calmly on out of the foggy northland into the warmth and glamour of tropical sunlight. As we proceeded we had to wear less and less of our British clothes.

I shall never forget those days of serene content and happy expectation of a future delight. I forgot all fears and was happy. I dreamed my dreams, and built my castles in the air as if I were once more the smiling boy in his teens that had long ago been me.

I remember the days of enchanting and lovely beauty that made one surfeit of delight. There was always some new sight to see, some fresh occupation to be engaged in, some pleasant friendship to enjoy. People have spoken of the monotony of a long sea voyage. To me it was, perhaps, the happiest time of my life.

The future was before me. It was deeply veiled; but I had convinced myself that I could pierce through the mists and see into the life that was stretching out before me, a life of hard work and of real enjoyment, of steady application, and of a safe reaping of the fruits of the harvest which I was to plant and tend until the time came to gather it in.

So I would rise in the morning and sing to myself as I dressed for every delight. I enjoyed every minute of my days, and passed my nights happy in meditation of the joys that were to be mine, and in quiet dreamless sleep, unless some happy vision of that future land passed softly over my mind. Truly I could repeat with the poet Wordsworth:

"Bliss was it in that dawn to be alive."

So far the voyage was my very heaven, although of brief duration. Then abruptly I descended from this heaven into hell, and was wrenched back into that dread abyss from which I thought I had escaped.

It was a beautiful sunlit Sunday morning as the ship steamed her way through the blissful ever-blue waters of the Caribbean Sea on her way to Caracas for re-fuelling with oil. My! What a hot place is this Dutch port. It was almost unbearably burning hot there, everything shimmering in the tropical sun. I was attending divine service. As I looked at the clear, worshipping faces of the men and women and little children around me, and listened to the tones of the captain and all assembled saying the Lord's Prayer, I felt a great surge of thankfulness, and humbly thanked God that in His great mercy He had delivered me from my enemies.

Hardly had I finished my grateful prayer than a harsh, grating voice, just behind me, made me go cold with horror. Oh, was I never to be free? I had caught clearly the words that this criminal said:

"I know, I know. He thinks he's safe now. But we will get him, never fear."

I swung round in the direction from which that voice of the past had come. I saw only the somewhat surprised faces of my fellow passengers. And there was nothing in the expressions of any of them to give me the least clue to the identity of the speaker.

I mentioned to an officer travelling on the ship some of my troubles. He was a widely-travelled man and very intelligent. He said he had come into contact with crooks a great deal. He said there are crooks who make the ocean liners their hunting grounds.

He confirmed my worst fears when he told me that the confidence crooks and cardsharps who worked the liners were men of international connections. At some length he explained that the men do not come under one central head, but that they all work in with each other. That is to say, if a London "fence" wanted the jewels of a wealthy woman travelling from Australia to England, he could arrange with a crook in Australia to make the voyage. Similarly, a criminal making a voyage from London to Sydney would be always willing to augment the proceeds of his trip by smuggling stolen property into Australia, where it could be more easily disposed of than in Europe.

This, of course, explained why I did not recognise the speaker on the day of the service. The international network of crime was now revealed to me in all its stark horror, and I knew that nowhere I went would I be really safe. I asked the officer if he was suspicious of any persons aboard, and he told me of three men whom he strongly suspected of being travelling crooks.

One after another I watched these men carefully, and finally reached the decision that they were all aware of my identity. Not a doubt remained, therefore, that these men had been instructed to molest me. At the same time they carried out their own crooked work abroad, and when we reached Auckland, they would doubtless point me out to Crime G.H.Q. in that city. In New Zealand, I feared, I should be subject to all that had driven me from my native land.

## CHAPTER VII

# Trouble at Balboa

I WAS GLAD WHEN WE REACHED BALBOA, OUR FIRST PORT OF call, for now that I knew my fears were so well-grounded, I felt the close confinement aboard the ship very trying. Accordingly, I laid my plains to leave the ship as early as possible after she docked, and take a long walk on shore. Walking has always been a favourite pastime with me, and it was this healthy exercise that had largely contributed to that bodily health which enabled me to enjoy life.

It was a delightful day, and a stroll through the streets of the old Panama city, with their cosmopolitan throngs and gaudy shops did much to restore my shattered nerves. After a time I hired a car and drove for some distance into the open country, intending to dismiss the driver, and continue my walk along the road. It was an old car, and as we jogged along the broad road, I suddenly knew that we were being followed. Peering through the rear curtain, I noticed another, very much larger car, which was keeping just behind us, about 150 yards away. What made this seem strange was that the car had a very much better turn of speed than mine, and there was no reason for its proceeding at such a low speed.

An idea swept through me as I thought. Balboa is well-deserving of its reputation as a "tough" seaport, and things have happened there which do not find their way into tourist guide-books. A swift, sudden descent by the men in the car, a few fierce blows to incapacitate the driver, and I could have been dragged to some thieves' den. Perhaps it would provide just another insoluble case, and the police would merely shrug their shoulders and forget the affair. My friends and relations would never know of my dreadful fate, and the underworld would have once more triumphed.

As rapidly as I thought, I acted. The driver spoke only a bad English, but I made him understand that at the next bend in the road he must slow up sufficiently for me to jump out. Handing him a roll of local notes, I slipped from the car and hid myself behind a fence, a few seconds before the second car reached the bend. I peered cautiously from behind the sheltering fence, and saw immediately that the car contained two of the men against whom the officer had warned me. There were three other bad-looking men in the car, but they were local gangsters no doubt, and, of course, complete strangers to me.

For the time I was safe, but I realised that the gangsters might at any moment descend on my car. Then they would learn from the driver what had occurred, and immediately retrace their way along the road. I could not hope to travel back to Balboa by that route, and decided that my best plan would be to walk through the woods by the side of the road, and take cover whenever I heard a car approach. I had scarcely come to this decision when I heard a car approaching just behind me. Instinctively, I made to draw into the shelter of the rock, but leaped back when I realised that this could scarcely be the enemy car returning so soon. I was right. The car was driven by a native, and had as passengers two young U.S.A. naval officers, who stopped the man when they observed my signals. I invented a story of having lost my driver while wandering in the woods, and they very decently gave me a lift back to the city. Immediately I went aboard the ship and remained there for the rest of our stay at Balboa. That night I saw the two travelling crooks come aboard, but neither they nor I betrayed in the slightest outward manner that we had seen one another ashore.

The events which had led to my decision to leave England had thus early changed my unconscious attitude towards humanity. That unthinking confidence in mankind which is in some part the heritage of our faith, and which to more happy men is in the foundation of communal life, had in me been considerably shaken. Later events were to destroy it entirely, but I could still take some pleasure in the passing friendly contacts of a voyage.

It was pleasant to feel that my fellow passengers and I maintained our mutual kindly attitude one to another for no other reason than the Christian fellowship of ordinary decent men, men from whom I was so soon to be separated.

These passengers were the salt of the earth. Many of them were artisans, with all the instinctive goodwill of men who work with their hands. My commercial experience in London had taught me to recognise the deterioration of character in great cities.

"Where wealth accumulates and men decay."

I had known the hardness which results from a life divorced from the immemorial tasks of humanity, in which lie the origin and perpetual necessity of man's future.

But these, my companions, were men who worked, not in the turmoil of our commercial bureaucracy amid the ceaseless strain of bargaining for the products of other men's labour, but were themselves the foundation of the State, and although they were not rich they moved and had their being in the pride of knowing that they were indispensable. Of them might the poet of the Welsh Marches have written:

"Their shoulders held the sky suspended."

With them I maintained a friendly intercourse which in great measure restored my confidence in humanity. Also the voyage was not without its social life, in which the ship's staff were not unwilling to participate.

But I will no longer allow my readers to deceive themselves. If my narrative were to have continued in this vein its purpose would not have existed. The blow was about to fall. It was said by the Greeks that "whom the gods would destroy, they first made happy for awhile," and the clouds of disillusion gathered quickly round me, although I was not aware of the bitter change awaiting me.

I have now the hard-won satisfaction of looking back and unravelling the interwoven threads of my life. As the voyage drew to its close, my confidence and interest in a new beginning in another land were accepted with foreboding, and a partly unexpressed wish that this journey among friends over halcyon seas might last for ever. But when we arrived at Wellington all my fears were forgotten, and I stepped ashore feeling like one who has been freed from bondage, and with the happy courage of the explorer I began my life in New Zealand.

## CHAPTER VIII

# Peace Broken

I ARRANGED ABOUT MY LODGINGS AND BEGAN TO SETTLE DOWN to this new life I was to lead. There is a different atmosphere about a colony, compared with an older land. There is less of the air of stability and conservatism which is apt to pervade the towns of the mother-country. More especially is this so with a seaport. And as I wandered through Wellington that evening, on the first day of my landing, and breathed in the fresh air I wondered once more what sort of life was going to be mine in New Zealand.

I decided to explore my new surroundings. Accordingly, as soon as I had my tea I went out for a walk. I had only intended taking a short stroll, and after about two miles I turned back to seek out my lodgings. That one movement of my body was the first warning I received of the recrudescence of my troubles in this distant land.

For, as I turned to make my way back home, I saw a man not thirty yards from me start quickly and with a gesture, whose suddenness belied its validity, sink into the sort of brooding stupor which so many idlers adopt as they stand motionless at street corners and at the side of roads.

I had to pass this man as I retraced my footsteps. And as I came towards him I felt a little quiver of alarm go through me. It is curious how some little incident stands out indelibly in the mind when one recollects the details leading up to some crisis. I distinctly remember that, just as I turned, my thoughts travelled swiftly back to the days when I was a young boy at school. I remember my master going round his class asking the pupils for the French idioms which they had learnt overnight, and remembered him coming to me and asking: "To retrace one's footsteps?" and I remembered my faltering and puzzling over it in my brain until I suddenly lighted on the correct phrase – "Rebousser son chemin." I was keenly occupied with these memories, and at the same time strongly, if intuitively, distrustful of the man who was so near me.

I came up to him and gave him a look a little longer than the casual glance one usually gives a passer-by. I was immediately shocked and horrified to discover his two eyes fixed darkly on me in a baleful stare. Another shock beat at my heart as I realised that I had seen this man before. I had noticed him that morning in the town. He had had that keen hatred in his eyes as he stared at me then. It was more than coincidence that he should be within striking distance of me now as well.

It was obvious what had happened. I had gone walking on with never a thought of danger, and all the time this loathsome spy had been tracking me down, finding out my destination, trying to learn my secrets, and rejoicing the while in anticipation of the praise and remuneration he would receive when he reported his information to his superiors.

For he was clearly one of a gang, perhaps the self-same gang that had forced me to fly from my established business in London. Indeed, as I turned it over in my mind, it seemed that it could be no other party of people. For what organisation could learn of my arrival and know that they could get much from me, all within the short space of those few hours since I landed from my ship, unless they were identical with, or had at least received their knowledge from, the ghastly fiends who had assailed and tormented me in London? Clearly I was a marked man again.

I walked numbly on. I do not know now how I managed to cover those two miles which lay between me and the comfort and shelter which Home – even a hired home – spelt. My mind was in turmoil and I felt weak. One part of my brain seemed to be repeating mechanically as a sort of ironic refrain, "Tracked again!" It was to this devil-chorus that I came back to my home.

It was getting dark now, but as I approached the already familiar house I looked back fearfully, yet under the compulsion of a force stronger than my own will. There he was, still a few yards behind me, no more than a menacing black shadow now, but the light of the street lamp set his eyes a-flashing, and I knew that he was still subjecting me to that cold, inscrutable stare of hatred.

I shuddered and went on. I came back to the house from which I had set out so joyfully, a very anxious man.

CHAPTER IX

# Life in Auckland

ALTHOUGH I WAS SOMEWHAT PERTURBED BY THE FIRST ATTEMPT at molestation, I was still too confident to despair in this new land. There were crooks and thieves everywhere, I reflected, and it might have been no more than an unfortunate coincidence. Indeed, it seemed reasonable to assume that any new arrival, who appeared prosperous, might well be marked down as a possible victim.

Not yet was I certain that this incident signified the doom of my fair hopes of peace, and I took train from Wellington to Auckland, where I obtained good apartments.

But no happy illusion was to endure; on that Sunday after my arrival I went to church, in the morning; that the vicinity of God's house could be the scene of evil intentions seemed impossible, and I left the church with the recollection of my earlier misfortune considerably dimmed in my mind. This calm mood, which I had not known since my adventures in London was rudely dispelled. Outside the church, mingling with the homeward-bound worshippers, stood a sinister figure. My attention was drawn to him by the dark colour of his clothes and features, which gave him a grim appearance. As soon as he saw me, he acted like one who has been waiting in anticipation of seeing me leave the church, for without hesitation he walked down the long entrance of a shop nearby, and stared fixedly upon me from the far end. The light behind his shadowy form outlined him as a silhouette against the sky, and he gazed at me as a venomous snake watches from a hole in the earth. With a violent shock of realisation, I knew in that instant that my fight had recommenced. I went home sadly like a modern Orestes, pursued by intangible fears and apprehensions.

A few days later my fears were confirmed only too well, for a similar molestation by two men, also dark, took place in a main street of the city. Apparently there was a definite technique employed by these people, for as on the previous Sunday, they sought a shelter as they discerned me approaching, by standing in the porch of the hotel just by and stared in the same silent, intimidating way. This was bad enough, in all conscience, but worse was to follow. My memory for faces is good, and business dealings make it a valuable faculty to recognise men after a lapse of time. It was thus, beyond doubt, that I noticed that one of these men was known to me. I had met him thousands of miles away, in the East End of London. He it was who, in the company of other abandoned villains, had molested me during my commercial career in the metropolis.

I was to see him again, for after a few days which passed in a comparative tranquility, I was followed down a street in which I was occupied with various purchases.

A man and a woman, both meanly clad, dogged my steps from shop to shop, and even had the temerity to enter after me and watch my purchasing transactions with the store keepers. The man was about 42 and about five feet seven inches tall, and had a dark brown moustache and a pale face.

After these preliminary attacks I was left in uneasy security for a few months. Was it to last, I asked myself anxiously, or were my foes plotting further evil against me? I was soon to be enlightened; the next attempt was so elaborately planned, and so nearly successful but for my refusing the trap, that it was impossible to doubt the truth of my suspicion that those months were nought but a respite, during which still darker crimes were being designed. No fewer than five people were employed in this plan, a fact which shows the determination of my oppressors. No ordinary criminal could have been responsible for such a deep-laid scheme, and I realised on this occasion that my unknown enemy (for a master-mind was clearly at the head of the organisation) was savagely determined to drive me, penniless and broken, from this far corner of the Empire.

I had been out for some hours walking alone, to enjoy the scenery in the Domain, and had returned to the city with a certain measure of equanimity. On nearing the corner of the road in which my lodging was situated, I saw the man and the woman who had some months previously followed me into shops. They stood on the opposite side of the crossing; with them was a powerfully built man of about 50, nearly six feet tall, and with face bronzed as by tropical sunshine, and with a brown moustache, which gave to his face an expression of cunning mingled with sensuality. This ruddiness of countenance suggested that he was a seafaring man. With keen gaze he watched me approaching the corner; as I drew near he made a sign in the direction of the road I intended to enter. From my position I could see no one to whom he might be signalling, but it was obvious that these mysterious gestures were connected to me.

My first impulse was to retreat; then I realised that in this peaceful street the worst that could happen was some plot to trick me into an invidious position. I, trusting to Providence to save me from harm, continued boldly down the road. On turning the corner I saw the person to whom the sailor had been signalling; it was a young woman who stood motionless at the road side. She was young, but her face had none of the fresh innocence of a young English woman. Already the marks of degradation were written indelibly on her countenance. Vice makes men and women callous and the inner hardness shows on the faces of those who have turned to evil. In the words of the poet Burns:

"I waive the quantum of the sin
Thc hazard of concealing,
Bude och, it hardens a' within
And petrifies the feeling."

But to continue my narrative. Opposite this unhappy girl,

standing on the other side of the road, was one of the criminals who had molested me in the past. These folk, in their blue suits and felt hats, looked to the undiscerning eye like ordinary citizens; but under the mask of quiet respectability were the faces of enemies of Society. This man took no apparent part in the scheme being enacted against me. In a moment I divined the plan; the woman was to dissimulate an attack on her by myself; the solitary criminal opposite would have appeared as her husband, while the others were perhaps to have acted as witnesses. Not yet were those who were seeking after me prepared to attack my life; they were content to wear down my resistance, and to endeavour thus to involve me in their toils (or the toils of the law). Quite possibly, as it was so near my home, a murderous attack was intended. Reputation, as Shakespeare said, once lost is never regained. They even might have thought to get me turned out of my apartments, they are such vile schemers.

It was such an ingenious scheme, this of ruining me by plot. However, having realised what was intended, I walked past the "witnesses" (enemy) and at my confident waiting in the main road, they after time dispersed in different directions and I proceeded home.

It would take too long, and would weary my readers, to recount all the misfortunes which befell me in New Zealand. Suffice it to say that I was followed on all my walking excursions, on my business activities, on omnibuses, trams and on ships; always pursued everywhere. My nerve and resistance were gradually affected and worn. Those who have never been an Ishmael with every crook's hand against him, will find it difficult to conceive how an innocent man may be oppressed and persecuted by evil men.

If I had not always now had an escort with me I should have been undoubtedly attacked, but I was molested incessantly. Violent attacks are daily occurrences, but who would imagine that criminals would pursue me across the world, and then use the most fiendishly subtle psychological assaults to unseat my reason and break my spirit. That they did not entirely succeed was fortunate, and due to my escort being always present. My object in writing this brief account of my misfortunes has already been stated; perhaps at this juncture I may interpose an answer to a question which is perhaps in the minds of those who have persevered thus far in my narrative. Why, it may be asked, should these, desperate yet cunning men have followed me across the ocean to a distant land, there to enrol many of their kind in the war against my soul.

I presume they communicated with their colleagues in crime in New Zealand, and instructed them to drive me back to London, where my peril would be their safety and also helpful to their nefarious designs. Perhaps, and probably even, the messenger of evil was on the boat which bore me in hope across the sunlit sea to a new country. Be that as it may, from this record the fact appears that I was, immediately following my arrival, subjected to assaults which were clearly aimed at making me so unhappy that I would prefer to return to London. No other explanation so easily explains for this persistent refusal to allow me any peace.

Any witnessed violence would have made it possible for me to claim the protection of the law. This was part of my tragedy; I was made miserable and oppressed and apprehensive, yet because no actual violence was done against my person, I was unable to complain. But looks can wound as well as swords, and perhaps these mental tortures, so pertinaciously prosecuted, were less easy to bear.

This digression from my narrative should answer those who wish for an explanation of these seemingly purposeless actions, and I will now resume my history by recounting some of the, perhaps, more striking of the adventures which occurred during the troubled time of my long stay in New Zealand. It is well that I should not describe all these incidents, for though the record of them is clearly engraved on the tablets of my memory, I can only claim the attention of my readers while I recount the most interesting of these misfortunes.

Oppressed by the evil occurrences and encounters which I have described I often determined to occupy my time by trying to escape from my Auckland molesters or, failing such relief endeavour to ignore their murderous looks and eventually their very existence. Thinking that this course would be out of the question if I were to remain all my time in the city, so causing encounter with my persecutors to be inevitable, I decided to weekly make one or two excursions to different places of interest. It was with this end in view that I arranged with some friends to make a railway excursion to Waitomo Caves. Surely I could not meet any of my molesters on such an occasion unless indeed my friends in whom I placed so much confidence had been betrayed into informing my enemies of my plans, my friends, as unwitting informers, deceived into believing the villains to be honorable men. However this may be, it was with pleasurable emotions and feelings of a certain measure of security that I set out on the Sunday morning for the Auckland railway station: but my happiness was to be short lived, for I arrived early at the station and before my friends had come I was the victim of another disturbing encounter. Idly wandering about the station, I was glancing, as one does upon such occasions, at the large, brightly coloured posters, some calling to my mind pictures of those places mentioned which I had visited, and conjecturing with regard to those I had never seen. Suddenly I became aware of one whose appearance took on for me an air of sinister threatening. He was tall, well-built, clean-shaven – qualities which I would have regarded in another without suspicion, but which were in this case overshadowed by the darkness of his eyes, his cast of countenance and his black suit, all contributing together with his evil expression to the general unpleasantness of his appearance. As I wandered from poster to poster, so did he, fixing me with a look of evil contempt, and turning now and again to others to draw attention to my discomfiture.

My friends arrived and we embarked upon the train, where I was again confronted by the "boring" evil stares of several of my usual molesters, who now stood upon the platform immediately outside my window. I asked myself why they should be persecuting me in this manner, and decided that there could only be one answer to this question. By their ceaseless staring and evil smiles, the cunning of which can only be likened to that of a devil's grin, they hoped to unnerve me, with the intention of forcing me to remain in the city rather than go on far excursions as this to the Caves. Once certain that I was in Auckland they could keep watch upon me and molest me in their usual manner of uncompromising persecution. Partly to defeat them in this and partly to rely upon the company of my friends for safety, I continued upon the excursion, confident that I should not be followed by my persecutors, who would be discouraged from any contemplated attack, by the presence of my companions. The pleasures of my journey, however, existing as they did through my belief that I had broken away, if only for a short time, from my enemies, were not to be by any means prolonged, for, on leaving the station at the end of my trip, I again encountered these malicious people. Indeed, their attempts to separate me from my friends, when we were entering the motor cars, in which we were to drive to the caves, were so very nearly successful as to cause me great worry and anxiety. Nevertheless, I was able to gain a seat with my friends and experienced some relief in my ignorance of the fact that far worse was to follow.

When we got to one cave that is known as the Glow Worm Cave (and it is interesting in that one travels silently upon a lake which is in the cavern) the lights of which are due to the light given off by the glow worms, which may so be the more readily observed; but one must not talk or make noise else the worms cease to glow! The idea of this unusual adventure appealed to me strongly. I looked forward with pleasure to my voyage. The cave remains almost dark until the party have entered the boats, and after some considerable jostling, I found myself on the end of a seat by the gunwale, very close to the water, the sides of the boat being very low. As I glanced to the man who sat next to me, a feeling of fear seized me and for a moment I was unable to think coherently: for this was one of the most evil and malicious persecutors – one who was clearly steeped in crime and given over to the following of every kind of vice and sin. A thick-set, powerfully-built fellow – he had cunningly separated me from my friends and now planned to do me some ill – even, perhaps, to deprive me of life. Cold with fear, I realised that this villain intended to take advantage of the gloom and of my position in the boat, to use his obviously great strength in plunging me into the water of the lake, where I would probably perish. Forcing myself back to normal thought, and concentrating upon my voice, I called to one of my friends, whose answer close at hand served not only to bring me reassurance, but also to discourage my persecutor from putting his plans to the test. He merely contented himself with whispering in slow and threatening tones, "I'll murder you." I say "merely" for though this was in itself sufficient to jar my nerves, it could not compare with the evil end I know he intended for me. The caves are situated upon the hillsides and sometimes energy is required to pass from one to another. It was in this way that many people were discouraged from visiting the last cave, which was situated considerably further down the hillside than the rest, and despite the very attractive descriptions given of the cave's picturesqueness and dignified splendour, it was with a very small party, mostly consisting of my friends, that I made the descent to this spot. I was certain that my persecutors had not attempted the walk down the hill to the last cave. We had a good inspection of this wonderful last cave and then returned back up the hill. As we were walking up the hill near the road where the motor cars were standing, seven of these Auckland molesters stood staring down at me and were saying loudly, "Look at fatty," "Fat guts," "Fish guts," and other like expressions. They were right near to the cars and all the rest of the people, except those from the last cave, were seated in the motor cars, and the crooks' buffoonery was done to make the public stare and also, perhaps, throw jests too and laugh. It was done to annoy me and disconcert and make me appear a public fool; and also to make my life in the place unendurable. When we got out of the cars and proceeded to the railway station, I went to the lavatory, where five of these same men jostled me and endeavoured to separate me from my friends so that I would be alone with them for company. Taking my seat in the train, I was molested again by two of these men standing under my window, staring evilly and smiling satanically at me until the train started on its return journey. When the train arrived at Hamilton Junction, after a few minutes another excursion train came into the station, I believe it was from Rotorua. Just after this last train had arrived, about eighteen youngish men, every one of them wearing a same coloured dark waterproof, filed past my window, and each of them stared especially at me; some of them returned, and for a second time "took me in" afresh by each giving me an evil gaze for three or four seconds. Was this a molest? They ignored my friends, not even looking at them. The men that molested me at the caves were between 25 and 35 years of age, and several of them had plenty of light brown hair and all were clean-shaven and respectable in appearance and were all strongly built and with an evil, don't care style.

So as to convey an idea of my unusual experiences (of daily occurrence) during my three years in Auckland, I will briefly relate some items, which are all done with design to disconcert, worry and intimidate.

One day, a week or two after the attempted "trap" was tried on me, I was walking along a main road at about my usual time when about twelve of the blackguards and toughs of Auckland passed me in a group, they were some of the most evil men of the town. All of them looked merciless and murderous in their gaze at me, and one clean-shaven man, about five feet three inches tall, and of about 50 years of age, said in brutal tones loudly to me: "You must not dodge us a second time or you'll know it." As they had approached I had a sense of menace. This fear was quite justified and there was now no doubt of their sinister motives.

One afternoon at the tram terminus at Mount Eden, a strongly built, respectably dressed man, with a light brown moustache and fair complexion, and of about 45 years of age and five feet nine inches in height, stood right in front of me, and gave me such an intense stare of mingled scorn, accusation and hatred that it really affected, disconcerted and discomposed me for some time.

It was a similar "stunt" the man at the railway station at Ilford, London, inflicted me with. I expect it was the "violence" or "attack" gleam that, coming unawares, affects one so.

A few days after my arrival in Auckland, as I was walking along at Three Kings, I passed near a baker's cart. The baker's carman stared evilly, maliciously at me and said loudly to a boy standing near (as this carman pointed at me), "He is mad."

As I was walking along by an Auckland park, two well-built, clean-shaven, dark-eyed and dark-browed, well dressed men, who might have been brothers, passed me, they were about five feet seven inches tall and about 40: both were wearing similar dark suits. As they approached they kept their somewhat sinister gaze on me. The next day I was taking my usual walk up the main road and passed one of these men staring designedly at me as he stood on the kerb; just as I had got by him he waved a white handkerchief as he looked up the road; I looked ahead as I proceeded on my way and observed his pal of yesterday who was about 150 yards up the road and looking in my direction and also waving a white handkerchief. When I proceeded by this fellow he stared threateningly at me.

This was done as a "monkey" trick to disconcert and intimidate me.

It was soon evident that some agency in Auckland was instrumental in putting all of those in the district that they could to be molesters and persecutors of me always; making my life there a continuous distracting trial.

I had not been in the city many months before most of the hangers about and hotel loafers, beggars and some hawkers and many suspicious-looking men and women were cognisant of me in some way. They made me aware of this by their acting. As they saw me approach they would nudge one another, or lean towards one another as they stolidly stared and got their companions to look at me too with jeering or intimidating gaze as they stood or passed me.

As I passed gangs of roadworkers and also as I passed building jobs very often, one of the men on the job would molest me by calling out some insult or looking at me with ferocious intimidation, or perhaps call out to his mates "That fellow is mad," or a similar sentence.

Some park gardeners and lavatory attendants that were very conversational and friendly to me became altered to anything but friendly and conversational.

When a tourist ship visited Auckland, and usually on all the arrivals of the passenger ships from Great Britain, Canada and Sydney, I observed that whilst these ships were in port I would be met somewhere or other on my perambulations by well-dressed, well-to-do looking men, sometimes wearing prominent "gold" watch chains and some wearing rings on their fingers. Generally their gaze at me was foxy and evil, but occasionally I would receive a confidential, engaging, friendly look, but usually the cast of these significant and stolid stares were accompanied by an evil cast of countenance (making it like the devil trying to look like an angel), but there was practically always cunning and devilry quite discernible.

Sometimes as I sat on the wharf at St. Heliers, a strong built, ruffianly man of about 40 would seek conversing with me, and whenever we talked together he would always ask domineeringly, "When are you going back to England?"

Once as I was walking alone in a very deserted part of the coast I saw him, and I noticed that directly he observed me his expression altered to a look of peculiar eagerness and staring "robbery and violence," and I could see that he was strongly trying to make up his mind to it too. Naturally, I hastened.

He was clean-shaven and always rather poorly dressed. He lived at St. Heliers and was about five feet nine inches tall. Often on my perambulations anywhere as I proceeded up a road I would catch sight of a man ahead of me or down a side street and as he looked at me he would behave designedly. He would open his coat (and also his waistcoat if wearing one), thus exposing a lot of white or light shirt to make himself conspicuous to me and make me look in his direction. When I looked, the man doing this trick would keep a rigid frightfully intimidating stare at me.

I was in the Auckland Zoo when a lot of Japanese sailors came off a visiting warship. Some of these men went to see the lions, and though no on else disturbed the lions when they looked at them, yet whenever these Japanese sailors looked at them the lions sprang enraged at the bars and growled loudly at them.

I met a working man on a beach at an Auckland district seaside resort. He told me he had brought his wife and family right from Auckland City in his motor car. He said that he was often out of work for a day or an afternoon, and he always then fetched his wife and family out right away just as they were, no "dressing up."

He thought his car a good investment as, though he could hardly afford it, yet it kept his wife and children in health, this time spent on the sunny sea beach.

An Auckland resident said that when he visited England and the Continent, a little time previously, he was driving his car in Paris when he was supplied with a Prefect's notification. He went to see this official, and was told that he had not obeyed the notice in a certain thoroughfare, and had exceeded the speed limit there notified. He would have to go to prison for two days. He said that he had to go on to Berlin in a day. He was told that he could not pay a fine for exceeding the limit as there was no payment allowable, as so many had disobeyed and paid formerly. He was also told to come back and do his two days in prison when he arrived back from Germany, so that after his Berlin trip he duly presented himself and did two days in prison in republican Paris. Equality and good liberty.

I went for a drive with an acquaintance, and then for a walk in some of Auckland's virgin "bush," and reckon it the most beautiful woods that I have ever been in anywhere.

Lady birds are very good for orchards, as are crab-apple trees, too.

I met a rich travelling American and he mentioned that the U.S.A. could not afford to give its citizens old age pensions. This was in answer to my remark that New Zealand does give old age pensions, and good ones, too.

A New Zealand doctor told me that on the average the men and women born in New Zealand and Australia are from a seventh to an eighth larger than those born in Great Britain and Ireland.

Another doctor said that life in large cities is to be deplored. He mentioned that those families that remain in London in about four generations become extinct. Were it not for the continual influx of country people, London would become depopulated. He also mentioned that a few miles out of London there are families that have been established for 500 and 600 years. He would like to take a million people from London and place them in New Zealand and Australia.

---

The tragic irony of my misfortunes was intensified by the fact that I journeyed to New Zealand to escape from my persecution, only to find in a distant land still further molestation by these men whose felonious skill was directed against me.

It would seem incredible that men should occupy the entire extent of their time and energy in tracking me down over those thousands of miles, only to pursue and molest me and to incite others to do the same. Human devilry could go no further. Indeed, I might have more easily endured physical pain at the hands of my enemies rather than the refined mental tortures they inflicted on me.

Those who have lived in harmony with their fellows may, in reading this record of misfortune, feel that the importance of such incidents is being overstressed. To them I would reply by saying that it is impossible for ordinary people to realise fully the hopelessness and frustration of a life such as mine when every crook hand is raised against one.

Gangs of criminals of the worst type, unsuccessful in their first attempts to despoil me, dogged me to my retreat in New Zealand, and there succeeded in making my life such a hell of misery by their tortures and psychological cruelties that I fled

This stunt was also practiced outside hotels, on beaches and in parks. Sometimes the molester who so behaved would be a quite well-dressed man.

One afternoon, as I approached a Victoria Avenue tram at Remuera, I noticed a man and woman observing me as though they expected me, and when I got on the tram they followed immediately after me and took the seats right in front of me with their backs to me. The pair of them gave me looks of contempt and evil and the woman held one of her hands upon the shoulder with the thumb pointing directly at me, the whole of the six or seven minutes of the journey.

From such a low and evil-looking creature this was a severe persecution. He was about 40 and was tall and fair, with light brown hair and was strongly built; he was clean-shaven; she was about 35, hefty and coarse and fair, also of vile expression.

Passing down Queen Street one afternoon, a short footpad looking man of about 30, really of the lowest and repulsive type and most awful to look at for his evil countenance, approached me, and as he did so directly he observed me he gave me a fixed broad smile of evil familiarity. He was dressed as a beggar.

As I stood on a refuge in the middle of one of the main roads waiting for the passing traffic to give me an opportunity to get to the pavement, one of the city bad men was standing about nine feet from me. He moved quickly and came right at the back of me right against me and had the appearance and gestures of intending pushing me into the traffic. I moved away quickly. He was frequently standing about on the watch and looking at me evilly. He was hefty, swarthy and about five feet seven tall and respectably dressed in dark suit and felt hat, clean-shaven and about 50.

One afternoon I was sitting in a waiting Corporation 'bus at Three Kings, when one of the blue-suited, light coloured felt hat crook molesters, who had been standing watching me, crossed over the road and went to the 'bus driver who was sitting at the wheel and got into a very subdued conversation with him; the whole of the ten minutes he was staring evilly at me and during this time the driver had turned round several times and looked straight at me; just as the driver was about to start the 'bus this crook, looking significantly and evilly at me, said loudly to the driver, "Let me know."

On another afternoon as I was walking out of New Lynn and proceeding towards Grey Lynn, I observed one of the blue-suited molesters approaching towards me and he also saw me just then. He at once stared at me very intensely and surprisedly, and then looked eagerly around and discerned a man up a side road, repairing the roadway. He hurried to this man and at once talked to him, meanwhile pointing at me and caused the roadman to look at me as I was proceeding on my way.

This sort of thing was done wherever these crook men foxed me to. They imparted some tale and these roadmen would, whenever they saw me again, stare at me and also call any of their companions' attention to me; and so the crooks caused these men to be an annoyance, and by so doing unintentionally serving the crooks.

During the several years (three) of my interminable unrelaxing molestation in Auckland, one of the gangs or sets of men working in the crooks' scheme was dressed entirely in black, and they included some women who were also dressed entirely in that sombre habit. This group of molesters was very persistent in their pursuit and some of them appeared perhaps more dangerous than the average miscellaneous molesters. They would wait for me and fox me about, very frequently following me on long excursions. There was about a dozen in this garb, which implied organisation behind the unattractive uniform, which included black hats and ties.

Perhaps I would be talking to a friend for some time and one of these (or perhaps two) would stand a little way off and stare at me stolidly all the while. Their faces and glances were all of an evil foreboding expression, showing unrelenting enmity towards me. They were generally in twos and were often loitering outside hotels or be watching standing on busy corners.

Living quite close to me was a giant of a man who was exceptionally broad and powerful. He was about 42. I fancy he had some connection with a motor repairing business. He had a motor car and he drove out every morning. He had brown hair and moustache and was always nicely dressed, and on Sundays he would be quite well dressed; often on that day he would ride out with several "flash" looking young women that lived with or near to him. He was friends with a lot of my constant molesters, whom he was frequently with. He undoubtedly was a leading gangster. Whenever we met he always looked at me menacingly and with a mouth made vicious (to frighten me).

## CHAPTER X

# New Zealand Notes

One enjoyable thing in Auckland is the large amount of sunlight and blue sky that obtains practically every week through the year, and another satisfying thing is that it is as green as Britain.

When on the finish of the journey we arrived safely at Wellington and the ship's engine had stopped, it gave me a wonderful peace, due to the absence of vibration and to the absence of "sound" of engines too. You could not at first account for this peace.

On Sundays the public houses are all closed (as in Wales) and I think this is a great blessing, especially to families.

In Auckland there is a rather small bird called *blighty*; the blighty flies very much like that much smaller bird, the humming bird of the tropics. The blighty hovers on the wing round the leaves, seeking insects.

There was no animals that are dangerous in New Zealand, neither are there any snakes.

Speaking to an Auckland bee-keeper, he said that before keeping bees he had had rheumatics badly for many years. When he started keeping bees he got stung by them a great deal, and this soon appeared to have cured his rheumatics. He had lost it entirely.

A cattleman told me that, providing you don't mind watching and being with your cattle and sheep days together, looking after them as soon as anything is the matter with them, you are bound to succeed. You must feel quite happy in their company.

once more, this time to the B.W.I. Nos. 1 and 2, whence I again set out to avoid them.

I left Auckland for being foxed and molested by all the underworld, and others acting with them, which made me acutely, painfully aware of the presence of persecutors and evil designers wherever I went, giving me continual anxiety.

Menaces threatened me in subtle ways until many things in Auckland became unbearable to me.

So I decided to leave the place, hoping to get where there would be none of this constant terror.

I bade farewell to my quarters. My landlord's daughter and son-in-law saw me off, and as we proceeded to the 11,000-ton ship trader which I trusted was to take me on my travels away from persecution, I felt full of hope.

I had settled on this boat a few days before.

I noticed, however, that as we approached near the wharf, there were three or four well-dressed and clean-shaven men observing me steadily.

My eyes had grown keen and were instantly aware of the colours of these men's suits. These were all very "smartly dressed" men, all wearing the same coloured suits and all the same pattern felt hats. This was not the last time that I was to see men in these coloured clothes.

It was not long before I began to recognise their features, their swaggering, blustering carriage, and the evil leering way in which they talked to each other, casting jeering glances in my direction. One of them in particular I recognised. He was tall and dark and his eyes were intolerable, he was indeed a nasty looking man and a bulge in his hip pocket betrayed his intentions and his profession. He had often been with my molesters in Auckland and in the district. While I am talking of these men it occurs to me that I should mention that when I was boarding the boat at Christobal (Colon) on the Panama Canal for the B.W.I. No. 1, a few weeks later on, several men wearing the exact same coloured suits and hats and clean-shaven, and employing the same foxy mannerisms of leering in a distancing way at me (they did not look so at anyone else), were standing about quite near the wharf of the ship that I was travelling by.

Hoping to leave this tormenting and distracting life behind me, I boarded the ship with my friends. After some time the farewells were said and the ship started its voyage. What a feeling of glorious freedom crept upon me as I saw the land recede into nothingness: a wonderful land of great beauty, but for me a land with many human vampires who live in the large spreading cities of busy humanity, where possibly no man is safe from the savage vermin of human foxes and jackals.

CHAPTER XI

# Colon

THE CLEAN, EVER-MOVING SALT SEA WAS ALL AROUND ME. MY soul was being filled with a great peace and I felt as if I was emerging from stifling darkness to a great light. I walked round the ship with joy in all my movements and in my heart an effervescent gaiety. At last I hoped that I had shaken the curs from my heels, and the dust of their molestations from my mind when, alas, turning a corner, I saw two of the crew working on the decks; they were two of those who in Auckland had with terrible persistency foxed me, and sought by their evil looks and presence to intimidate me always.

One gave me a cunning, knowing, foxy look of evil recognition. Though this persistent malicious pursuit was taking away from me my habitual ability to decide upon a course of action, and depriving me also of any power to carry it out, yet I made up my mind to ignore their presence. It gave me agony and fear through, at first, yet afterwards I forgot their being on the boat.

Hence, though the sea was rough, and the rain swept the decks and lashed my cabin window, the voyage passed quickly and happily. I made a point of being pleasant to everyone I met, and the pleasant company filled me with good spirits. Upsurges of *bonhomie* made the whole world of the ship seem good-natured. I was especially interested in the young men – fresh and clean limbed, who were undergoing training as the ships' officers. The efficient kindliness of the ships' officers in training these young men gave me exceeding gladness. Some of them were excellent fellows, who spoke to me with a smile on their lips, when I told them that from my observation of them, I was sure they would preserve their manliness against taint of any kind; that they would uphold honor and integrity, not only on their ships as part of their profession, but also in the wider atmosphere of human conduct; they never failed to greet my remarks with laughing eyes, or else, merrily they would retort, "You don't say so." One of them – he had clear blue eyes like the sea for which he was so ably fitted, went to the trouble of telling me that some time previously, they were in New York Harbour when the Prince of Wales was there, and the British Ladies kindly persuaded the Prince to honour them with a visit. In this way my simple, pleasant voyage to the Panama Canal, which lasted three weeks, passed with lightning rapidity. We did not sight land once.

I met an American gentleman on board during this pleasant time, and his interest in me flattered me. This gentleman told me about his life, and he was not loth to chat with me for quite a long time at a stretch. He mentioned the wonderful glaciers that one sees in a voyage along the Alaskan coast. They go grandly right into the sea precipitously. He told me of his life at Seattle during the Klondyke boom. He was a "mining engineer by profession and a student of human nature by inclination," as he put it. During the boom he had come into contact with all the strange types of humanity which drift to these mushroom settlements. The flotsam and jetsam of mankind were there, "Though I wouldn't give tuppence for your civilisation," he said. His smile was broad and tolerant and lit up his mature, understanding features.

"I'll tell you a story," he said, "though I'm not a lot of good at it."

"Go on," I replied, "I'm listening."

He had seen so much of life "in the raw" so to speak.

"Well, do you know Seattle?" he asked.

"No," I replied.

"Just don't, if you want a quiet, east life."

"That's a rough spot is Seattle, I remember one night speaking to an American judge in a saloon there. Judges in America aren't quite like yours in England, not so distant from people.

They know their place, of course, but they're more approachable, sometimes not in quite the right kind of way, if you see what I mean," and here he smiled.

"I think I do," I murmured.

"Hey, but I'm wandering. To come back to the yarn. An Irishman came into the bar, obviously with plenty of cash. A big, fine, rough fellow he was, with a voice like a prairie bull. Well, they all had a good many drinks together, and were in their half-way state, you know, ready to fall on one another's necks or quarrel. The Irishman got up to go, and the American said to him as he was departing, 'Well, I wish you all that's good in Ireland, and I hope they'll have the sense to make you a judge. More good husky fellows like you they want. Good mixers make good judges, look at me f'rinstance, eh!'"

"They'll never make me a judge in Ireland, surely," the big fellow retorted, "and they would not have you for a judge, either, in Dublin or Cork, or any other Irish place."

At this point the American gentleman sighed deeply.

"What's the matter," I asked.

"Don't ask me, it was too horrible for words," he said in a whisper.

"Why, what happened?" I asked.

The American gentleman looked at me. "You really want to know?" he asked.

"If you want to tell me, and if it will do any good to tell me," I said.

"Well, they both drew, but the judge was quicker'n the Irishman. He got him through the belly. Died in the Sanatorium. Of course, he got the chair – couldn't get anything else."

I stared at the monotonous sea. Suddenly I felt that I hated being compelled to voyage about. I wondered all kinds of things. These fits of abstraction sometimes enveloped me, in which whole worlds of horrors seemed to, and of course did, surround me. The Captain told me of a German submarine and of a dog, too. I can still remember the queer story he had to tell. "You see, sir," he was saying, "it was in the war. Well, as I was telling you, sir," he proceeded, "my ship charged a German submarine. I don't remember much about what happened after. Woke up in hospital. They told me my ship had gone to the bottom. Of course, nothing like peace and the rolling ocean for setting a man up."

"You see, it was like this. The dog had committed a nuisance as we passed Ushant, a misdemeanour as you say, and I hate a dirty deck. I gave the dog a kick. It squealed and ran away. I thought this was the end of the incident, naturally." He paused, dramatically, and I woke up sufficiently to murmur.

"How can I know?" I murmured that I was vastly entertained.

"I don't mind telling you, sir, it wasn't. Not by a long chalk. Do you know, this dog acted almost human. He used to follow me, dog me, as it were, but he was not in a hurry to revenge his indignity, until he had to leave the boat at Hong Kong, when he slyly bit me viciously on the leg." The Captain came near me, and continued – "Ran like merry fire down the gangway he did. I never saw the brute again."

I left the ship at Christobal and walked along the wharf to the motor-boat which was to take me from Christobal to Colon. My mind was running over the events of the voyage, when I noticed the peculiar stare of the negro owner of the launch. His black eyes were examining me all over in a repulsive way. When I returned his stare frankly, he averted his eyes and left me and went to the ship's gangway, and after a time he motioned to the two crook members of the crew who were at the top of the gangway to come down to him. This they did before my eyes, knowing that I saw them, and aware of my suspicions concerning their intentions. He had a long whispering with both of them, besides some general talking. The negro from my launch, speaking in a broad Irish brogue, spoke in a voice which carried with ease, "The old fool can't fool us much longer, I'll see to that." One of the members of the crew laughed like a hyena, and said, "That's right, the old fool can't get away from *us*." The last word "us," was heavily accented, and as he uttered it he pointed with his thumb over his shoulder at me, waiting in the launch, with my eyes watching their every movement. It was as if I was fascinated by snakes. When the launch owner returned he gave me an intolerably evil stare, presaging trouble and danger.

However, we arrived without accident or event at Colon. It was a Sunday. My state of mind was wide awake, being all the time on the *qui vive*.

The Ship's Agent had advised me to go to a certain hotel at Colon, and immediately I touched terra firma I got a carriage to take me to it. This was one of those places where it is packed promiscuously; where the scum of the earth congregate to consummate their lawless passions and designs. I drove through the town, noticing, without being particularly interested (for my state drove me in upon myself), that though it was the Sabbath, places of amusement and theatres were open and in full swing, and the whole place was full of people of all kinds of nationalities – all shades of skin, white, black, yellow and the in-between colours of the mulattoes and other half-castes. The strange atmosphere of wanton gaiety oppressed me. After the negro hotel clerk – whom I hardly noticed, had given me a room near to his office, and I had eaten a good kind of meal, I went to bed. I closed my eyes and waited for the flood of sleep to drown me in its healthful waves, when loud noises began in the corridor and on the stone stairs outside my room. I listened for them to stop, but for hours there was tramping up and down stairs and sleep was obviously impossible. I began to wonder about the nature of the hotel at which I was, for a number of people seemed to be floating in and out at all hours of the night. The trampings certainly destroyed my sleeping possibility. At about 2 A.M. – the luminous dial of my watch showed me the time – the noises seem to get more spasmodic, less continuous, and indeed seemed as if they were going to die away altogether. I was just sinking into a doze the relief silence gave to me, when I fancied I could hear someone snoring quite near to me; an extraordinary experience. Its proximity was puzzling. Then I became certain of its nature. It definitely was a *man* – or a woman, who knows, snoring in a most vicious and determined way. He was in the next bedroom to mine. The snoring had this peculiar, almost aggressive, quality, which made it obvious that the performer was not sleeping. I held my breath, and a strange thing happened each time. The snoring stopped. Then I breathed through my nose (which was only just audible to myself). When I breathed so the snoring recommenced. We played this game for, it seemed like, hours, until I thought I was snoring myself when I breathed through my nose. One peculiar problem presented itself to me; insinuated itself into all other thoughts which occurred this awful night through, and that was, how did he hear me breathing through my nose, for it was as much as I could do to hear it myself. As a result of this peculiar way of molesting me, I could only think that he was a crook bent on reducing my alertness or destroying my combativeness. In addition, it struck me that he used some listening apparatus. Of course, my molester was awake all night, meticulously listening to discover when I opened my mouth to breathe inaudibly.

The same experience, I am sad to relate, occurred again, a fortnight later, when for two nights running I was molested (and who knows, perhaps by the same individual?), by a man in the next bedroom to mine who snored loudly and vibrantly whilst I breathed through my nose – stopping with alarming rapidity when he could not hear my breathing (when I breathed through my mouth). Anyone who has not had this experience cannot imagine the debilitated state of nerves which it produces. All I know is that I have been through hell, and that all the fantastic horrors of Dante or Virgil are nothing to this more subtle and insidious experience.

For, speaking to a cashier in the bank next morning concerning the nature of the hotels in this place, I was accosted rudely by a completely unknown man, who, after eavesdropping in a most blatant way, he looked straight at me and said "You stay in the hotel you are in at present or…" He broke off and laughed evilly.

"Or what?" I asked, not to appear frightened by his coarseness.

"Or it will be a sight worse for you," he returned. The whole incident suggested all kinds of suspicions to my mind. My molester was one of a gang. I went to another hotel and stayed there for some days, during which time I rested. These days were spent in comparative quietude. When I had returned to my former hotel to collect my luggage a negress was in the office, a particularly evil, low type of woman. I asked for my bill and told her that I was leaving. She shook her head and replied, "No sar, you just can't." She then called out to someone in a raucous voice that was quite unlike any other woman's voice I had heard; "*He* wants to go," she bawled.

A man's voice called her away. When she returned she said: "Yes, sar, you can just go now."

She gave me my bill which I paid, and I left, under her mocking and malevolent gaze.

The new hotel was quite pleasant, and I was able to escape from the torments of actuality to some extent – for short periods. The food and accommodation were excellent and at night a Spanish orchestra generated, with its splendid harmony, a romantic atmosphere of make-believe, which suited my condition. It was like heaven compared with the horror of the other hotel. The whole atmosphere was different. Some U.S.A. officers and ladies dining in my hotel, added to the pleasant appearance of the place, and perhaps as Nietzche says: "The happiness of existence is only possible as the happiness derived from appearance." Talking of appearances, it struck me very forcibly, that the American ladies in Panama looked very white – fragile and bloodless almost – and not at all robust, whereas the Spanish women walked with ease and vigour and grace, and were always alive with energy.

This little dream world of mine was soon to be shattered, for (alas!), when I was out visiting several officers in Colon, I noticed an evil faced mulatto peering through the windows. I had seen this mulatto before on several occasions, keeping step with me on the other side of the street, stopping when I stopped, and proceeding when I proceeded. He was of respectable appearance, about five feet eight inches in height, about 52 years old and exceedingly well-built.

From this time on my entire organisation was in a state of strain, for I was foxed wherever I went, by respectably dressed coloured men, and one day, finding that I was never off my guard and never went to unfrequented spots, my molesters tried a novel scheme.

One afternoon a really pretty negress, about twenty years old, walked in front of me, with all her graces and charms evident. This made me immediately suspicious. In addition she kept looking back at me and half-smiling, nodding her head. She was a decoy of theirs.

The persistency of my molesters was extraordinary, for two nicely dressed negroes kept continual watch, day after day, standing in the street outside my hotel. My intuitions concerning my pursuers had by this time made me an excellent judge of some kinds of men, and these negroes were professional crooks. They had even – consciously or unconsciously I do not know – the smart, alert, "gimlet" look of some of the London crooks which it had been my misfortune to have had as molesters.

In the hotel I was molested by a new arrival – a vicious, scoundrelly-looking white man – tall, dark, and cadaverous features, with clean-shaven, brown face. It was his by no means pleasant habit to mutter as he passed me, and though I was unable to pick out the actual words he used, the tenour and import of them could easily be imagined. They were between a snarl and a sneer, with a dash of something more aggressively threatening thrown in.

Despite these molestations, however, I used to amuse myself for a short time – in watching the great number of U.S.A. airplanes which patrol this part of the country; conquest of man over the elements; the use man has made of his environment, instead of allowing his environment to make use of him, the grace, beauty and power of these bird-like machines. I used also to allow my eyes to rest on the details of the many shops kept by coloured people; to ease the strain of perpetually listening to the attackers by paying attention to the loud ringing bells of the Catholic

Church – bells for worship and bells for schools. The industry of the Spaniards also took my eye and the vigour with which they overcome the scorching heat, did not tally with stories I had heard of the laziness of the Spaniard – the alleged "manana" temperament of the Spanish race. I was even aware of the climatic conditions of the country. I distinctly remember that it rained once or twice during my visit and that it made such a noise in its downpour that I was filled with child-like surprise and wonder. In truth one must avoid in a genuine narrative, at all cost, exaggeration, and this narrative is as true as I am writing this with pen in my hand.

I took a walk through the streets of Colon on the next morning.

At one shop I paused to inspect some gaudy native handiwork in a shop window. As I had done so I just looked round, when, to my despair, I saw two coloured seamen standing on either side of me. There was no mistaking them, even without the exulting, fierce grins they bestowed on me. One of them fingered his belt and I saw the dark hilt of a jack knife.

He dare not use it in the main street of Colon, with a policeman not ten yards away. He did not need to, for the poisoned dagger of molest, already deep in my heart, had been given another vicious turn.

These two coloured men, of course acting under orders, followed me back to my hotel, using abusive language just loud enough for me to hear. A complaint to a police officer would have meant indignant denials, and a dismissal of the charge on the grounds that the words of two men were better than the unsupported testimony of one.

A Spaniard had a conversation with me, and in the course of it he remarked that he hoped that the U.S.A. would have a war with the British. I told him I did not think this would happen. He said perhaps they would not as they were both thieves. I said to him that the Latin races had quite their share of the earth's surface (just as the Slavonic races have), so what had he to complain of.

Perhaps the most pleasant recollection that I retain of Colon is that I was extremely delighted with some white or light-coloured pineapple. It seemed larger and far superior to other kinds. A candid New York citizen complained that the British had had help in the Great War from even little New Zealand, where he had some interests. He thought this help bad business. He little appreciated the Empire's dire need, neither did he think where America would have stood if we had lost! Since the War I have been informed from German sources that the U.S.A. would have been conquered shortly after Britain's collapse, and this "item" was looked upon as most essential to Germany's overlordship.

Some days later I went by boat to what I call B.W.I. No. 1. It was a speedy American steamship, worked almost entirely by negroes. One negro was obnoxious. I knew from his peculiar ways of foxing me that he belonged to the underworld and was in the service of the crooks. He was a crook, and from his desperate, careless nature, a dangerous one. He used to stand so that I could not help seeing him, his eyes fixed on my face, and when I met his violent horrifying orbs he would quickly avert them. So would we play, I, like a fascinated rabbit, and he like an overfed snake, playing with me before he destroyed me. Alternatively would he and I gaze at each other; he malevolently, and I with enquiry in my eyes. My temples seemed bound in cold steed bands getting ever smaller and tighter on my skull.

Occasionally he would vary this criminal pastime by employing one of his associates to make up a triangle. They would signal to each other with ocular and bodily movements and gestures of "molestation," and would flash similar significations to me.

I could perceive that the Americans, gentlemen and ladies, were quite as reserved and dignified as the English, as they danced to the music of an electric gramophone on the deck of the ship. I was thus able to collect my thoughts to disabuse my mind of the myth of the blatancy and vulgarity of some Americans. These Americans were also "stand-offish" with one another in quite a British way. Alienists are fond of saying that the first sign of mental disintegration is fierce and fond introspection on the part of the potential lunatic, while I (praise be!) was still able to look out upon the world and find it interesting and sometimes very beautiful, and, "any justification of the world," some wise man once said, "can only be an æsthetic one." It is the fact that men make themselves and the whole world so ugly, so loathsome, that sickens me.

CHAPTER XII

# British West Indies No. 1

THE NATURAL BEAUTY OF THE SKY, ON THE VOYAGE ON THE blue sea, to B.W.I. No. 1, deserves mention. It was the most fairy-like scene – the morning sun shining upon a mass, a vast expanse, of clouds – resplendent in the magnificence of a whole spectrum of colours. It was a most transcending experience. Never in my life have I come so near to what is called "inspiration." As the sun blazed stronger I saw these clouds slowly but surely disperse and melt into the infinite glory of a deep blue sky, and a rugged mass of mountains was uncovered, towering high in the blue. It was quite a surprise to me, was this unveiling of the mountains.

Peculiarly striking was the atmosphere generated by the prevalence of negroes. I proceeded to an hotel recommended by a negro, drove in a car driven by a negro, and was shown into my room by a mulatto. Everywhere there were examples of this African race, many of them evil and vicious from long and evil contact with the white crooks. The negroid atmosphere was preserved also by the music, which I heard as I sat in my room. It came from somewhere near me – the haunting melodies of the negroes, the old plantation melodies, simple emotionally, primitive rhythmically, and rich in lovely low swinging sounds. In the plantation melodies the mystical elements predominated over the purely erotic. I was very thankful for this old music, for I felt utterly alone and deserted. In the same way I welcomed the presence of a kindly gentleman who sat at my table. We soon became friendly. He was one of those that bear you no ill-will.

We chatted together and amongst other tales he told me the following interesting story.

"I don't know as how I like men much. I like bears well, I think," he said.

"Bears?" I queried.

"Yeah," he replied. "I've often slept all night in the Canadian woods – I come from up there you know. And the bears have come sniffing round me. Nothing more than that. Smell me and go away."

"What! without hurting you" I asked.

"Sure," he said.

"In that case bears certainly seem better than many men it has been my misfortune to come across."

I liked this man very much and the story gave me a considerable amount about which to ruminate upon. I grew fond of this Canadian gentleman who preferred wild beasts to men. It was a great pity for me that he had to leave for his Canadian home some weeks later, for he was one of the most charming men it has been my good fortune to meet. He was an accomplished musician, and though of Norwegian descent, yet he was very British in his outlook and allegiances. By the way, he was the violinist that played so charmingly.

It would appear that there were hardly any limits to the surprises my wandering life was to give me. For instance, I had taken the precaution of not giving my name at my hotel, but I had not been staying there for more than a day when the landlady called me by a name which, except for the initial letter, was identical with mine. Now as my portmanteaux were all securely fastened and closed, and were without name labels – this knowledge of my name could have been no accident. Coincidences of this nature simply do not happen. I recalled the knowing glances of the hotel proprietor and family. There would be no doubt that they knew not only my name but also whom I was and why I was moving about from place to place. Someone of course had been there to track me in my wandering and to give my hotel landlord the knowledge of all my credentials soon after my arrival at this hotel.

I got my negro hotel waiter to show me what there was to be seen in the town. As we proceeded along the sidewalks numerous glances were shot at us, and negroes stopped and stared straight at us. Indeed, one of these, who was apparently a friend of my waiter, stopped him and engaged him in conversation. This "friend" seemed to be a nice man to me at first, but after some whispered conversation with the waiter his face seemed to become inflamed, as it were, with cunning and thief-like viciousness; his open, simple countenance became overcast with a look of wily trickery. As soon as we arrived at the Botanical Gardens my waiter left me with a hurried excuse and moved about the gardens talking to the negro workers. With these he had a hurried, whispered conversation, during which glances full of vague threat were directed at me. I continued my inspection of the gardens with considerable curiosity, and I examined the tropical plants, the humming birds, the cacao bush, the sugar cane and a great variety of tall palm trees and beautiful flowering plants of many kinds, and heard some sweet singing birds.

An incident later in the day only served to excite my fears still more. I observed two white men, dressed immaculately in dead white from heel to helmet. They were both clean-shaven, and their countenances could be read with ease by anyone accustomed as I was, to being forced to seeing the facial features of men. They stared fixedly at me though they never moved from one spot. They simply swivelled their heads and bodies in my direction. In addition, the negro workers went to the trouble of pointing me out to fresh arrivals, without attempting to hide their actions. I was becoming more and more convinced that these molesters, white and black, were all probably members of the underworld. They gazed at me so long and so closely that I thought they had been sent to examine me thoroughly. Since this time I have had visible and vocal proof of the criminal natures of these two white men. I do not exaggerate my fears or speak without sufficient proof. Indeed to complete all these manifestations of molestation and insult, a tall, lithe, ruffianly mulatto followed me from the gardens. He stopped when I swung on my heel to gaze at him. He stood quite still and gave me what was meant to be an intimidating stare. When I proceeded on my way, he followed me through the coloured crowds, which were in the street. Only his eyes and mouth would betray his evil intentions. He was not difficult to recognise, for he had a slight moustache, discoloured with alcohol and was poorly dressed. Things were not simple, they were most obviously indirect. The subtle machinations of this gang of crooks could not have been combatted by the whole police methods of this fairly primitive and lawless part of the world. In addition, I could not lay my finger on anything definite. The methods of my pursuers were not illegal – they were worse – they were demoralising.

When I revisited the Botanical Gardens the workers – mostly negroes – always pointed me out to any of their "friends" who "happened" to be visiting the gardens. Occasionally indeed, one of them would say, when I was within earshot, "I know that man all right."

I made mental notes of faces and dresses and physical features wherever I went, and those who I had seen "introduced" always had their eyes on me, in the gardens or elsewhere ever afterwards. Again, I was walking down a quiet road a few days after, when I saw two white figures approaching me; they were not difficult to recognise, even at a distance. They were the two men I had seen in the Botanical Gardens. Both stopped when they came level with me, and one said to the other in a high pitched voice: –

"He's dopy, you know."

"Quite," replied the other.

They passed on with their swaggering gait. There was to be no solace. An old game was to be played again. One that, until experienced, can hardly be imagined. It was the old "snoring game." For two nights a visitor to the hotel slept in the bedroom next to mine and when I breathed nasally, however noiseless and softly, he would break into a raucous snoring (to describe it properly). When I breathed through my mouth the night was filled with silence. It was quite apparent that he could not have slept all night – for two nights in succession. Of course, this might have been the same man who was so adept at this game at the Colon Hotel. "How did he hear me," I asked myself over and over again, "Had he an apparatus or what?" No human ear is sensitive enough to hear through a brick well and the intervening space between the two beds. He would also stop snoring when I gave the least movement, and some delicate instrument was surely essential for the detection of this.

There seemed to be two ideas – in the heads of those who so intently and ingeniously pursued me. Their actions and minds were those of the insect, for in all kinds of cunning and assiduous fashions they demonstrated these two ideas to me, to wit, that I was mad, and that I was not wanted. For instance, one day, about a week after my arrival at B.W.I. No. 1 two mulatto ladies came into the tram in which I was travelling from one part of the town to another. The Conductor of the tram – a mulatto – came up to us. He said to the two mulatto girls in a harsh sneering voice, "He's mad."

"Batty, Buddy?" queried one of the girls.

"Sure, mad."

"Mad? Who is, buddy? Us?" asked one with a look of horror on her brown face.

"No, not you."

"Who then? persisted the young mulatto. By this time the whole tram was in a state of excited curiosity. I was burning all over with the shame and indignity of it all. The tram conductor shrugged his shoulders and walked away whistling a stupid mob-melody of the day. All this the passengers seemed to consider a huge joke for the tram was soon filled with titters and rough laughter. I could not stand it longer and amidst the jibes and jeers of everyone I got up and walked out of the tram at the next stop – though this was far from my destination. Bitter, burning thoughts rushed through my head as I stood on the thronged sidewalk. I had only been here a week, I mused, and already even a tram conductor was obeying the dictates of the crooks, who had been busy as insects publishing descriptions of my appearance to all, and making it their nasty business to point me out wherever I ventured into the streets.

This, then, was one of their ideas. The other – that of making it plain to me that I was an undesirable, also exercised their crooked minds and I experienced, many times, this form of molestation.

I very soon found that all the riff raff of the place molested me and were in the crooks' service, and knew that I was their victim.

Near my hotel a gang of negroes were repairing the roadway. They were thus engaged for about a fortnight, during the whole of which time a negro of the gang looked at me malevolently every time I had occasion to pass by him. He would stare at me and, speaking out of the corners of his mouth in a way that betokened long practice and misspent youth, he would say to his friends, in a loud voice: –

"Say, and when is he going back to England, where he belongs?"

And another would chip in, in a kind of sing-song, saying: – "Sure, why does not that man – we all is acquainted with – go back to England?"

To which the negro would reply, spitting in his leg-of-mutton hands, "Why, you's right. It beats me. Say, do I want to be alone? Do I? I bet I do."

Again, one would have thought that in the House of God the garments of molestation would melt away; that the holy sanctity of the church would be proof against even the brazen action of my "foxers." But not so. I made a point of going to church each Sunday – and to the same church. After my first visit there was a little knot of smartly dressed young men in nice suits and English straw hats who stood outside the church after the service, generally right in my path when I emerged from the church. As I approached them they would all, as if the whole thing had been carefully arranged and rehearsed, start laughing, jeering at me, looking contemptuously and threateningly at me. I did not deviate from my path. I walked straight towards them, and when I came near to them one of them would say, "We'll kill him if he stops here."

"Of course," "Quite," "Naturally," the others would say in a matter-of-fact determined kind of way, calculated to demoralise me. These men belonged to a particularly bad set as I afterwards discovered. They could always be detected because of the coloured bands, of a certain pattern, which they all wore around their straw hats – a pattern identical with that worn by a gang or two in the town and by some at B.W.I. No. 2.

They lost little opportunity of demonstrating my undesirability to my self, though why they wanted me to go from this place I could not then understand. Perhaps, of course, they did not desire this, that is, for me to understand the reason. Maybe the whole idea was simply to destroy any confidence I had in myself and put me to confusion. If this was their intention they certainly went about it in the right way. For, once – it was about 3 A.M. – I heard a man's voice come suddenly out of the darkness – a well-known voice – its owner was attached to the hotel, related somehow or other to the proprietor. The man was apparently talking to himself in a loud voice – practising "free association" at the top of his voice. He was saying, in his penetrating way: "He's Mr. —— from London. He's Mr. —— from London. I know he is. I'm sure he is."

Here he would pause. Then with awful suddenness he would break out again: "He thinks we don't know, the poor wit. Why does he think we don't know?"

If all this had not the air of being deliberately planned I might have thought this man was a madman, but he was only mad in the sense that all this molestation was the maddest thing, apparently, that a human being could do – but it was methodical and it was done with such fiendish persistency for a criminal purpose. This man was in the room directly beneath mine. Perhaps, again, with some automatic listening apparatus he had heard me wake up in the night, after having somehow or other, awakened me. In this way he could practise his long silences and his sudden shoutings. I don't know which were the worse. The silences kept me restlessly awake often in nerve-straining expectancy, and the shoutings were like hammer-blows on my tired brain.

At my table at breakfast there was a white man – whom I immediately recognised from his murderous look, his hard, set, cruel mouth, his dark straight eyebrows and dark eyes. He was wearing a white suit, and a white helmet was resting on a chair at our table. He was, without a doubt, the evil man in the Colon Hotel. Luckily my breakfast was not entirely spoiled for me, for an American with whom I had struck up an amiable acquaintance soon joined me.

"Men like him," I said, alluding to the dark man, "make men like me think that men like Rousseau weren't so far wrong."

"Who's that guy and what did he say?" inquired my companion.

"All that comes from the hand of God is good. And all that comes from the hand of man is bad," I murmured.

"Oh, snap out of that. Let's walk."

And walk we did. Our steps led us to the Recreation Ground, where we sat down to enjoy a conversation. We had not long settled ourselves comfortably when a mulatto woman – young and of striking figure and gait – walked slowly and deliberately up to us. She looked at me and out of the corner of her eyes – not at all unlike some women I had seen on one of my rare visits to a film-show. She sat down next to me, and as naturally as the violet is modest and beautiful, this woman was bold and inviting, and she is no "rara avis." She started talking mostly about the weather and the colour of hair and eyes, the grace of walking women. Soon she launched herself out upon self-confession.

"What are you," she said, "I'm a Roman Catholic. I don't mind telling you. Why? Well why not? I meet lots of swell guys from being a Roman Catholic. I'm no ordinary girl. I've been all over the world. I can say what I like to two broadminded gentlemen like yourselves. Can't I? or can't I? I haven't got anyone to bury, you see. Nor do I believe in having anyone that way. Marriage, I mean."

"As she was babbling on like the proverbial brook in this manner, almost as if she had been would up – she was molesting me in a most insulting manner, that is, she was looking at me vilely and slyly. However, she and her like are not at all difficult to understand ordinarily, but she was now working under crooks' orders. I noticed also that there was a man sitting on a seat quite close to us, who frequently gave this woman occasional sly signs. He had the coloured hat band of the same pattern as that worn by other crooks mentioned before. I had had about enough of this woman and I hastily excused myself and dragged my American friend – who was very much amused with everything – away with me.

A few days later, my American friend and myself visited the same place again. We had not been seated any length of time before two well-built mulatto girls, or "ladies," as they are sometimes called – though why I do not know – approached us and sat down right opposite us. With their dark eyes – full of deep tropical lights – they stared at us in a fashion, calculated by what such a procedure revealed and suggested, to arouse admiration in a man. Needless to say both my American friend and I felt nothing more than slight amusement and pity. Looking away from the mulatto girls I discovered two men – mulattoes – nicely dressed, observing us slyly through some bushes. They wore the same patterned hat-band that I have mentioned before. I was becoming almost literally sick, and I left hurriedly with my American friend. We walked quickly along the streets until my eye caught sight of a large old church. My suggestions that we should enter was enthusiastically agreed to by my American friend. The anticipated coolness of the interior of the church had no difficulty in seducing us from the tawdry heat of the crowded and miscellaneous street. I had never been in this church before, and I wanted to see old monuments; but the two or three negresses who were sweeping the floor seemed to recognise me immediately. As I passed near to them they looked evilly at me. One of them murmured an indecency, and another replied "Ah don't like him neither." It was a niece of pure effrontery. I left the church, followed by my friend. He urged me not to allow my imagination to get inflamed unnecessarily.

They were only too devastatingly real to me for me to be able to ignore. Several times whilst I was in London women had been put on to decoy me and some remarkably deceiving ones at that, that is, apparently genuine people, and the same thing had been tried many times by the New Zealand crooks.

They (the crooks) seek to put upon you the character of sexual abnormality and sexual perversion. This insinuation was always being reiterated upon me by my molesters, whites and coloured and negroes whilst I was in the B.W.I. Nos. 1 and 2. It is the means employed by the crooks to get their intended victim helpless, to get the victim in disfavour with the authorities, whose business it is to preserve the cleanliness of public morality. Again, these crooks, by suggesting these things to me hoped to get me either in their direct toils or perhaps into prison, or hospital, or even the madhouse, and then somehow to fulfill their evil designs on my property. How they intended to rob me in this way I do not know, but that they so intended they lost no opportunity in informing me in one way or another. This suggestion or moral undesirability is brought out with exceeding clearness in the following incident – which will also show how thoroughly the crooks prepare all the details of their scheme and the trouble they take to perfect them in action.

One night about 1 A.M. I awoke, started into hurried life by a piercing scream, which rent the night air. This was repeated three or four times. I was struck dumb with horror. Somewhere outside in the street an act too horrible to contemplate, I felt, was being perpetrated. Loud voices came to me through the night – drunken, raucous voices – intimidatory voices – the voices of men and women become beasts. I struggled to my window and peeped out. To describe what I saw would be unprintable – to retell what I heard would be unbearable – even in retrospect the whole episode seems incredible. I can only give the barest outline of the scene. There were about 50 people around a cart, in which an almost naked, middle-aged white man was standing, amid the jeers and raucous laughter of the villainous mob. The language – that part which I could understand – was of the foulest, and the gestures and actions of the negroes and negresses were the lowest species of unbridled evil imaginable. Where were the authorities? What were they doing? They were nowhere to be seen. Not a single policeman anywhere near. As they came under my window a voice – like the scream of a steam-saw – screeched out – the voice of a huge negro: "There's another of the B——s. There he is, another sodding Englishman up there. Don't think you can escape us, you white-faced Scandinavian Count!"

What he meant by the last phrase I can only conjecture, for these people have a special jargon of their own, in which the filthiest and lowest forms of abuse are capable of utterance. For awfulness of linguistic obscenity and molestation I have never met its equal anywhere. This incident left a vivid mark on my mind, and I lay awake thinking of what they had done and would do to this victim of the crooks, and also what they would do to me, as one of their victims, if they ever had the chance.

We decided to travel to what I shall call B.W.I. No. 2. We told no-one of our plans, but, as had happened before, and was to happen again, our intentions and movements seemed to be known. The day of our departure, we took the trouble to avoid ordering a private conveyance, and decided to travel to the ship by tram. As we were waiting, with a large number of other people, for the tram to arrive, a vile-looking, angular negro of immense height came and stood on the opposite side of the road. He stared at me. I stared back. He shifted his gaze slowly to a negro who was standing near me. Deliberately he shaped his wide, ugly mouth and thick lips as if he was saying "Mad," and he pointed at me so that numbers of people gazed at me to "enjoy" this piece of public buffoonery – nay, worse, public affrontry of the most blatant order. This was a definite attempt to inculcate in me an inferiority complex – to use the jargon of modern pseudo-scientists – the leading crooks make the mind their great study. It was indeed a trying and disconcerting piece of open molestation. Of course this helps to get their victim an easy prey and more and more nearer into their prepared snares; he becoming nerveless and with no combativeness – helpless.

However, we boarded tram and boat and started our voyage to B.W.I. No. 2.

My American friend, who was one of the gentlest men it has been my pleasure to know, leaning over the rail of the boat, was deeply shocked by the way negro women were allowed to take heavy burdens of coal on to the ship. He said that it was a disgrace to the British Empire – which he always held in the highest esteem.

I soon became aware of a specimen of this negro race watching me. He was a member of the ship's orchestra, and his eyes followed me from my first day on board. He always gave me evil glares, quite impossible either to ignore or to misinterpret. If a man can look robbery and murder – and it is my sad experience that he can – this man certainly achieved such a look. But I had become so accustomed to this kind of thing that familiarity had bred the proverbial indifference, and though I was not aware of it at the time, this man was undoubtedly in league with the underworld crook organisation which had made it its business to harry me from pillar to post, using for this purpose its deep, universal, subterranean ramifications. This negro was, as it were, "speaking" for the "bosses" of the organisation. His was a "voice" properly interpreted, crying out their unscrupulous, criminal object of pursuing to the death, for robbery.

But it was not only the negro who was the slave and instrument of the master minds behind the organisation, for one of the passengers on the boat was a white man – dressed in immaculate whiteness from heel to helmet, and I discovered, when I got to B.W.I. No. 2, that he was a Government servant there. It was a sad thought that even such an honorable profession was not free from the underworld influence, for he was one of those who took a leading part in B.W.I. No. 2 on all possible occasions, with the molesters who made me their special object of persecution.

CHAPTER XIII

# British West Indies No. 2

If I imagined that I should be free – at least for some time – from my trials and tribulations, I was mistaken. It was only an hour after landing at B.W.I. No. 2, when I was passing an hotel frequented by U.S.A. tourists, a negro carriage-driver called out loudly: "He's all alone from England." Surely, I thought, he could not mean me, for I knew no-one. But there could be no mistake, for he was pointing his whip at me in an unmistakable fashion, and six or seven other carriage-drivers then started staring at me.

Maybe, I thought, this was an accident, surely it could mean nothing. In so short a time they could not have set the machinery of "molestation" in motion. This thought, however, was soon to be abolished completely from my mind, as the following incident will show.

It was about half-an-hour after my first experience at B.W.I. No. 2, when I was walking along the sea-front in the vicinity of the "fashionable" shopping quarter, that my next exploit was to occur.

Two clean-shaven, smart-looking white men, both tall and about 60 years old, passed me. They deliberately stopped and stared at me and one of them said: "We shall know him by his beak, what!"

"Quite," said the other, looking me up and down and allowing his gaze to rest momentarily and insultingly upon obvious parts of my anatomy.

"Quite what?" asked the other in a jocular fashion.

"Oh, just, quite," replied the other.

These two were evidently leading gangsters, though their suits were sun-faded – they might have been either black or brown originally.

My American friend and myself were struck at the beauty of B.W.I. No. 2 when we arrived. We went to get our dinner at a restaurant frequented by white people. As we were dining two well-dressed white men walked in my direction. Although there was plenty of room for them to pass, both of these men bumped into my back just as I was eating and nearly made me choke. Instead of apologising, they both glared angrily at me.

One of them said: "You damned sod. Do you want all the —— dining room?"

I protested, but the other one said to me grimly: "You've got mighty bad manners for an Englishman (?). We can handle that though, and you too."

With this bluster they walked to another table, after their studied molest. I was simply a target for all persecuting crooks. It was a continuous campaign of studied molesting everywhere and wherever I was. It was becoming increasingly vile.

An incident that made me think there was something sinister and peculiar in the underground working ways of the crooks was –

My American friend and myself were walking on the sea front on the morning of the third day in this place when two mulatto nurse girls or maids passed us, both of them wheeling perambulators.

One of these pointed to me and said to her companion quietly, but I just caught the words: "That is the one we must all try to get a hold of. He's wanted."

The very next day my American friend and myself took a two mile walk out of the town to a much frequented beach. We had turned about and were just proceeding to walk back home when, turning a corner, we passed about a dozen men and women, all of the negro race. One of the women shouted, "He's all alone from England." All these people stared at me very markedly and observantly.

Our apartments were comfortable and quite near the sea, about ten minutes' walk from the principal part of the town. It was far better to be a little off the beaten track than to be in the middle of things. For there seemed to me to be less chance of wholesale molestation where we were, than if we were plunged in *medias res*, so to speak. Alas for all my plans! They were doomed to fall about me like those of the "mice and men" of the Scots poet. The second day brought its usual train of terrors. Negroes wearing the, to me, well-known pattern hat-bands, were among the motley crowd. Wherever we went these men were to be found there too – smartly dressed most of them. I was recognised on more than one occasion and the customary glances and gestures were brought into operation. And what "foxy" eyes they had! I remember this second day for those eyes. I saw them peer at me, while I was listening to the band in the park and their looks mingling with sweet music filled me with a strange nausea.

The next experience was not with negroes, but with white men, the worst types of whom seem to stick like dirty glue to all parts of the world. My American friend and I were sitting in a large hotel, idly watching the movements of the well-dressed crowd, musing upon the character of individuals and groups, studying the features and dresses of the male and female – who visited the place – most of them travelling from U.S.A. We were seated quite near a group of white men – all quite young and spotlessly clad in tropical white. They were playing "poker" and drinking "whisky." And when they aren't hardening their features with poker, or destroying the linings of their stomachs with whisky, they pursue other vicious and criminal ends.

All these men wore the – by this time – well-known hat-bands on their English boater hats. In this, as in other characteristics, they were in no way distinct from the negroes who aided and abetted their crooked schemes. As we rose to walk in the night air, they all jerked their heads, almost like one man, in my direction, and one of them said: "See him, he's mad. Bats in the jolly old belfry."

"Sh," another said, with his fingers to his lips, with mock

seriousness and caution, "Sh, not so loud, you'll wake the baby and he'll hear you."

To which another added in an ironical tone: "And after all, boys, he's wearing the old school tie, too. It isn't done, you know."

This, and a good deal of equally fatuous conversation of the same nature, was merely veiled molestation, and these *soi-disant* white men all seemed as if they did not care in the least what they said or did; their features seemed to approximate to a type, and not a good type either. They looked, in addition to being vicious and criminal in a large desperate way, petty card-sharpers and "sharks" of the meanest variety.

No type of man, however, seemed to be untouched by the ramifications of the underworld in this part of the world – that is, if we can speak of "types" of men. But I refer generally to the occupations of men when I speak of their type. For instance, one would naturally not expect the Pope of Rome, or the Archbishop of Canterbury, or the Chief of the Salvation Army, or a Professor of Moral Philosophy to be in active co-operation with the crooks and robbers of society. This account, however, is not concerned with a diatribe against the ecclesiastical powers that be, though I am bound to recount a particularly unsettling experience I had with a man whose position would not induce one to expect the kind of actions in which he indulged.

Some days after our arrival at B.W.I. No. 2, my friend and I were lazily meandering along a principal road, when my eye caught a sign in the grocer's shop, "Postage stamps sold here." I entered the shop to purchase some. The grocer was a negro, with a soulful, brimming face that did not deceive me. His eyes denied the piety of his other facial features. He looked at me with orbs that emanated savageness – cannibal optics, eager and murderous. Nothing better could be said of them, and they looked subtleties far worse. He said to me, in a loud, sonorous voice, filled with cupidity and envy: "You are English, aren't you? You've got plenty of money, haven't you? I wish I had some. Real money I could see...and feel...and use."

He cheated me in my change, but to show my utter contempt for the man I merely smiled when I counted the coins he gave me. He blushed – as far as he and his skin could be said to be able to blush – to the roots of his oiled, black hair. If looks could kill, I would have been a mangled stick of red flesh on the floor of that grocer's shop. Such looks could only kill the sensitive plant of the human soul. I know this word is out of fashion, but that is because that for which it stands is also completely obsolete. There are very few of us who could not afford to be a Dr. Faustus – for nearly all of us could cheat the devil of his reward. Mephistopheles would have to employ extra cunning to extract a soul from many of us moderns. The devil has almost gone out of business for this reason – and his successful and triumphant competitors – men and women – have driven him out of the market, and, sad to relate, I had discovered in this negro grocer one of the most successful rivals of the "defunct" Devil!

But this is not all. Not by any means. Prepare yourself, you believers in the integrity of human beings! This negro grocer was a Baptist deacon. He preached hot sermons, gentle sermons, sermons on temperance and chastity, sometimes to large audiences of more or less simple-faithed people, and yet it was his hypocritical and iniquitous habit to speak behind my back in a way that would have gained the delighted approbation of His Satanic Majesty. Sometimes he would be so carried away with the fullness of this crook stunt that he would shout after me, "Get back to England, you sod." "We don't want you." "Get out." "Sod you." "You bum shit," and other much worse language too.

How he knew me I do not know, but his actions betrayed his alliance with the rest of my molesters and so an alliance with men of robbery and murder.

I am, partly from circumstances, a lonely man. I have, however, recognised this and have tried to discipline myself to be never less solitary than when in solitude – but also only with partial succcss. I was filled with deep regret at the departure of my American friend to New York. I was now without a visible friend in the world, and to cap my misery the molestations increased from the day of his departure.

Two days after he left me the landlord of the apartment-house came home from one of his voyages as a captain of a trading vessel running spirits into the U.S.A. I had my back turned to him, and a large mirror was in front of me. In this I saw him reflected. He was looking at my back with the gaze of a thief – malevolently, craftily. The same day a dark, evil-looking white man, standing outside a liquor "bar" stared at me evilly, and as I got level with him he shouted to someone inside the "bar:" "Here he is."

A negro – very fierce and villainous of countenance – emerged.

The white man said: "Follow him, and hands up to him. And make it damn quick, see."

The negro looked at me, and followed me for nearly half-a-mile, but as I kept to the crowded thoroughfares he was unable to accomplish the designs of his master, which might have been said just to intimidate me, though the white man looked a villain.

At B.W.I. No. 2, the first signs came when burly natives (negroes) sometimes jostled and pushed me as I walked along the footpaths. This was very noticeable as the blacks treated the other Europeans with respect and got into the roadway for them if the footpath was narrow. Whoever instructs the negro and other molesters must tell them that I cannot hit back.

These are only a few instances from many, and they may be monotonous to you, but it was their very frequency which gave them their peculiar significance, and also the fact that sometimes the molestations came from unusual quarters. For instance, I had only been in B.W.I. No. 2 for a week when I made enquiries at two shipping offices, concerning their ships, in case I should want to leave the place. At each one the white (or apparently white) clerks of the Agents called after me as I left the offices: "He's a big sod."

The full connature of this truncated term at the time missed me, but not so the terrible accents in which it was uttered. It was as if a steam hammer had hit the top of my brain, and corrosive acid was eating away the base of my spine. Often as I passed a large house on the sea front whose occupants were white people of influence, I was molested by someone shouting from it, "Throw him out."

Upon the heels of this public insult and attempt to demoralise me, another peculiar incident occurred.

The negroes, who occupied small two-roomed houses on the opposite side of the road to my apartments, started persecuting me in no uncertain fashion.

A horrible looking negress used to sit on her front piazza and talk loudly, long and lewdly to the various men who visited her. She, it was true, was talking *to* them, but *at* me. One well-dressed, moustached negro "friend" of hers – for the link of purpose is terribly binding – and the shackles of felony are even more binding than those of fidelity – used to stand outside her house and carry on obscene conversation, full of intimidations and indecent gestures, all of which were directed *at* me to *her*. I had proof later on that he was one of the ringleaders of the crook scoundrels who haunt the place. When this negress was alone the insults and insinuations would still continue as long as I remained within earshot. Sometimes the game would be a little varied. Two negroes (one was the vicious, snarling brute who obeyed the white man outside the liquor "bar") would sometimes aim with their insinuations at me through the negress, who was all that is evil and base. From morning to night these and a host of other negroes would keep up their shameful antics – including with their obscenities, indirect threats of murder and robbery – even of abductions and ransoms and such like intimidating and sensational matters. On several occasions a car arrived, in which sat a young white man of about 28, clean-shaven, with evil, cruel, dark eyes and dark hair brushed well back from his forehead. He seemed to be the "chief," and his associates in the car were, a good-looking, round-faced, nicely dressed negro of about 30, and a poorly dressed negro of about 28. The entire time, perhaps over an hour, during which the car stood outside my window, these three kept up an unbroken flow of filth and threats of kidnapping and murder or ransom.

There could not be the least doubt that these were all part of a syndicate of crooks and allied to the international crooks.

One morning I was out walking, when four negroes with malevolent intent written on their criminal faces, stopped within a few yards of me. Their demeanour was quite threatening. One of them, looking murderously at me, said: "Hey, mister, I think better yo' no stop longa here. Yo' go back England. This town is not healthy for yo', I can tell yo'."

Somehow or other the whole atmosphere seemed unreal – like a very "uncomic opera" – and the threats of immediate murder and robbery not feasible, but it was not long afterwards that this element of make-believe was entirely driven from my mind.

I was sitting near the landing stage one fine evening. My thoughts were among the ships and other craft, conjecturing concerning their occupants and the strange lands from which they came. Suddenly I heard a low moan, and saw a sinister-faced white barman of about 30, supporting a helpless white man, who seemed quite young and respectable, but who was hopelessly drunk or doped. His head kept falling like so much inert matter on to his chest. And each time this happened the barman viciously pulled it erect by the crisp hair of the unfortunate man, both of whose trouser pockets were hanging out pathetically, telling their own unmistakable tale. Eventually, the barman got the man down by the waterside. There were some muffled sounds. Then silence. In a few moments the hurried steps of the barman could be heard as he almost ran into the nearby bar. Later on I looked, but could see no trace of the young white man. I walked to my apartment bathed in a freezing perspiration.

Day after day, night after night, they foxed me – the same negroes, the same white men, using the same language and the same tactics of molestation, though sometimes, as in the following incident I was unable to understand the nature of their threats. This kind of thing had the additional horror of the unknown.

One night, I heard a man and a woman call out to me, as I was lying in my bed, that they were busy with "a piece of paper." On other nights the same allusion was shrieked at me. Once the man said, "You don't think I have a paper. Well, that's your mistake, not mine. And it's all written out I tell you, do you hear?"

To this he added in a queer, jibing voice: "I have got it from the white man. You know him – or you ought to by this time."

I was, however, completely mystified, and I sank back on my pillow to toss wakefully through many nights, pondering over this mystery and all thc molestings and strange happenings and evil looks of practically everyone.

In some ways an equally mysterious happening occurred. It was near the fine house of a negro member of the House of Representatives. I often passed this residence on my way to my apartment, and one day as I was walking in this vicinity, I saw him on his front piazza, talking to several well-dressed coloured men, who were hanging upon his words, uttered in a loud, oratorical fashion, as if they were veritable pearls of wisdom. As soon as he saw me his whole manner changed. He lowered his loud voice and the group of men grew more compact to catch his words. I saw him deliberately incline his head towards me, and as he did so the other men, as if in a theatre chorus, turned their eyes upon me, like one man. Suddenly he stood to his full height, and, using his powerful voice to the uttermost, he said: "Well, boys, I would not take two thousand dollars for what I know of him, and you have never known me make a mistake, have you?"

The question was literally hurled at the heads of the coloured men around him, for his right hand suddenly shot towards them with the impelling gesture of a practiced demagogue.

I walked home, lost in wonder as to what it was this negro politician knew of me. I wondered what was his scheme of villainy.

For days I went about thinking of these two mysteries, and during the whole time I frequently heard phrases, from whites and negroes, directed at me from the people in the streets, and the loungers in the hotels. I overheard on more than one occasion the remark that if I did not go to England "we shall get nothing, so make him hop it damn quick, because we want our share." This kind of occurrence only complicated things and made them even more obscure than before, for I could not understand why my return to England could in any way benefit them.

Some nights after the "piece of paper" episode, I retired early to my bedroom – about 9.30 P.M. – and fell into a deep sleep, from which I was rudely awakened about midnight. I heard someone trying to open the door in my room, which joined it to another room. Of course, I had locked it. I heard my potential intruder walk on to the front piazza and run down the outside stairs. Soon the sound of a woman laughing came to me – the kind of laugh a low woman has when she is discussing matters concerning the private affairs of men. A few moments afterwards the woman was joined by a man, whose heavy footsteps rang on the quiet road. In a loud voice he cried: "Go and give him this piece of paper."

My heart seemed to leap within me at the mention of the "piece of paper." At last, I thought, I shall clear up this mystery.

The woman replied: "I have been up to his room, and what do you think? It's locked."

Again her irritating laughter rent the night air.

More heavy footsteps approached, and the first man addressed the newcomer in a loud voice; then molesting sentences came clearly through the silence of the night, "We'll put him in the sea and salt him," said one.

"Sure, we'll out him," replied the other. Then both in chorus yelled out: "Get home, you big b——." (Mind you, I was in bed).

As they walked away one of them said to the other: "I want to see his landlord. I sure like his landlord. He's one of us."

Peculiarly enough, apart from myself, all the boarders were out this night, and did not return until after one o'clock. The landlord's son returned at the same time. When I told them, they thought nothing of the whole exploit, which betrayed an utter lack of interest in the sufferings of a man – or worse – though I am not suggesting that any of the boarders were actually crooks. Even my landlord and landlady, who occupied the room beneath mine, and who could not have failed to have heard the whole incident, denied emphatically that they had any knowledge of it. They spoke as if they wished to suggest that I was imagining it all. This I could not tolerate, and, to show them that I was in grim earnest, and also because I was a little frightened by the growing frequency and intensity of the molestations – I determined to have recourse to the law, trusting that this would rid me of my pursuers.

The next morning was Sunday. I requested the landlord's son to call at the Police Station (which he passed on his journey in his car that morning) to ask that a detective should be sent to my apartments immediately. In about an hour a negro detective arrived. I gave him my correct name, and it gave me a queer feeling inside me when I used it again after the three months I had been using the name given me by the B.W.I. No. 1 hotel people, foolishly thinking to put the trackers off my track. He listened to my story of the molestations with an unmoving and unsympathetic face. At the end of my story – I was nearly in tears – he got up suddenly and left me. He went to my landlord's room immediately beneath mine, and I confess to eavesdropping by putting my ear to the floor of my bedroom, after dragging back the carpet. I heard the detective narrate my story. I overheard also the allegations of my landlord, abetted by those of his wife, that the whole story was utterly false, and was entirely a figment of my imagination. The landlady's most important part in the conversation was: "Of course, he's mad, and as you know, completely harmless." The utterance of this last thought brought a choking sensation to my throat, so that I was unable to hear any more of the conversation. Hurriedly I went to church. As I entered, people stared at me, and when I was seated the entire congregation turned round to gaze at me. A negro man said quite loudly, "He's a law man," as he scowled at me. But I took little notice of him or of anyone else, for I had fallen into a deeply abstracted mood, generated by the soothing, sweet church music, for I ever loved the soft flute notes of a great organ. And I thanked God with all my soul, that somewhere, at least sometimes, there was still peace and solace for the aching heart and the tormented brain.

---

The people in the shop below and the negroes opposite now also molested me for hours each day by playing a gramophone and singing gross abuse *at* me "tuned" in with the records.

After this the white landlady started throwing insults at me on every possible occasion, and motor cars containing sometimes coloured people and often whites would have one of those inside the car make a noise by knocking the inside of the car as they passed me wherever I was out walking.

It was from now that the negroes and others started their gesticulating antics to befool and to persecute.

As I was walking along, a party of negroes, or perhaps one only, would be approaching in my direction. One or more of them would stretch out both arms horizontally each sideways and would then turn towards the sea and move their lips as though saying some hateful or angry words to me and would accompany this with very murderous looks.

---

Later on, some weeks or so after, they started calling out, "Get out," and other sentences whilst gesticulating as above. Practically every negro was a molester.

But peace is among the rare, exquisite things of earth, both in its duration and its occurrence. Even where solace ought to be expected – in a cool church – the irksomeness of the outside world often penetrates to smash the bliss of peace to sharp-edged fragments. Very frequently, as I approached the church on Sunday mornings, an evil-looking white man in a car would be by the curb of the sidewalk almost opposite the church, sounding the four notes of the "bugle hunting" call as he saw me coming along. During the several years of my stay in B.W.I. No. 2, this nicely dressed man would come after me in slow gear, as I walked about the district, and he would continue his sounding of the harriers' call in the loud strident tones of his "special" motor horn. Often I would awaken from a reverie or reading to hear the faint but unmistakable notes, far in the distance, growing louder and coming nearer. Also, occasionally negroes would drive their cars near me, sounding this "call" on ordinary bugles. It was done to intimidate me. All this "bugling" was done so cunningly that I felt that my molesters were sometimes signalling and urging others to molest also, besides being done always with the purpose of intimidating me.

As natives signal on their barbaric tom-toms – each tribe taking up the call and passing it on with dreadful monotony – so these sometimes urged others to molest me more abominably. Frequently, this monotony would be harshly destroyed. For instance, a mulatto girl – young and pretty – would come alongside and deliberately point in my face and say to her companion, who as often as not was a brutal looking negro: "Look, he's the one we've got to get at. Isn't he a sod?"

Or again, I would be kept wide awake and the whole of me desiring deep sleep – by the upstairs tenants of the house immediately behind my apartments, and also by negroes who stood in the street outside. Sometimes pandemonium was let loose *all* night long. It was quite indescribable. Threats, accusations, filth, were hurled into the darkness of the night, until daylight scattered my molesters to their beds or occupations – if they had any other occupation except that of molesting me. Indeed, it seemed as if this must be a "full-time" job of theirs, as some of the same negroes were employed nearly every time – and for the entire period of my stay at B.W.I. No. 2.

It might seem that molestations at such a distance could not harm me, but I ought to say that, in addition to the nerve tension of these actions, the negroes used, of a night, to get a ladder and put it against my window-sill. This action they accompanied with threats of coming up into my room, of shooting and strangling me, etc. Naturally many nights I was unable to sleep at all, and I often kept all my clothes on, ready for eventualities.

Thus commenced the more serious acts of molestations which

kept me on the *qui vive* at all hours of the day and night, and, during the rest of my sojourn in the apartments I occupied. If I was at the rear, I was ceaselessly troubled by a mulatto woman in her early forties, a very fat, vicious specimen of her kind. She would sit at her window and keep up a continuous flow of the most shocking and obscene sentences and lies and abuse, accompanied by indescribable gestures and postures which revealed her utter villainousness. If I was at the rear of the premises at night a "white" man with dark eyes and a murderous expression on his countenance would startle the darkness (and me) with a very bright acetylene lamp, which he would shine dazzlingly upon me, picking me out of the darkness, and giving me a feeling of being utterly alone in a dangerous place. Perhaps he was that fat woman's "husband." He was probably the same man who had instructed the negro to "hands up" me, and he spoke in tones of venom, hatred and contempt in all his sentences of robbery and murder.

The occupants of the shop below me joined in the general abuse of my person. I overheard the landlady, talking to one of her friends, say quietly and with deep and unsympathetic conviction: "Of course, in the finish, they'll make mincemeat of him. They'll get all he's got, and that's as certain as my name is what it is and that we will get our share of it."

Inadvertently and unintentionally, I overheard many scraps of such conversations – sometimes when I was miles from the town – far does the barbaric, threatening tom-tom of the London crooks' underworld beat out its unmistakable message. Out of the mixed noise of talking would emerge scraps of underworld jargon, such as "Get out," "Get back to England where worms like you belong," "Big sod," "He's the one. He's in the book." Coloured men and whites – there was no distinction between them in this respect, nor in many other respects – used these and other words, every day and wherever I happened to be during the whole time I was in B.W.I. No. 2. Sometimes, in an attempt to lose myself to get from the molesters, I would mix with crowds in the centre of town. But, alas, my presence was always detected.

On one of these occasions, an organised molestation was set up with frightening rapidity, and out of the mouths of those gathered about me came references to the "book," or "the big, black book," or to the taking of my "photo." This was more disconcerting. The same references respecting photographing me had been made when I was in Auckland, sometimes, too, by persons who were apparently quite gentlemen.

After I had called in the detective I thought that the "arm of the law" would at least help to decrease the force and occurrence of my molesters. But this was not so. Indeed, the "arm" seemed a very palsied one, for even in the Public Library, and in my own apartment house, the abuse and mockery showed no abatement. To escape, I would go to the very top room of the house, but this was soon discovered. Negroes would climb to the tops of the boat masts so that they could see me in this room and view me in the only morsel of privacy left me. These boats were 150 feet away. From their vantage points they would hurl their usual slogans.

I again reported these incidents to the detective, but the molestings increased even more after this interview, and I came to the conclusion that it was quite useless to rely on the police in this part of the world. My heart went out to the English "bobby," who, for all strangers in a foreign land, is a symbol of safety and human feeling.

---

I now entered upon one of the strangest periods of my life, and I still look back to it with some bitterness, every remembrance of it brings a feeling of deep resentment and mortification. I will, however, attempt to set it down in the plainest terms without exaggeration, or to interpret the actions of others with undue harshness and prejudice.

All this molestation distracted me to the point of making up my mind to leave B.W.I. No. 2. I went to the shipping agent to see about taking a boat to Canada. He asked me to call again when the boat arrived. On the morning of its arrival, I took my baggage to the shipping office, which I found was closed, as the hour was too early. I then took my baggage to the nearby Central Police Station, and stood by it, intending to go back to the shipping agents when open. After a while a negro sergeant arrived. He gave me a quick, keen glance, and asked me to wait to see the Inspector. I waited for some time, and when the Inspector arrived he in turned asked me to wait for the Commander. The Inspector and Commander were Englishmen from the London Colonial Office. The Commander duly arrived. I was ushered into his office, where he cross-questioned me with an air of smiling doubtfulness (which at the time I could not understand) writ large on his face. As I briefly told him my story his incredulity became more and more obvious. Of course, I was not aware for some years after this that my landlord had been brazenly lying to him about me, and I was unable to appreciate the importance of the Commander's believing the real truth of the matter at the time.

Leaving these befooled police chiefs – I was not then aware of their being befooled – I proceeded to the shipping office, only to find to my great consternation, that the boat had sailed. Filled with a horrible sinking feeling, I returned to my apartments, not knowing where else to go. I was shut in, surrounded by enemies and unsympathetic police. As I proceeded along, passing negroes upon the road shouted at me: "Pooped out." "Pooped out, yer can't get away from us." They looked at me with malevolence and contempt.

The mind is considered sometimes to be so overburdened with anxiety that it becomes numb, incapable of further sensitivity. I thought mine had reached this stage; that my molestations had attained such a pitch of ceaselessness and cunning that no further miseries would touch me. But this was not so. For I seemed to pass into a patch of sensitivity beyond description – sensitivity to each and every happening that came into the ken of my experience.

One kind of happening in particular I well remember. If I sat down anywhere, in a park or other open-air place, a coloured person would drive his car near to me, stop, and keep his engine roaring furiously and hooting his horn in a perfectly fiendish, maddening fashion. Or again, a disconcerting, peculiar "monkey trick" practised by my molesters was to employ about a dozen cars, which would make a quick, mad rush past me and close to me. These cars were always occupied by my habitual molesters. They came at great speed and obviously without much warning, so that sometimes I could see their occupants still settling themselves more comfortably into their seats as they drove rapidly by me. This usually occurred a short time after I had started a walk.

Fatigued, and yet in a state of chronic excitement of the most unpleasant kind, I would return home, only to find no rest, no peace there either. On one occasion I returned to find my landlady talking to a white woman, who was employed on a ship that touched a U.S.A. port. She was saying to my landlady as I came silently and unobserved into the apartment house: "Buster (I did not catch the name) told me he means to 'have' him. And you know Buster, as well as I do."

There could be no doubt that she meant "having" me, for immediately she saw me she stopped speaking and looked away.

---

I felt that things were working up to a climax. The very air was thick with threats of immediate action. Many had been the threats, for instance, that my bedroom would be raided, and one night about 10 P.M. I was in my bedroom getting ready for bed when I heard footsteps on the front piazza. A man's voice came to me. Then someone tried to open the inner door of my room, unsuccessfully, of course, because I had locked it. A woman's voice whispered – though loud enough for me to hear: "I'll show you the way to get in."

These two then walked through the front parlour and two other rooms. Fear gripped me as I heard them coming. I departed, in some haste I must admit, from my room and proceeded to the top landing, where I sat on a bed which was there.

I had no desire to meet these intruders face to face in my state of mind. The two entered my bedroom and I could hear them rummaging about in my belongings. Suddenly I heard a loud snap as they burst the lock and fastenings of my trunk. As they took out the contents and were examining them I could (though only indistinctly) hear them commenting on their nature. They (this man and woman) seemed to know where I was, and also that all the other boarders were in their rooms and had locked themselves in – though on other nights the lodgers never went to bed until at least an hour later. The man intruder in my room occasionally called out in a loud voice, so that I could distinctly hear him, sentences of intimidation and abuse. One of my letters that he read caused him to be particularly angry. Perhaps it was the one containing particulars of some of those who habitually molested me. He shouted – almost shrieked – at the top of his voice: "I'll see the sod about this. You see if I don't, the soft swine that he is!"

This letter they purloined. They stole my birth certificate and other papers including a letter I had written when I was in Auckland, relating all the particulars of my molestations and stating when they had commenced; also that I had spent £1,000 on guards. I had written this in case anything untoward should happen to me at any time, and I kept it in my portmanteau. I had addressed it to "The Police."

About midnight a negro came up the back outside stairs leading to my bedroom and joined the marauders. He spoke to them. I recognised his voice at once. He was the negro who had frequently molested me in front of the house. His name seemed to be "Jack," a tall, bold villain of the worst type. This man was employed on this occasion to take my things downstairs and into the road, where they were examined by someone – perhaps in a car. He returned with various messages, which were delivered by him in a low voice so that only unintelligible scraps came to me. This went on till daylight. My landlord and landlady slept in the room beneath mine, and I am quite sure that they were aware of everything that was happening. Just as daylight broke the burglar said loudly: "I want to see him. I'll have to go upstairs after him."

This aroused me. I thereupon knocked on several doors and at last one opened. I asked the occupant of the room if he would admit me. He said, "Oh! It's you, isn't it? They won't be long now. Come in, and rest awhile."

I felt sure that if I reported all this to the police I would be disbelieved again. I kept my mouth shut about the whole mysterious and annoying episode. I presumed that the two intruders were real "whites" – man and woman – as distinct from the apparently "whites," for their voices had the peculiar "timbre" of the "whites," as opposed to the coarser and different style of the various coloured peoples. Of course I assumed both were crooks.

The next day, as I was walking into town, I saw two tall, smart, white crooks that wore sun-faded suits, whom I have mentioned before. As these rogues saw me, one said viciously to the other: "He thinks he's damned smart. We'll bull-dog him." Both glared at me dangerously.

They also made a remark which told me that they were aware of the burglary in my room.

---

The molestations continued unabated. I could put my finger on many and prove that they were acting in a definitely criminal and felonious fashion to me. I suspected many others, but everything was so vague, I could not definitely say I knew their object, so that at this time my mind was in a perpetually distressed state. I suppose that the hot climate which does not aid or abet cold reason, was not aiding my mental activity, and, in addition, the molesting was accomplishing its intended design of distracting and distressing me. Threats of violence were continuous.

One night it was in such a nervy state that I went up to the son's bedroom – he had just come in at about 1 A.M. – and I asked him to allow me to sleep in his bedroom, on the floor. He gave me permission, so, fully clothed, I stretched myself out on the floor and went to sleep. O blessed sleep that it was! I awoke just after daylight, about 5.30 A.M., and I immediately heard a man's voice saying (even now it seems incredibly horrible and unreal): "He's ————." (He mentioned something unprintable).

"He's done it," he went on. Turning in the direction of the voice I saw, framed in the window, three white men looking steadily at me. The assertion and accusations considerably upset me. I was stunned. My brain ceased to think. The world seemed thick and wooden. One thing only reiterated itself inside me: "You must get a doctor – and quick." I asked that a doctor should be telephoned. He duly arrived and examined me. He was a white gentleman.

"Of course," he said, his face wreathed in smiles, "Of course, you're all right. Quite in order. Nothing unusual."

His smiles were caused by the landlord and his wife – though it was years afterwards that I discovered the deep duplicity of these two people. They had given all kinds of lying reports to the doctor, who believed them.

If you think I have reached the depths of humiliation you are mistaken, for yet another shameful happening was to occur.

A little while after the doctor had departed, a gentleman came in his car and told me that he had instructions to drive me to the hospital. I told him that I would not go.

"Very well," he replied, in a reasonable tone of voice, "if you won't come with me, you know what will happen."

"What?" I asked, and the tears threatened to burst from my eyes.

"You'll be taken to prison," he replied shortly.

After a little while (I cannot say after a little consideration, because I was too flustered to "consider" anything), I went with him in his car. I was taken to the Lunatics' Department adjoining the Government Hospital and lodged in a building with a negro attendant as a companion all day. At night he left me and I was locked in the building. This was the procedure until I was released. "My" building was about 120 feet from a boundary wall.

I had hardly been in this place – of all places – for more than half an hour when the usual molestations began to commence. A lot of people peeped over the wall. Some even climbed trees to see me. Though I could only recognise one or two by sight, I recognised numerous voices, which now commenced their vituperations and calumniations. In addition to the usual words I picked out some new ones. They were: "You Jew thief," "You rook," "You crook," "You bester," "You skunk." There was also a new voice, though I could not see its owner. It was an awful, dreary, hopeless, wretched, melancholy voice: I cannot find sufficient epithets to describe its utter "world weariness." It was a woman's voice, which kept on repeating in a maddening way: "Pooped out of England." "Pooped out of New Zealand."

This outside molestation went on for two days, after which it stopped and the attendants took it up. All the time I was there they did their level best to upset me and keep me in an unbalanced state of mind. Several nights, for example, an attendant came to my room about midnight, and flashed his light full in my face. This was a very unsettling thing to do and the attendant knew it. Again, a very tall negro attendant said he had obtained all my letters, and had "got my bank" (what he meant precisely by that I do not know). Every day something of this nature occurred. One of the attendants, who wore a different uniform from the rest, and who carried a stick with a flat club end to it, occasionally used to hold this obtrusively before me and he always gave me an evil stare of menace.

The lunatics' building was a little way from the one in which I was incarcerated, and the dangerous lunatics were kept near their buildings and also close to the attendants, when they were being exercised. This, I discovered, was the practice, but on several occasions after my arrival, the attendants allowed one very bad case to come near me.

He was a nightmare of a man – an ape-like creature with long, twitching fingers and powerful hands and arms. He would walk towards me like a loping wolf, his bloodshot eyes almost popping out of his head, his hands outstretched before him. As he came he was muttering and blaspheming most foully. Suddenly he threw his mis-shapen head back and would shout out. Then he began circling round me, jerking his head and his whole body in a way terrible to behold. He would stop from time to time and cry out: "I'll strangle you. I'll tear out your throat. I'll nip your guts out and stamp on 'em."

On one occasion I saw the negro attendants staging something. They had withdrawn the "light" cases from my vicinity. I was left with this anthropoidal madman, who, in attitudes of crouching and leaping, acted like a wild animal about to attack me. He landed up between me and my room, my only possible means of escape; and looks of insane cunning kept coming and going on his face. He kept repeating: "I'll do him now. Now is the time, my lucky lads. Rip and tear. Tear and rip. Bite and claw. Claw and bite," and so on.

All the while he kept extending his long fingers in a mad fashion. After about half an hour of this, one of the attendants came along with a knowing smile and the demented man was led away like a new-born lamb. As you can imagine, it distressed me.

I spent my time in this place thinking that the attendants must also be connected with my molesters in the outside world, though why they should be I could not imagine. When the Doctor discharged me I went back to my apartments, through sheer force of habit, for I was very weary and sick at heart.

---

I had experienced the whole gamut of mental and moral sickness, and nothing, I felt, of a worse nature than that which had already happened to me, could happen in the future. The molestations again occurred, and I was aware of them, but for the moment I had no room for fear. A negro shouted to me the name of the ship which had brought me from New Zealand to Panama, which he could only have learned from the international crooks and the leading molesters. One day a tall negro knocked my hat off in the street with a deliberate gesture as I was out walking.

One day I happened to be passing near the Police Station and

I dropped in to see if the Commander could help to lessen the numerous persecutions. I saw him, but before I could complete a sentence, he rapped out in an angry voice: "Clear out of this place."

I turned away, not quite with that "calm of mind, all passion spent," but an utter indifference and lack of feeling.

As mentioned before, the crooks endeavoured to get me into disfavour with the authorities by spreading defamatory lies, and this was proved, because I was in a bad odour with the Commander, and I also had proof that the crooks and all their abetters had been vilifying me to the people of influence. They camouflage the fact that they are crooks by defaming their victim. It is done as a blind to mislead any honest people.

The network of espionage was so fine and complete that all my actions were known almost as soon as they were done. The following is an example:

I had decided to go to the U.S.A., to visit my American friend. I went to the U.S.A. Consul to visa my passport. As I was waiting in his office, I saw one of my molesters just leaving after a consultation with the Consul. He looked at me with triumphant, leering eyes. The U.S.A. Consul refused to visa my passport. No reasons were given. Simply a blank refusal. And for years after this a common form of molestation was: "We pooped you from U.S.A." "America won't have you." "Pooped out of America." This was just to harry me and intimidate me, like the more usual phrases, used by all my persecutors – including my landlady and landlord, and the boarders of my apartment house. I never grew accustomed to people saying, "He's done it," or "He's a big sod." Familiarity had not bred contempt, nor indifference.

My heart sank when the U.S.A. Consul refused the visa. When I arrived home in England, I enquired about it. It was explained to me by an authority that it may have been handled by any one of a number of officials in the Colony. They were the cause of this refusal.

I was being treated like a pariah. Once more the crooks had scored. Was it official hostility? or working with the crooks?

This sensitiveness was in part engendered by the fact that so many seemed to be implicated in the machinations of the underworld, or that those who were not seemed to regard the molestations as a slight of no importance, or wink at those doing it.

For instance, I was walking along a main road and the passing negroes were indulging in their usual insults, such as "Sod," "Get out," "Pooped out." Two English Colonial Department officers (both were captains) were walking in the other direction on the other side of the road and overheard some of these remarks. "This is a piece of good luck," I thought, but the two Englishmen simply glanced casually at my molesters, and one said to the other in a jocular fashion: "Pooped out."

Both of them laughed as they continued on their way.

I wonder whether they in any way realised the underworld's dark and obscure ways of obtaining their ends. These "insignificant" molesting words may be the steps that lead to robbery. And, when all is said and done, murder might be the end attained (that some "undiscovered" crime is intended is a certainty).

After some other experiences with cab-drivers, and even negro policemen, I decided to leave B.W.I. No. 2 now, because, though every place was as bad as any other place, there may be some virtue in movement and possibly some alleviation.

---

I went to the shipping agents and paid my fare back to B.W.I. No. 1. In the car, on my way to the ship's launch, two nicely dressed white men passengers to the ship (they looked as if they might be father and son) eyed me nastily. One of these men was about 60 and the other about 40 years old. The younger man said to the older: "I know he's got the goods, I tell you. Property and cash, and I'm going to have every little bit of it. If not – well, drowning's as good as any other way, and you can see to that. It won't be the first time, eh?"

They broke into a guffaw.

A white clerk belonging to the shipping agents asked me for

my home address in England, and in a fit of absent-mindedness I gave it to him. I soon discovered that he was one of the leaders of the underworld in this place.

If I thought that I should at least have a change in the personnel of my molesters, by leaving B.W.I. No. 2, I was, in no small measure to be disappointed, for the launch which was to take me to the ship contained a number of white men and women whom I recognised as continual molesters of mine; "the old familiar faces," as Charles Lamb called others, much dearer to him than these, though not more well-known. I heard one of these men say, as I was getting into the launch: "Here comes our man. Here he comes. All dressed up and nowhere to go. Poor sod."

And I felt like a sacrificial lamb prepared for the slaughter, for as soon as I had boarded the ship I sensed that I had walked into the middle of my enemies. I saw the "ship agents' clerk," who was talking to a bevy of bad, fast-looking, young white women; the clerk was saying: "Here he is, girls. We've got him."

Proceeding a little further along the deck I met an evil-looking white couple. As soon as I caught sight of them I knew them for what they were, and after overhearing a bit of their conversation, there were no doubts left in my mind. The man said to the woman: "How can we miss him. He's easy money now."

Wherever I went on the ship the usual forms and phrases of persecution met my eyes and ears. Whilst in the lavatory, even, I heard a woman, who had seen me going in, use the most foul, lewd language and some of the more usual molesting words. I also heard the voice, like a dirge that "rings the dead seaman's knell" of the woman who had stirred me at the asylum. She was using intimidatory and obscene sentences.

Some hours later I sought the comparative privacy of my cabin, where I reviewed the events on board and ran over in my mind the various characters who had followed me. Some of them, I felt, meant bad business. They were probably professional crooks – real desperadoes. As I sat there meditating and reflecting, molesting words reached me in my cabin. I then went to the officer and obtained my papers and boarded the lighter which was alongside. There I stayed until dawn, when the launch came to take the "unloading" and "staff" men to shore. And so I got back to B.W.I. No. 2.

---

I went to look for new quarters. These I found, in a nearby district, where I hoped at least for some time, to avoid the "storm and stress" of molestation. But, alas! my persecutors were upon me like wasps on strawberry jam at home in England. I wondered what was coming next. My mind was a welter of futile prophesies. I seemed to be surrounded, not only by international crooks, but by a multitude of their fry. For example, the proprietress, one of her sons; her grandfather, an old man of eighty; a negro who haunted the back garden, and many others in close contact with the house. They employed all the old means of molestations and one or two new ones. The son, mentioned above, was a particularly obnoxious piece of work. His chief form of amusement of a night – for himself – was to "crawl" pieces of iron for hours upon the roof over my room, mostly immediately above my head. He would do this with satanic persistency for hours on end, keeping me awake. The old man of eighty was also a nasty morsel. His tongue was among the filthiest in my experience.

But these and their like I expected to be more or less maliciously minded, their whole training and upbringing was conducive only of evil states of mind, and they are brought up with the purpose to aid and abet the crooks. It was, however, when those who ought, from their training and profession, to have known better, employed these mean, diabolical manners, that I felt then how complete and devastating was the system built up by the marauders and evil birds of prey masquerading as human beings – the leaders of the underworld. These felons "run" the place.

There was a lay reader at an important Anglican church near my quarters. He was a tall mulatto. This church attracted a lot of apparent "whites," besides many coloured people. I say "apparent," for some of these with white faces are very much negro by blood. Often this is shown in their limbs, which are often considerably brown or dark. I must say that I *do* expect something better than malevolent molestations from professing and leading Christians. I feel that we have a right to expect more. And yet this lay reader was often in the company of my molesters and was altogether a quite discreditable and unworthy person to occupy a post of spiritual responsibility, as the following account will show.

His particular form of molestation of me was to stand outside the door of my room, and, as though talking to someone downstairs, he would shout: "He's ——."

He used some of the most shockingly lewd expressions of obscenity known. His acquaintance with the Six Anglo-Saxon monosyllables was intimate, deep and perverted. Sometimes he would pretend that he was answering a telephone call when he was downstairs. He would employ the same kind of language for this purpose. The frequency of this man's persecutions startled me as much as the fact that he was a lay reader. There was something so monstrously foul and fiendish in the repetition of the same lewd phrases. How one so important in his church – for he not only read the lessons, but also led the congregation in singing – could molest me, shows how the crooks subvert these inhabitants.

This was not the only pseudo-religious man who took part in my persecution. The old negro of about 65 years of age, who was a Government servant, also indulged in numerous fits of molestation. His particular kind was exceedingly cunning. If there was a service or children's class in the adjoining chapel, he would sing also, but he would bring into his singing all the obscene and other sentences generally used by my persecutors. It was only with considerable difficulty, and after a long while, that I was able to trace this man, for he could "falsetto" his voice to blend so perfectly with the singing children that he seemed to be actually one of the singers in the chapel. This kind of malicious insult seems to be a universal accomplishment brought to a fine art in B.W.I. Nos. 1 and 2. This particular man could make up his sentences to fit the rhythm and length of the song with conspicuous ease and success.

About a fortnight after I arrived in my new quarters, a man and a woman, both of whom I had left on the ship, bound for B.W.I. No. 1, came to live near me. The woman was the melancholy-voiced individual whose tones had harrowing effects upon me. Often during the day this dirge voice would be mouthing the most vile sentences, and sometimes the man would talk to her about me in such a way that I could not possibly help overhearing what they had to say. The voice would drearily reply *to* him, but *at* me. And this went on continuously for hours each day.

To escape, I would sometimes go to the chapel when a service was proceeding, but even there I was molested, both by those near and those inside the chapel. Those of the congregation sitting near me would utter obscenities during the service, and those outside the door, or by the open window would follow suit. But the remarkable part about this molest was that only one at a time would be so engaged. It was a molestation under strict control – almost as if it was an orchestra obeying a conductor's baton – and this has always pertained by my molesters. These persecutors always had the cunning of the devil and worked together like well-ordered machinery (this must be due to plenty of practice), so that amid all their threats of murder, shooting, violence, drowning, or other consoling things, there was never any jarring or ineffectiveness in the molesting. Once I saw a mulatto gentleman talking to my landlady. I overheard them talking about me, and I discovered that he was her lawyer, and a man of importance in the place. He was saying: "If only so-and-so (I did not catch the name) got hold of him, what a glorious share-out there would be for all of us."

One day, I went to a Chinese restaurant frequented by whites, with an acquaintance. As I was sitting at my meal an intolerably evil-looking white man, about 40 years old, clean-shaven and well-dressed, opened the door of the room from the outside and stood in the doorway, staring inimically at me. He announced to all present: "He's wanted in London," and though he did not actually point at me, there could be no doubt as to whom he meant, for immediately this man had disappeared through the doorway, another man, sitting at a table near mine with two well-dressed "ladies," who looked all that they should not be – addressed his companions thus, looking at me with sinister, evil glances: "Look at him girls, he's got no manners. Why doesn't he get back to London and learn them from the Queen."

This might seem harmless enough, but accompanied, as it was, with all the intimidating tones and gestures of the practiced molester, there could not be any doubt as to its significance, or to that of the incident which occurred when I left the restaurant, when a tall while man, dressed immaculately in white duck (he was about 60 years old and was standing at his office door) called out loudly to a group of negroes as I was passing him: "Sod him out boys, if you want your pickings."

Some days afterwards, I met the Baptist deacon of whom I have spoken. He was walking behind me, with some negro companions. He overtook me, and, getting in front of me, said in his rich, lowered voice to his companions: "If we don't get him back to England we'll get nothing, and that, brothers, will never do. We must worry him out."

To this a negro replied, "I don't mind, sir, what we does, nor what we tries. It sure don't matter to me."

And another negro interpolated in tones of utter disgust: "He's soppy, he can't *do* anything either. Who cares for him?"

This was correct, I could do nothing. I was quite helpless – shut in and around by my enemies who chose their own weapons and fought the unequal battle according to their evil, dastardly criminal mind's desire. So, thinking with Landor, that "silence is the ante-chamber of God," I kept my mouth shut and attempted to do nothing. I was bewildered, in a tangle of molesting that I seemed unable to get away from. Sad to say, I learned to hate many "forms" of religion and many so-called religious men. I have mentioned some above, and I must mention also the mulatto builder who lived at the rear of my house. His voice was like a devil's roar, powerful and out of tune. His face was evil and always satanically smiling; it was a countenance of falsity, obvious to all with eyes to see and a mind to understand how the canker of the soul is manifest on the face; he was one of the leaders of prayer in the adjacent chapel. He was typical of the place, for frequently he would bellow at me the usual obscenities and some extra vile ones. For an hour or more at a time, and very frequently, he would be roaring at the top of his voice: "Sod him." "Pooped out of America." "New Zealand won't have a big British sod like you." "We've seen to your passport," and so on.

All this persecution was fantastic – an extravaganza, though purposeful and relentless and dastardly in its aim. It was pandemonium for me night and day, week in and week out, month after month. To be anywhere was to be in the midst of my enemies. The B.W.I. Nos. 1 and 2 population is trained in the fine and cruel art of felonious molestation. They sucked up my peace of mind as a cat laps up milk. Practically the whole of the population is clearly in the service of the head crooks of the world. And this is a bald statement of fact, and no figment of an over-heated imagination. My landlady and her female intimates knew me as one pursued and hunted even to the death.

These were all definitely antipathetic to me. For instance, one day I overheard a "lady" talking about me to the landlady, and when she remarked how well I was looking, the landlady answered, "Mark my words, he'll soon be a complete wreck. I've seem them too many times before not to know what I'm talking about."

Almost every time I was out walking I was molested by fresh people whom I had never seen before, in addition, of course, to the usual molesters – who comprised practically everyone in the district, man, woman and child – yes, even the innocence of children was distorted. I remember one day I was walking down the road, with which I was completely unfamiliar, occupied by shop-keepers and other merchants, and composed of large well-built houses, when I was peculiarly molested. I could see no one, and yet as I passed down the road from each house and from behind each hedge came out words of insult and vile abuse, such as

"British sod," "Get out," "English sod," "British skunk," "White sod," "Get back Sod of Hell," "Jew," "Go back to England," and so on. A real co-operation by the population in the crooks interests.

As I saw no-one in the road, how were they aware of me walking along?

I met one of the residents of this road. He was rather a prominent man in the place. After a little polite conversation with him I turned from him and said good-bye. I had not walked more than a few feet away from him, when his wife, who was with him, said in an acid voice – the voice of maliciousness – "Pooped out!"

I turned on my heel and faced them. I stepped back to them and asked her the meaning of what she had said. They both only looked at me, in what was meant to be a contemptuous silence.

In addition to these, there were many government officials – both active and retired – young and old too – who seemed to be in the pockets of the crooks or were themselves crooks who had made me their special victim. Two old mulattos – they must have been seventy – used to molest me. Both wore sun-faded suits and one a straw boater hat. On many occasions I heard them say some-what as follows: "I keep on worrying him. I try till I die, so to get a share of what he's got."

This man was a pensioned Government servant.

Occasionally I would see standing by the road-side a big, very stout, broad white man, about fifty years old, in white suit and helmet. On each occasion he would be looking toward me, waiting for the negro who was always following me on these occasions. When I drew level with the white man, the negro would dart forward and shout something to him, usually to the effect that he had "pooped me." The white man, I discovered afterwards, was a Government employee.

---

One morning I had a very strange and disturbing experience, in which an accident, which no one could have foreseen, involved me. This experience taught me that my molesters were always on the look-out for the slightest excuse for involving me in their molestations. I had unfortunately tumbled into the water while walking by the side of the sea. This did not unduly disturb me, and I called a carriage which I ordered to take me home. We had not driven more than a half-a-mile before we were stopped by the Government Hospital ambulance. I was induced to get into it and be taken to the hospital.

I was put in a ward containing four or five negroes. The resident white Doctor gave me a sleeping draught, which sent me to sleep for the next nine hours. Waking up at about 9.30 P.M. I became aware of the dazzling white powerful lights. A man was talking about me as "the white sod." I felt quite fit and fresh. I turned over in my bed and saw a white man of about sixty-five or so standing in the doorway to the next ward. He was grey and unshaven, a stubby beard stood all over the lower part of his face. He was looking at me. As soon as he perceived that I had noticed him he began to speak directly at me.

"Sir, you are numbered and photoed," he said, "and you are minutely described in our books all over the world. Wherever you go to there is no peace for you. Your every journey is telegraphed and you will be followed wherever you go, until we get you."

For years I had wondered at the real motive of this molestation. Although the revelation was upsetting, it also was a kind of relief. I felt that the old criminal was actually telling the truth.

Perhaps I should explain that part of my anxiety proceeded from not knowing the origin and aim of my persecutors or the real idea of the master brain behind the molesting. I had often been puzzled as I had recognised some of my molesters in illustrations I had seen in the illustrated papers which I took regularly in Auckland. On several occasions I had seen their pictures in which they were mixed up in a leading capacity with some labour disputes and in labour demonstrations there. But this old crook's words seemed to give me enlightenment. Something definite and probable, too.

After this little monologue I fell into a slight doze, from which

I was awakened by the sound of a negro's voice which I knew very well. I was able to envisage him completely – his excellent clothes and his good car – as he was an habitual persecutor of mine. It was midnight by the ward clock. I rose myself up. I looked through a door and recognised the man. A little while afterwards I heard this man and a woman talking about me. I must state that this man was a negro, whom I later discovered to be a doctor, and the woman was white and a head Hospital nurse. Their conversation lasted for about half an hour, during the whole of which time I was the subject of their remarks (!) which were to the effect that if I did not go back to England they would get nothing at all. "We must sod him out," he said once or twice during their conversation. This man saw no one else except the white head nurse when he departed. This conversation was utterly astounding to me in that I was the subject of their talk. I had only been in the place about four months and yet I was so much an object of attention. It was truly disconcerting, to say the least.

What a mess some people make of their minds and their lives that they should be such dastards; but they were only typical of practically all the inhabitants.

The next day three more negroes were admitted into the hospital and placed in the same ward as myself. One of them I recognised. He was not long on his "sick" bed before he began vigorously insulting me. He kept his large coal, black devilish eyes on me for hours, watching my every movement and making riling comments. "Look at his eyes. Like a sick cow's," he would say, and "He's moved his arm, and his leg and his soft belly, the silly cow." In addition he referred lewdly to other hypothetical movements of my body. I have no doubt in my own mind that he was put opposite me to aggravate me and so to worry me out and "help" me to leave or to my "exportation" from B.W.I. No. 2. I overheard him telling one of the patients that he came to the hospital whenever he liked – which sounded very suspicious.

The next morning I awoke to hear the white head nurse talking to one of the negresses, who acted as nurses in the hospital.

"We've got to force him to go back, you know," she was saying, "or else there's nothing for any of us. He's no good to us as he is. He's only for himself."

Later on the Head Nurse, noticing that I was awake, assumed her blandest most benignant cast of countenance, and then came to my bed. She seemed to be very kind to me, and said that as a special favour I should be put in an upstairs ward by myself, where I would not be troubled by visitors. I thought someone may come into the ward in which I was at the moment, to whom I could safely make certain complaints, or of whom I could enquire concerning the reasons for my treatment at the hospital. Her talk of a quieter ward was a molest. I felt that there was more safety – if more direct annoyance – in numbers. She did not lose her composure, but simply patted my hand and smoothed my pillow and advised me in a "friendly" manner to go back to England "to get over it."

The same afternoon a very tall white man, about fifty-five years of age, well dressed and wearing a creamy "Palm Beach" plus-four suit and diagonally patterned stockings, came to the head nurse and said to her, "He must be pooped before he leaves, get me?"

It was not only in the daytime that these molestations took place. Every night a mulatto attendant would sit in my ward, quite near me, and keep up a running fire of lewd and suggestive remarks. He also used some of the usual B.W.I. No. 2 molesting too, and one night – the last before I left – I was given a particularly nerve-shattering shock.

The night-silence was unbroken, save for the breathing of my fellow-patients, and even those noises were swallowed up into he vastness of the hot night. I was not sleeping very heavily, when suddenly, without any warning, a terrific crash took place, and for the moment I was undecided whether it was inside my skull or outside it, that it had taken place. My wits came back to me slowly and I gathered that the noise was caused by the dropping of a huge weight on the floor of the ward above and right over my bed. All this, of course, fully awakened me, to discover that the lights were full on in my ward, and that all the patients were staring at me! The mulatto attendant was talking in a loud voice to several of them, and he was saying "He's done it again, the big ——— that he is."

I was literally sick at the sight and sound of this man, and the terrific shock I had just experienced. I looked at the clock; it was 2 A.M. I remember thinking, in a half-dazed kind of way, that it was not without its significance that none of the other patients seemed to be worried by the loud noise. I cannot explain this, I only know them as hyenas, and that is all that I can say. Of course, this was the "poop" ordered by the tall white man in plus fours, who was in a situation in a Government office. This population is toughened, calloused, by the desire of material gain – tenderness metamorphosed to greed, cupidity, desperation and viciousness, and the complexity all these bring in their horrid train.

---

I love children to have that soft upbringing, prolonging their child-period, keeping from them the bitter wine of rancorous disease of mind and body. Nothing hurts me more than an old head on young shoulders. Sad it is to relate that they employed children of the tenderest years, and, alas, given the toughest tongues to molest me. For example, a little white boy – with the shining face of a fat cherub, and the soul of the nastiest gamin – would stand by a chicken-house near my apartment, and use all the Anglo-Saxon monosyllables and local words of utter lewdness. This he would do when he knew I was in my room. He would even come beneath my window to do this, often standing upon the chicken-house, with the foulest abuse, uttered in a shrill, piping, childish voice. Pity at the cruelty of it all. His parents were crime-sodden and therefore he could not be expected to be other than he was. In these moments I cursed with the deepest sincerity the fiends that cursed these young morsels of humanity, turning them into pimps and prostitutes, thieves, murderers, vice-sodden tricksters, provocateurs and procuresses, before they were out of their early years of life. What can you expect a population to be like when such upbringing is in vogue.

Eventually, as a last resource, an idea struck me and I thought that I could possibly get some help from the Anglican Bishop of the Diocese, who was from Great Britain. I hoped that by his knowing the facts he would be able to influence the authorities.

I called to see the Bishop therefore, but as he was away at the time, I enquired if I could see any other Church dignitary.

A few minutes after a typical knight of the Church came to see me and he kindly consented to listen to me. He was the Bishop's secretary.

I had never, to my knowledge, seen him before, and yet I could see by his manner and look (both of which suggested) that he was acquainted "with" me or "of" me somehow or other.

As I related some of my experiences it soon became easily apparent that my relation did not appeal to him at all, and that he was a quite unsympathetic audience. He had prejudged my statement before I made it. He made one or two attempts to interrupt me, but did not.

Seeing his lack of interest and that it did not make him see any grimness, but rather the reverse, and that it had made no impression upon him at all, I cut the narrative short.

Of course, he had made up his mind beforehand to disbelieve it, and when he said that it was "all nonsense," I had almost expected it.

That night whilst I was endeavouring to read some book a molester loudly related the whole of this interview, word for word. I had asked the secretary to keep it a secret as he did not believe a word of it, so the next day I called upon him and said to him that he must have told someone. He was very indignant at my suggestion. It follows that espionage had been used. Of course, the explanation is that he had been befooled by "doctored" accounts of me. The lying tools of the crooks, or the crooks themselves, had done it. It was necessary to their intents and purposes that I should be given a defamed black record. Some of the "society" people of this place are in league with the international crooks.

They "blacken" the intended victim also to deprive him of honest friendships and decent people.

That this sort of experience, as related above, at the untender hands of children was not accidental I was also convinced, for everything was too premeditated, too planned, too well ordered, to be the invention of these little ones.

They were the instruments of those who had had a similar upbringing and training to that which they were subjecting these children who were molesting me. Sometimes the power of mimicry possessed by these negro and mulatto boys and girls and the adults also would be used. A boy or a man would bark like a dog, and a companion would accompany it with an awful lewd word, with such reiteration this bark and word would be repeated that I was sickened by its mere repetition.

Again, perfectly innocent children would very frequently be "used" in a most diabolical fashion. These children would be playing or standing together in the animated groups which children alone are able to form, without strain or artifice. I used to watch them and enjoy their natural grace and vivacity, when suddenly my enjoyment would be dissipated by the foulest of the usual molesting expressions, uttered in treble voices coming from these children. I could not understand how such innocence could be so suddenly changed into such obvious and blatant viciousness. But one day I discovered the secret. A man or woman would be standing at some distance from the children, and by the use of ventriloquism, would produce the horrible phenomenon. I discovered it in this way. One day, unable to stand the horror any longer, I walked over to these children and reprimanded them. They looked at me in blank astonishment. While I was thus talking to these children, I noticed that one of the boys seemed to have said, "He's pooped out," but actually his mouth was shut with a long piece of sticky toffee. At the same time I noticed the man. When he saw he had been discovered, he laughed and said, "Sod you." He then walked away.

In another way, also, the very young of the district were taught almost from their cradles to abuse me. If a baby cried near me the mother or father would immediately begin a savage incantation with words such as, "What has he done, my darly, Oh what has he done to you. Never mind. We'll poop him. We'll poop the British sod for you. Don't worry, we'll sod him, the white sod. He's only a big, soft, silly old white sod," and so on.

There was no rest from all this; even at the old Post Office I was molested like dirt, and when out walking with the one white man who seemed at all friendly to me, companions of his would meet him and stop him in the street to say, "I hear that he's a big sod."

Sometimes I sought solace by reading the Bible, and it was my occasional custom to read some Psalms to the old man, who was over 80. But every time I did this, his daughter would burst in upon us, and in her loud, raucous voice she would bawl out, "Hypocrite! Hypocrite, do you hear?"

As if by magic, all my doings and sayings of the day were known, and to indicate the extent of their knowledge, and to vex and try me, my persecutors would always repeat to me every night, the different conversations I had had during the day, and all I had been doing.

Whenever, for example, I sat on a beach, perhaps for two or three hours, I would talk casually to several people. These talks were generally of no consequence, simply remarks about the weather, or the state of trade, or one or two events of outstanding importance in the newspapers. In fact, the usual topics of conversation in which one indulges with a stranger. When I returned at night, and I had settled down to read, I would hear the whole of these conversations reported verbatim, and repeated in a mock-mimic of my own voice, interlarded with blasphemics delivered in the natural voice of my persecutor. This kind of thing occurred during the whole of my sojourn in B.W.I. No. 2, and also in B.W.I. No. 1 on the occasion of my second visit there. My molesters were obviously concerned with my knowing that I was being perpetually shadowed, and this was equally obviously a part of their endeavour to drive me back to England, by making my life unendurable.

An equally peculiar and annoying form of persecution was that of having a white man or a coloured, apparently with some culture, "read" his newspaper aloud, if I happened to be sitting on a bench in a park, or some other similar place. His "reading" consisted of nothing but the usual sickening words of molestation, and if I continued to sit where I was, he would go on with this form of persecution for hours, even turning over the leaves of his newspaper to give the whole "performance" an air of reality.

---

I was persecuted in these apartments by a negro who used to stand in the road below, outside my bedroom window, at 7 o'clock every morning, calling out filth and threats of all kinds until I went out, and then someone would follow me everywhere in the usual way. After some months of it I could stick this no longer, and I went to stay at a house nearly a mile further from the town, and quite near the sea. But this was actually of little use, for my molesters stuck to me like leeches, and some of them transferred their activities to my new quarters, with all their old ardour unabated. Indeed, after the first few days this new place was in every way as bad as the former places had been, all the neighbourhood becoming molesters.

The proprietress was a pseudo white woman, whose 15-year-old son used to disport himself under the piazza, or under the floor of the room in which I happened to be. He would, with the usual "crook" ceaselessness, keep up the customary flow of abuse, using the usual sentences and adjectives. The way in which these inhabitants of the B.W.I. persevere with their persecution was always amazing. It is true that this particular example of a molester broke the monotony occasionally, but it was only to change his position, so that he would be under my window, or by a door wherever it would be more convenient for him to make me hear it. On all occasions, however, he remained out of sight.

All my molesters collected again and focused their attention on my movements. There was no cessation, merely a change of *personnel* in my attackers. For instance, a more or less coloured man would occupy himself for hours and days on end, leaning against a fence near my apartments, and while I was sitting on the piazza with a book which I would attempt to read, he would keep up an everlasting jabber of filth and the usual adjectives. Or again, an old man, a neighbor of mine, of about 70 years of age, would sit on his piazza or in his front parlour, whichever happened to be more convenient, and he, again, in his weird, aged voice, would repeat, like a broken down cockatoo, the same insulting sentences. There was a certain harrowing pathos about this old man, for he had achieved old age with a heart of unworthiness and devilry, instead of the compensation of goodness. His sagacity was that of a precocious and dirty-minded adolescent. The mellowness of age had missed him. He was merely desiccated. All this was put upon me by the master-brains behind the organisation of my molestations. They had calculated to a nicety the effect on me of one who should have been a ruminating sage, and was merely an obscene, thief-minded man. This old man (as all B.W.I. Nos. 1 and 2 people are) was quite aware of the object of his molesting tactics. Almost all the population are slaves of Satan (and crooks).

But the main part of the molesting here seemed to be organised at the house of a mulatto family who lived next door to me. The woman of the house would start molesting each morning at about 7.30. Her son, a strong boy of about 14, would take on when the woman's energy or invention began to flag. At other times of the day, negroes would arrive and keep the performance going, working it up to a grand climax of lewdness at about sunset. All this amounted to an assault of the most fiendish nature upon my privacy and peace, and one would have to be Goethe's *"ideal spectator" par excellent* to disengage oneself from these persecutions, and view them as a dramatic performance in which one could not possibly be implicated. No, these molestations were too direct, too pointed, too manifestly meant for me. I could not escape feeling a good deal of the horror they were meant to inculcate. I was one of the performers implicated in the tragedy.

It was rarely that my persecutors troubled to be hypocrites. They showed their contempt for me openly, but sometimes, as for instance with the white Government sanitary inspector of the B.W.I. No. 2, a thin veneer of civilised manners would be preserved to my face only, of course, to be shattered immediately behind my back. This man was always molesting me in this particular way. He always wore a white suit and helmet, and was the gentleman incarnate to look at and speak to. But when I had left him for half a minute he would shout out (especially if there were negroes in the street): "Get out." "Go back!" "Go back to England!" "We don't want you and we won't have you here!" "You are pooped out," or some other insulting phrases, such as "You are pooped out to England. Pooped out!"

Other men in responsible and official positions in the B.W.I. No. 2 did not bother to preserve the externals of politeness.

For example, adjoining the house in which I was living there lived an "apparent" white man. He was an assistant in the Hospital, and was in the service of the white doctor. This assistant passed my apartments four or five times a day, on his way to and from the hospital, and with that "crook" assiduity – of which you must be tired of hearing by this time, he would shout out to me, as he passed by, in a most venomous and suggestive manner: "Sod him out." "Sod him in." "Get out, sod." "Get back, sod." "Go to hell, you sod." "You sod, you…"

This is the kind of B.W.I. incantation that under certain circumstances cannot leave you unmoved, to say the least of it, and generally it succeeds in driving you eventually to distraction and distress.

I do not want you to imagine that only the flotsam and jetsam of B.W.I. Nos. 1 and 2 were employed to practice these fiendish molesting tricks. Indeed, I think I have given you sufficient evidence to the contrary. Often the most highly-respected citizens (sometimes, it is true, in more discreet ways) would employ forms of molestation.

I well remember a wealthy and respectable (for indeed these two do not by any means always go together) tradesman of the town, would visit the proprietress of my house. He would sometimes bring his family with him.

A few days after I had arrived at these apartments, I was sitting in my room, when I heard this tradesman talking to the proprietress in a fairly loud voice. The proprietress replied in a similar tone. Then the tradesman dropped his voice almost to a whisper, so that I could not catch all of the conversation. The proprietress followed suit. I caught such phrases, however, as "We'll sod him in." "We'll worry him out."

This ceaselessness of molesting was a special study of the inhabitants of the B.W.I. Nos. 1 and 2, and most of them seemed to have graduated with very high honours in this art of molestation.

This tradesman came two or three times each week, and after the first occasion he brought a mulatto man with him each time, whom he always posted outside the door of the room in which I happened to be, whether it was the door of the parlour or of my bedroom. This he did always. He himself had private conversation with the proprietress for an hour or two. This man outside the door would keep up a course of molestation until his master had completed his business. He used the most shockingly lewd and abusive sentences imaginable, and all of them absolutely unprintable, and in addition he made hair-raising threats.

One day the proprietress suggested that we should go to one of the beaches and take meals with us. This I agreed to do for her convenience. When the party was ready to go I discovered that it was composed of the tradesman, mentioned above, and his wife, the proprietress and myself. We all sat in a large motor car and drove off. Behind us was a truck, full of children and driven by the man who was always posted outside my door by the tradesman to molest me.

He did not break his habit on this occasion, for he molested me during the entire journey, using the most vicious and obscene language, which did not in any way seem to upset the rest of the party. Indeed, at each new vileness the "ladies" laughed quietly and intensely. I was very sorry for the truckful of children, and glad when we arrived at our destination.

As I got out of the car I noticed a well-dressed gentleman, who was sitting in a very good motor car, looking at me. About a hundred yards away there was a long line of cars parked facing the sea. The occupants of these cars were either sitting in them or quite near to them. I walked by this "gentleman," and I had proceeded about fifty years towards the cars when he stood up in his car and shouted through a megaphone, "We don't want him! We won't have him!" Immediately the whole line of cars was filled with people who shouted in an organised way, in batches of two or three: "Get out sod, we don't want you." They call this a "poop."

I got away from these as quickly as I could, but, alas, I was unable to escape altogether. I was walking near a large hotel on the sea front. Two negroes and a white man were repairing the electric lights, which a recent hurricane had damaged. The white man wore a helmet and a khaki uniform. He seemed to be in charge of the job. The whole of the two hours I was trying to read, sitting on a seat near the hotel, the white man molested me in an exceedingly malignant tone of voice, incessantly vociferating, "Get out!" "We don't want you." "We won't have you." "Go back to England."

Also, he introduced some vile, filthy sentences. It is not without its significance to remark that the white man and the two negroes were all Government servants.

It was my idea to resist their attempts to move me. Although unhappiness came as a result of my staying, I felt that to accede to the threats and demands of my persecutors would be to court worse disaster, and that, as long as I showed them that their molestations were ignored, I would, in some measure, tire them. But, alas, these hunters of human blood were never tired, and one morning I decided, in a fit of acute dejection, to go to B.W.I. No. 1. There, I thought, as I lay in that seductive half-sleep just after dawn, I would be sure to get a little relaxation, even if it were only while my pursuers were adapting themselves to my sudden change of location.

CHAPTER XIV

# British West Indies No. 1 Again

IN THIS FRAME OF MIND, THEN, I TOOK SHIP FOR B.W.I. NO. 1. The ship moved and the dreaded place was fast disappearing from view. In a comfortable cabin I could look out upon the speeding waters and dream. One of those rare moments of bodily and nervous ease came upon me and my soul was irradiated with happiness – from great distress to great trust. The ship pressed on its course and my face was framed in the porthole of my cabin. The winds of the sea seemed to be sweeping away the horrid nightmares of B.W.I. No. 2. I cannot adequately describe the feeling of intense elation which had come upon me. To understand it, you must be able to sympathise to the full with me, tortured in every nerve and brain-cell over a period of years. You will then be able to understand the relation between what I felt on my way to B.W.I. No. 1 and what I felt before I left, for it is the relation of things that brings their significance to light – from *great* distress to *great* hope.

In this frame of mind I began to settle down for the night – the first night out, feeling that many hours of happy solace in sleep "the balm of hurt minds" – was in store for me.

But the balm was sour. For I overheard some men talking in some place near my cabin, – they were in a cabin or lavatory. One was saying in tones well known – the destructive tones – harsh, merciless tones, "We are going to get him this time. We'll sod him out of every hotel that he goes to."

"Sure," the other replied, "we've got the big bum on the run now."

Needless to say the amount of sleep I got that night was conjectural. From that time on I realised that I could not give myself up to day-dreams, that pleasure and dreams of happiness were not yet to be my lot.

I could not sleep. I got up at dawn and went to the smoke lounge to try and amuse myself with an illustrated paper. The lounge was empty. I sat down. But I had not been there more than a minute or two when I heard voices. Old familiar voices, using the old familiar terms. They came from a cabin adjoining the lounge. There were four different voices, all easily recognisable. Their owners, with that persistency which we have already mentioned as an accomplishment of the inhabitants of B.W.I. No. 2 talked for about an hour and a half – all the time, in fact, of my occupation of the lounge. They were talking at me in the old well-known fashion, recounting incidents of my life in B.W.I. No. 2. Such as my seeing the detective, my absconding from the ship in the dead of the night. One of them related how I had been taken to the Government Hospital, and he mimicked the gasping noise I had made when I fell into the water. They kept repeating this noise in a most disgusting fashion, varying the monotony of its repetition only with phrases such as "The bum-shit!" "Arse of hell." "The rotten sod!" "White sod."

My short-term dreams were shattered. I was thankful for that small oasis in the immense desert of my persecution, and I steeled myself against further molestations, for now I could see that my life on board was to be in no way different from my life on shore – except perhaps that on board, living in a small self-contained community, the molestation might be more frequent and its nature more intense.

I will recount a few experiences – though by no means all of them – which show to what lengths my malefactors were prepared to go.

For instance, a peculiar form of molestation consisted of the utterance of the well-known, well-worn phrases – "Poop him out!" "Sod him out!" "Go back to London, we don't want you," "Pooped out of America," in a tantalising way. The voice seemed to come from above me, when I was walking up and down the deck. I noticed that if I increased my pace the voice seemed to lag behind me, and if I walked in a slow meandering fashion it was directly over me. I suspected some form of ventriloquism, as I had had some experience of that in B.W.I. No. 2. However, to make absolutely certain, I dashed up the stairs to the upper deck – not expecting to find anyone, but merely a process of elimination, to discover the probable method of this kind of molestation. You see I was becoming a bit of a connoisseur in these forms of persecution by this time, which means probably that my sensitivity was less than before, and that I could with an effort attain a certain degree of impersonal interest in the molestations, from the point of view of their being well-constructed.

I did begin to be interested in the *form* of these molestations, and the form of the one I have been describing was not without its interest, for as I got to the upper deck, I saw a white man prone on his "embonpoint" with his eye glued to an opening in the deck. He was trying to see where I had gone. No doubt this was the man who had been literally *pouring* the persecutory sentences upon my head. He became aware of my presence. I stood near him silent and watching. He got up and I knew I had seen him before at the B.W.I. No. 2 where he lived. In fact we *recognised* each other – I with silence, he with a very little shamefacedness of a man caught red-handed in some indecent indecorous circumstances. He brushed his well-cut jacket and trousers with elaborate perfunctoriness, and slowly meandered away from me. He could be said to have *trickled off*. Like some stream that could not make up its mind how straight or how fast to move, he disappeared around the corner of the deck. He ought to have known better, I thought, a man of his age, for he was well over fifty. But I had given up expecting not only the magnanimous, but also the decent behavior of the large mass of those who call themselves human beings in the B.W.I. Nos. I and 2. This had not made me less interested in, or observant of, my "fellow creatures." On the contrary my life, with its incessant torment, had taught me to see in people what others, whose lives had been less eventful, could not see. I can say, with more honesty than many who claim the same accomplishment, that I seldom forget a face. I noticed, for instance, a man with a limp, who dined at my table on the ship once. He seemed a harmless ordinary creature, but he had made an impression on my brain which was ineradicable, and some time afterwards, as you will read, he molested me as I was driving along the sea-shore at B.W.I. No. 1.

Perhaps not unnaturally from the physical and nervous depression occasioned by the presence of unfriendly people all around me, in the circumscribed space of the ship, I was violently sea-sick on many occasions, and those alleged psychologists who claim that there is no recognisable interaction of mind and body simply do not know what they are talking about. On one occasion after sea-sickness, I went into the dining saloon considerably after the usual dining time. I was amazed to see, sitting at "my" table and dining too, four men whom I had never seen on the ship before. This was strange, for one soon gets to know by sight all the passengers on a ship like the one on which we were travelling. They did not observe my entrance, and as I turned to speak to the Steward I heard one of the men say quietly, but perfectly audibly, "He doesn't know we're here, of course. He mustn't, get me? We are to surprise him when he lands."

But if this section of the gang depended upon their invisibility for their ultimate effects, there were some on board who, whenever I was on deck, made the usual threats and loathsome phrases which were bandied about and hurled at me. The ship became, in fact, a replica, on a small, but not less intense, scale of my existence at B.W.I. No. 2. In my opinion, there were several crooks whose usual "beat" was in B.W.I. No. 2, who used this ship with no other end in view than of molesting and robbing me. Doubtless also, I was not the only "pigeon" to be plucked, otherwise it is difficult to understand why so many crooks should be employed for myself.

I looked around me for help, and at last an English officer on board, who was travelling from the London Colonial Office to take charge of the police in some Crown Colony, seemed to me to be the only available source of help. He had to report at B.W.I. No. 1. I knew this before I approached him. Just before the ship touched the wharf at B.W.I. No. 1, I spoke to him and said "Excuse me, sir, I would like to make a statement to you."

"What's the charge?" he shouted loudly enough for all around to hear. Surely, I thought, there was no necessity for roaring like this. My face must have shown my utter amazement, for he was looking at me in a most puzzled kind of way. I could not reply. I could not find the least spark of sympathy in his official face. I saw that it would be useless to say anything to him in quiet confidence. He looked as through he would want to make everything immediately public, and that I knew from bitter experience would never do with any statement of the matter of the molestations and threats. Once again I had been baulked by officialdom. But I had little time to muse on my situation, for the ship had touched the wharf of B.W.I. No. 1.

I was startled by one of the passengers, an alert, clean-shaven man, who called out in an exceedingly loud, penetrating voice to those congregated on the wharf, "We don't want this man. This English sod!"

He was standing right outside my porthole, and I could see him plainly. He was, in fact, one whom I had often seen at B.W.I. No. 2. He had the appearance of a Boston American. Also, he was one of those four who had occupied my table in the dining saloon. He was well-dressed, about 60 years old, about five feet nine inches in height, and well built. I had the feeling, as I was standing by my luggage on the top deck, as if the whole world was in the hands of the underworld. Negroes, most of them smartly dressed in dark suits, who were disembarking, appeared to me to resemble professional crooks, and the knowledge that they worked hand in glove with my white molesters, "foxing" me about and performing the usual molestations, became almost insufferable. The mulatto customs officer gave me a lot of unnecessary trouble, turning out all my trunks and cases and generally making himself an officious nuisance, whereas the other passengers had little or no attention of this kind paid to them. At last, however, I freed myself and my baggage from the crowded Customs House, and took a car to my hotel. All went well until I got out, when I heard a man's voice say "Furrage him out!" "The skunk!" "At him, boys!" They stood near the Hotel.

Looking round, I saw on the other side of the street two of the smart dark-suited negroes, whom I had observed leaving the ship about an hour previously. This might have been coincidence, as you might think that I am exaggerating these details beyond their true import. Such, however, is not the case, for these two negroes destroyed any chance of accident or coincidence by their manners. They glared over at me viciously, as only men of their kind are able to glare, and one of them said "We'll hustle the skunk out!"

"Sure we will, and now," replied the other.

My hopes of some – if only slight – respite were dashed to the ground. My movements were known and the organisation of the crooks was elastic enough to accommodate itself to my change of quarters with conspicuous ease. Indeed, I had hardly arrived at my hotel when molestations were set afoot. The first night, from a house quite near, someone started to play a gramophone. That night they played some of the B.W.I. No. 2 early molesting stunts with word accompaniments. It was about 9 P.M. Between the records a man's raucous voice split the intervening space with threats, insults and obscenities of B.W.I. No. 2. Worked up to a furious ecstasy by the horrible music of the gramophone – mostly depraved rhythms – there was nothing too indecent for him to utter. He was an adept at chiming in with his obscenities so as to fit the time and rhythm of the record. In this way he sang to me for hours, boasting of his success and the "happy days" that were to be his, of my defeat and the feast it was to be my lot to give to the worms or the sharks; with monotonous frequency he would inform me that I was trapped. He would sing out over and over again:

"In a trap you are, you ——!
In a trap-trap, trap-trap.

You're a ——, yes, you ——.
In a trap-trap, trap-trap,
And when I get you on my knee!
In a trap-trap, trap-trap,
Then I will see-ee, see-ee you,
In a trap-trap, trap-trap, trap-trap,
In a trap you are, you noble English ——!"

This kind of thing went on the first night until 1.30 A.M. The next day the gramophone was played without intermission from 9 A.M. until one o'clock the next morning! Sixteen hours of the same molesting tactics. Sometimes a women took her turn with the gramophone and used the same molestings.

This lasted for the first fortnight of my stay in B.W.I. No. I. No-one in my hotel ever referred to it, but all could hear it. It was devilish torture to me.

After the fortnight, when this gramophone molest had ceased, a man's voice proceeded from someone right under the roof of the stabled on the opposite side of the road and opposite my window. This voice – and other voices from this roof in their turn – used to inform me: "We won't lose you, you big beautiful fairy!" "We follow thee, o'er land and sea just like the busy, busy bee – you big buzzing ——!" "You're radioed, my dear, to every country in the world; aren't you too, too popular – you lousy swine?"

I often saw some smart negroes enter these stables, and I have no doubt in my mind – though of this I have no definite proof – that from their position these negroes could see, through a chink in the roof, my every move and action when I was in my bedroom, for nearly every day I would hear as I moved about the hotel:

"What do you think I saw Archibald?"

"I'll buy it, buddy."

"I saw him put his panties on."

"And allee nicee dirtee shirtees?"

"Sure, and how."

"You don't say?"

These men would burst into loud laughter when they would see the shame or aggravation written on my countenance. They were revolting specimens of human kind. These things were in themselves small, but the feeling of being perpetually watched, that no part of my existence was private, irritated me; for instance – whenever I took a bath – and surely in one's bath, as in one's bed, one has a right to expect a modicum of privacy – someone at once used to occupy the room immediately beneath the bathroom, and make the most awful lewd remarks and noises. Again, every time I used the lavatory, words of filth were shouted at me by some person in a room quite near. My life was becoming a cesspool – filthy and nauseous – and I wondered how long I should keep my mental balance under the ceaseless fire of these persecutions, which began about eight o'clock in the morning and went on till well after midnight. If I attempted to escape it was always in vain. Even in the bar of the hotel, which I visited infrequently, for I was not given to alcoholising, a man would shout about and at me, as soon as he saw me enter. Brazenly he would hurl forth vile abuse and intimidation. He would proceed somewhat as follows:

"We'll drug the beastly b——, see! Drug him! Dope him! Down him, the sod! You know what we'll do to him? No? I'll tell you! I'll tell the world. We'll bull-dog him!" He would wail at the top of his voice, "Blast him! You know who I mean – the dude, the skunk, the big white British sod! To hell with him. Down among the dead men, down among the dead men, let him lie," he would sing. I wondered why he was never turned out of the bar, for his exhibitions, besides being in the very worst of filthiness, were loud and obnoxious to all around. I can state truly – as much as I dislike it – that all these people were in league with each other, all co-operating and working for the international crooks against me. It is a sad thought – and this itself is one of the saddest thoughts, for we were not given this life to be infected with the poison of human malice and molestation for obtaining robbery with violence and murder. It makes us quite devils.

All that is truly decent and consoling forsaken for devilry. This round-faced man who molested in the bar was one of those that dined out of hours at my table in the ship's dining saloon.

When I went to the bank on the second day of my arrival at B.W.I. No. 1, this well-dressed white man with a very large, round, clean-shaven face was there, sitting on a seat near the Enquiry counter, where my business was to be transacted. He was a man of about 63 years of age and he stood nearly six feet high. I had seem him often at B.W.I. No. 2, where he was generally in the company of two young white women. As I entered the bank, his eyes followed my every movement, and I am quite sure from the looks he gave me, that he had been expecting me. Doubtless he had posted himself there to learn all about my business arrangements with the bankers. He concentrated all his attention upon me, his lips half-closed and his eyes staring straight at me, as I was talking over the counter to the clerk. During the time I was carrying on the conversation a voice, apparently coming from one of the bank clerks some distance away from me, said "We won't have him, sir. He must go back to England immediately. I'll see to it without fail. We certainly don't want him, sir."

This was, of course, ventriloquism. Round-face was breathing irregularly and his lips were moving a little. It was also very cunning to make the bank clerk talk in this particular way. I had never been in this bank before. I take off my hat to Round-face for this. He was no brainless crook. The clerk was speaking apparently as if to the manager about a customer and not particularly about me, and yet I know that no-one else except myself could be meant by the ventriloquial Round-face. It was a very disconcerting molest. On the next occasion when I visited the bank Round-face came rushing in just after me in a most hurried fashion. His rapid entrance left him a little breathless and he stood quite still, looking at me, at a loss as to what to do next. At this moment a good-looking well-dressed mulatto came into the bank. Round-face, perceiving him, hurried to him and touched his arm. A whispered conversation followed, and the mulatto turned his dark, velvety eyes on me. I returned the stare in a determined fashion. He averted his eyes and looked at Round-face, a signal from whom sent him to me at the Enquiry counter, where he endeavoured to overhear all my business by standing at my side.

Round-face, I am convinced, was staying at my hotel, through he kept out of my way, usually with complete success; but from his voice, which I heard one day outside the bank, I am led to believe that it was he who sometime performed the obnoxious molestations upon my person during the moments that should be most private in a man's life. His voice also used to issue from the bar when I was in my room, uttering awful lewdness, unprintable obscenities, which, in England, would have meant prison for him. Whether this was ventriloquism or not I was not able to discover.

One evening, Round-face was sitting on the hotel piazza. This was one of the rare occasions when he appeared to me in the hotel. He and his companions were sitting in deck chairs. When Round-face caught sight of me he bellowed tremendously, "If he does not go I shall have to go. Do you know who he is? He's the three B's. The Big British B——."

After this encounter I had no doubts as to the intentions of Round-face. He was definitely one of the leading crooks, and one who had been deputised to get rid of me, to get me on the move. This ageing crook was an underworld leader and he was endeavouring to lead me, eventually to get me in toils for robbery and probably murder too.

I went also to another bank several times during my stay at B.W.I. No. 1, and every time I was molested grievously there, a voice issuing apparently from among the clerks at the rear, saying: "Get out, go!" "You are pooped out!" "We don't want you!"

In addition, there were also some awfully lewd, B.W.I. No. 2 sentences used all the time I remained in the bank.

Each time I had occasion to make use of this other bank, a negro, well over 60 years of age, followed me or preceded me. I knew him from B.W.I. No. 2. I recognised him from his grey hair, grey stubbly moustache and beard, and the criminal, indescribable, murderous expression in his black eyes. He always carried a sheaf of papers. This was mere camouflage, to preserve the semblance of his being a business man. Actually, I knew him for what he was – a crook's foxer and watcher and molester. He always made a point of getting as close as possible to me in the bank. He did no business there. Perhaps this negro was responsible for the "clerk's voice" – for a surprising number of the inhabitants of B.W.I. No. 2 were ventriloquial in their habits and inclinations.

On the second day after my arrival I had occasion to visit a barber. His shop was empty when I went in, but in a few minutes it was packed with negroes, mulattoes, and broken-down "whites." All of them began molesting me as I was being attended to, and the barber himself treated me with some molesting sentences too. The air was blue, as it were, with the filthy B.W.I. No. 2 epithets and lewd suggestions that were hurled from mouth to mouth in the confined space of the barber's saloon. How did these men know the B.W.I. No. 2 molesting sentences? When the barber had finished shaving me and I had paid him, the other "customers" began to push themselves in front of me as I attempted to leave the shop. They did this in an organised way, with the barber looking on, a cunning smile on his face, until I was left alone in the saloon with him. When I departed I had to run the gauntlet of my molesters who had stationed themselves in the doorways of the nearby shops. They called from these places as I passed, and uttered the usual B.W.I. No. 2 molesting words and sentences with which I had become, by this time, so accustomed. I walked down the road to the "sanctuary" of my hotel.

But this hotel – like the others – offered no real sanctuary, for men's voices, using the customary jargon of molestations, came to me at all hours from all kinds of places. When I took a walk in the hotel garden, a man's voice molested me – appearing to come from a certain upstairs window – with such phrases as: "If he does not get out we'll kill him, disembowel him, scatter his entrails on the garden path – the bum-shit. We'll have all he's got, the hell-damn Englander."

This is a very much expurgated edition of his speech – which, in actuality, was freely sprinkled with shocking obscenities.

A day or two after my arrival at this hotel, a most horrible looking ruffian of a negro – about 50 years of age – stood under my window shouting madly, using the most violent and intimidating flow of language, and this he did ceaselessly for many hours a day, for two weeks. Need I say that this was no accident, no coincidence, but a piece of organised persecution, consequent upon the crooks knowing my hotel and, indeed, my personal habits. I felt towards the crooks as a character in one of Shakespeare's plays felt towards the gods, "As flies to wanton boys... they kill me for their sport."

I rapidly came to the conclusion that walking was unsafe, and involved me in too many opportunities for being followed and molested. I determined, therefore, to hire a motor car. One day, as I was being driven in this vehicle – which belonged to my hotel – the chauffeur suggested that we should return through the Botanic Gardens. I immediately ordered him not to do so. He affected not to hear me, and proceeded quickly through the main entrance. I was, of course powerless. When we approached a large lawn in the Botanic, where a good many motor cars were parked, men in them leaped to their feet, like so many mechanical toys. They shouted, "Get out," "Go back to England," and glared at me with hatred in their countenances. There could be no doubt that this was all prepared for me, and that the chauffeur was in league with my molesters. Indeed, he even slowed down as we passed along the lawn, so that I should receive the full blast of this organised persecution. Probably several of these molesters actually stayed at my hotel, and, knowing my habits, were able to adjust theirs to suit mine. They were thus able to stay in when I stayed in, and follow me or ambush me when I went out.

One day, I arranged for a motor car to drive me to a certain place along the seashore. All went well for some time and I began to enjoy the fresh sea air and the beauty of the afternoon. But my dreams of contentedness had hardly begun when they were shattered, for, when we approached a narrow gateway on the road, we found it blocked by a small cart belonging to a negro, who, apparently, had had a serious breakdown. I say "apparently," because I am afraid my mind was prone to suspicion "as the sparks fly upward." This breakdown held up traffic and there were about forty cars standing on our side of the gateway, waiting for the obstruction to be removed. As we waited, I observed many of the cars, much to my surprise, were filled with some of my molesters, whom I was beginning to recognise. My chauffeur drove his car slowly alongside the other cars until we came to near the obstruction. Then he began to "back" his car, and, as he did this, the owners of many of the other cars bawled out the usual B.W.I. No. 2 molesting sentences. I complained to my chauffeur, who smiled at me and said "No, sir, it's not you. It's the fellow with the cart."

But I knew this was a lie, and the queer smile on my chauffeur's face confirmed my opinion. Besides, phrases like "Get out," "Pooped!" "We don't want him!" "The beast," "Pooped him out," "Sod him in!" I knew these phrases too well, to think they would be applied to a man whose cart was broken down.

When we got to the end of the queue I perceived a white man, who was lame, paddling in the sea, with some children who were bathing. They appeared to be his children, or, to judge from the familiarity with which they treated him, to be closely related. He was clean-shaven, rather stout and about 45 years of age. I was greatly astonished when I discovered that he also was keeping up loudly spoken utterances such as, "Get out," "Go back to England!" "We don't want the dude!" "Blast him!" This he kept up for half an hour, until the obstruction on the road was removed. I then perceived this was the lame man that had dined at my table on the ship.

Turning this incident over in my mind, I have been unable to come to any other conclusion than that the whole traffic block was pre-arranged, so that I should be forced to listen to the persecutors, and so that I should think the place all "against" me. Apparently they had only one desire, to remove me from B.W.I. and send me back to England. It was beyond me why they should want to do this.

I still continued to drive around in a motor car, because, as long as we were moving there was less chance of ceaseless molestation than if I were walking or sitting down. Nevertheless, even when I was being driven in the motor car, certain professional white crooks, and some crook mulattoes, too, whom I knew from my experience in B.W.I. No. 2, and some of whom I recognised, often stood on the roadside as I drove along, and called out threats and directed intimidating looks at me.

I was at a loss for a time as to how my molesters discovered my plans, and were always stationed along the particular route which I happened to take. But I noticed, after a time, that whenever I went for a motor drive from the hotel, the chauffeur always had occasion to call at a garage near the hotel. There he would get out and converse with the attendant. Doubtless my chauffeur explained in some detail the plans for the day's drive. My molesters would then call at the garage and follow me. The drivers, or chauffeurs, of these pursuing cars would drive alongside my car and call out such things as, "Get out," "Go back, sod," Bum-shit." I noticed that some of my molesters were using motor cars belonging to my hotel and some of them were driven by chauffeurs from the hotel. On occasions even the chauffeur who happened to be driving me would torment me by "throwing" his voice to the back of the car and making use of B.W.I. No. 2 sentences and also obscene phrases. When I taxed him with this he looked at me in "innocent" bewilderment.

"But I heard nothing, sir," he would say.

"Pooped him out," would come from the back of the motor car.

"There you are," I would say.

"You are imagining things," he would reply.

But there was no imagination about this, as I can prove, for often when I returned to the hotel I would overhear the chauffeurs talking together in the hotel yard, and they would repeat the molests happened to me during the day, and they would repeat also phrases that they had used ventriloquially in the car, so that I had a double dose of molestation each day. Once, in actual fact, and then by proxy, for generally the chauffeurs would speak purposely in loud voices so that I could hear everything as I was changing in my bedroom, or as I was reading.

This seemed to have a bad effect on me – I was not a bit hardened through frequent inoculation – and the chauffeurs in the hotel yard increased the intensity of the molestations, beginning every morning before breakfast. Also, the negro servants and waitresses, the entire hotel staff, and some of the boarders, molested me frequently, and on several occasions some of the staff of the hotel congregated in the evening and let off "gun" fireworks with alarming suddenness and frequency, right under my window. After a display of this kind, someone would shout out, "See, that's what we'll do. We'll shoot the guts out of him, the big sod."

Several times during my stay at this hotel the chauffeurs would "repair" a motor car under my window. For hours they would keep the engine running, rattling like a machine gun. When they were "repairing" the engine, the chauffeurs would indulge in the usual molesting sentences, threats and lewdness, and one of these, a negro, was more disturbing than others, on account of his superior braininess. His malevolence was always well directed vituperation and he succeeded in disturbing me on more than one occasion. His vituperation was fiendish. It is a great pity that such intelligence should be put to such a base urge.

Though I was perturbed by their persecutions I continued to employ these chauffeurs whenever I wished to see the surrounding countryside. On one of these occasions the chauffeur had a "dummy" breakdown some miles from the town. As I knew a little about motor cars I could see that the efforts on the part of the chauffeur were not *bona-fide*. Whilst these *soi-disant* repairs were being carried out, three or four negroes stood at the entrance to the village near to which we had stopped. They gesticulated with their arms by extending them horizontally (as at B.W.I. No. 2), gesturing and intimidating, too. They pointed to the harbour and docks, and shouted, "Go back to England," "We don't want you," "Get back to England," "We won't have you," "British sod!" "Get out."

When the natives had accomplished their performance to the satisfaction of my chauffeur, he completed the "repairs" and drove through the village. When we returned an hour or so later, the whole village came out to meet us, though I had never been there before. Many of the population went through the same motions as those mentioned above, and uttered the same intimidating phrases. To facilitate this organised persecution, the chauffeur slowed down and drove in bottom gear through the village street. In this way I was able to get the full "benefit" of this pre-arranged "stunt."

To illustrate once more the intricate and universal ramifications of the crooks, who were causing all this to be done to me, so as to eventually rob me, and probably for my destruction too, eventually, I will recount the following incidents...

I was visiting the biggest general store in B.W.I. No. 1, in order to purchase some neckties. As I entered, the chief shop-walker hurried to me and treated me obsequiously. He had observed that I was a stranger of some means. When I had explained to him my needs, he called an assistant, who, equally polite, conducted me to the proper department. As I was examining the neckties, a white man and a woman (perhaps his wife) entered the store. They perceived me and signed silently to each other with their eyes and eyebrows. The shop-walker approached them and his politeness to them was tempered with familiarity. They had a whispered conversation, a little after which the shop-walker approached the assistant who was attending to me, and said in a loud authoritative voice, "Take those ties away. They are not for that dude."

Then he turned to me and said, "Good day to you, sir."

Having said this, he swung on his heel and left me. This was a nasty piece of molestation, quite uncalled for and completely unexpected, for I had never been in the shop before, nor had I seen the white man who came into the store with his wife. I was, however, to see more of him. A few days later he molested me as I drove along in the motor car. He and some confederates shouted after me the usual expulsive and indecent phrases. I must say that the crooks made up in frequency what they lacked in originality of utterance

I had a most peculiar experience a few days after this molestation in the store. On several successive evenings the motor car in which I was driving passed the Mental Asylum. Every time I passed it I had a queer sinking feeling in the region of my solar plexus, as I remembered my experiences of a similar institution at B.W.I. No. 2. On each of the evenings, after the first one, a number of the inmates of the asylum congregated at the gate, though it was getting late and they should have been safely inside the building according to the regulations. Out of the gathering dusk their hoarse voices and mad looks came, and my chauffeur almost stopped, so that I should miss nothing of the offensive nature of their language and gesticulations. Their lunatic – though ordered – malevolence simply oozed from them to me, and my heart was filled with a great hate for those criminals who made use of them in this way. Who had been able to make use of these poor mortals to molest me in this obnoxious way? I am certain, from what I knew of a similar institution, that the attendants and warders, being tools of the underworld, were responsible. And, this being so, it was a great betrayal of public trust. It is equally distressing when great wits and great lack of wits are used for nefarious purposes, for great intellect is given to man for good and noble ends, and lack of intellect is a sad accident to be succoured by society. Everything that one should be able to trust is no good and of no value in B.W.I. Nos. 1 and 2, apparently where the crooks are concerned.

I want to mention that I seemed to be well-known to the B.W.I. No. 1 police, for, a few days after my arrival, I happened to be taking a walk towards the theatre, outside which was a queue waiting for an afternoon performance. There were three or four negro policemen on duty outside the theatre, who as soon as they saw me, began to look evilly at me, and one of them said in a loud voice to his colleagues, "He's pooped out."

"Who did yer say?" enquired one of the policemen.

"Him, just him," replied the first, cocking his thumb at me in a most irritating fashion.

"We know him," chipped in another.

"Say, what don't we know of him?" cried the last.

All this was most annoying, because people in the queue began to take notice of me, and to look offensively and make remarks at me. It is a sad thing when abuse springs easiest to the mouths of men, and molestation comes from the official arms of the law.

To escape from the abuse which had arisen I boarded a street car, but I had no sooner taken my seat when two smart looking negroes, dressed immaculately, if a little flashily, boarded the car and sat behind me. I thought I was not mistaken, for they began almost immediately to use all the B.W.I. No. 2 words of molestation. They did this until I could stand it no longer. I gave them an angry glare and got off the car. This I knew almost at once was a mistake. It showed my enemies that their tactics were taking effect. The two negroes simply burst into loud raucous laughter, which seemed to be catching, for the whole car was soon rocking with cruel mirth. Really, I cannot understand these people; they are so criminally vicious.

It was soon impressed upon me that I had not escaped from B.W.I. No. 2. Indeed, I was made to feel that I could never escape. My enemies reminded me of this by sometimes playing the "hunting" call on the bugle, just outside my hotel, when I was getting up or eating my meals, or getting to bed. They must have been informed of my personal habits by the staff or the proprietor of the hotel.

---

One morning I was reading a book, and after a little while my reading (quietly to myself) was slightly disturbed by persistent talking in the room below (right under) me. I later noticed that he was talking in monologue. I did not pay attention to this talking for some time; but afterwards my hair "stood up," when, with surprise, I comprehended that what was being said by the negro (who was the hotel's factotum) was every word of what I was reading. He was almost simultaneously repeating practically with my reading for some time, so that I heard him *say* quite loudly the very words that I had just *read* only a few seconds before quietly to myself.

At the time I felt considerably disturbed and mystified by this conundrum, but I never thought of it afterwards until I recalled the peculiar circumstance at Aberystwyth three years later.

I looked suspiciously at the mirror on the dressing table and also even at the electric light glass, thinking, perhaps, they had use of a periscope and a magnifying glass. Eventually, I settled it in my mind that it was by means of a periscope!

---

Another incident which showed me that I had not cast off the nightmare of B.W.I. No. 2, occurred one day as I was passing along the corridor to the upstairs lounge and my bedroom, which was near the lounge. I heard voices, one of which I recognised. I passed through the lounge and there perceived the negro doctor who had conversed with the white nurse about me in the B.W.I. No. 2 hospital. He was sitting at a table with two white men, nicely dressed, who looked like "confidence tricksters" in appearance. When they saw me they began to talk loudly and "invitingly" of the best bonds to buy. They looked at me "expectantly," but if they expected me to indulge in any speculations of which they had the handling, they were sadly mistaken. They were all big fellows and they looked hopefully at me as I walked by them with total indifference on my face; then they scowled at me.

I became thoroughly sick of the town and all its unhappy incidents. I longed for the quiet of the countryside, where, at least, the objects of nature would be indifferent to me. They would only be able to "speak" to me of their essential purity and liberty. This longing became so acute that I determined to run away from my molesters at least for one whole day. This I did. In an hotel motor I drove a long way out into the countryside. There I wandered and gathered flowers and became almost "as a little child." I gave some pence to a mulatto cottager who was talking to my chauffeur, and started to get into the car. As I was doing this, the mulatto, who had thanked me in profuse terms for the pence, howled at me, "Go back to England! We don't want you, son of an English bitch."

As he said this he gesticulated wildly and disappeared into his cottage. His head reappeared at the window, which was open.

"Sod," he said, and disappeared again.

Of course, my chauffeur had instructed him to do this. Practically all the population obey the crooks and their agents in the B.W.I. Nos. 1 and 2.

We returned quietly to the town, my dreams obliterated, my heart hardened again against these fellow creatures. As we passed through the main shopping centre, just about closing time, three "apparently" white men, all well-dressed, came out of a big store. They saw me approaching. My chauffeur saw them; recognised them and slowed down. One of them said in a loud voice, "He's got to be worried back to England."

"Yes, sir," replied my chauffeur, and drove on.

All this, I must confess, was getting a little too much for me, and I determined to take fresh apartments. I despaired, of course, of eluding my pursuers, whose "foxes" were everywhere and well-informed. My new apartments were two or three miles away, in a less busy locality. My new landlord was a Spaniard.

As I was about to leave my old quarters, a big negress, a servant at the hotel, ran in front of me to the "strange" car I had hired to take me. Her design was obvious, but before she could engage in conversation with the chauffeur, whom, in any case, I had not informed of my destination, I ordered her away. She came back meekly, although there was a sly look in her bold countenance, and impudence in the movements of her proud body, which talked more loudly than any words she could have used. Of course, she had been told by her mistress to tell the chauffeur to molest me.

---

If there is any part of the world which tends to make one lose one's respect for mankind, it is this half-savage, pesudo-civilised robbery-mad B.W.I. Nos. 1 and 2 section of human society in which I happened for the moment to have cast my lot. Respect is earned by those who respect themselves. Self respect is not a virtue with the B.W.I. Nos. 1 and 2 people. I am not, of course, saying that all the women of this part of the world were not right. It would be unnatural not to find occasional goodness, even in the midst of such all-pervading, foul depravity. Alas, the good ones never came my way. On the contrary, the dregs seem to float into my life, annoying me fiendishly, but disgusting me more. This contact it was my lot to make almost as soon as I had settled into my new apartments.

That night I had no sooner tucked myself into my strange bed, when I heard several young women talking together and tittering as some women can. Suddenly they began calling out the molesting phrases of my ill-wishers at B.W.I. No. 2.

"Say, cutie," one was saying, "don't you know him? Oh, you must."

"Who d'you mean, baby?" asked and commanded another.

"Who? Nobody but him – the big bum-shit," replied the first in a most piercing falsetto.

"The British skunk," volunteered another.

Then they started to shout out, obviously knowing that I was within earshot: "Get out!" "We don't want British sods here." "Pooped out of America!" (I gathered by the intonations and sounds of their voices that they were white young women).

Several nights I was serenaded by these "ladies," whose voices were like viragos, and who showed absolutely no self respect – to say nothing of their utter lack of respect for me and my peace of mind and comfort.

One morning after having experienced a performance of this kind, I perceived a mulatto, wearing a very faded suit of some material which may have been black at some time or other. When he saw me he immediately began gesticulating with his hands, arms and body in an exceedingly unsightly fashion. His movements suggested that I was right down, "down among the dead men," almost, so to speak; that my case was hopeless, that I was helpless, and that all I had was soon to be lost. All this was to inculcate an "inferiority complex," as our pet psychologists would put it. He turned to talk to the proprietor of the hotel, and kept pointing to me as he said, "I put the babies on him last night again. They'll get him going – the fat swine. He can't resist the ladies, oh, la, la, the big-nosed sod!"

As he said this, he kept crushing his two hands together, to suggest that they had me where they wanted me, and that they could crush easily when the time was opportune. It was up to me, my soul whispered inside me, to postpone the "opportune time" with all my intelligence and might.

For some time the proprietor and the family had treated me well, but soon after I had seen him with the man in the faded suit, things began to go not so well. Indeed, they went very badly, as you will soon see.

A few days after the conversation reported above, the proprietor's son-in-law brought a dog into the garden, where I was taking a walk. The dog followed him around the garden, and after a little while, he began to molest me, using his dog as an excuse in the following fashion several times.

He stood up, and, pointing to the gate while he was looking at me, he said to the dog, "Get out! Go back to England! We don't want you here, do you hear me?"

I did, for he was shouting loudly and standing only a few yards from me. Needless to say, the dog knew that the absurd commands were not meant for it, and stood stock still, wagging its truncated tail. The son-in-law then walked up to me, smiling, and greeted me, saying, "Hullo, I didn't know you were here. What do you think of my new dog? I was just teaching her a thing or two. Mustn't let the dogs get out of hand." He gave me a quick, superior kind of look and went into the hotel.

Later in the day, when I was sitting in the garden, which was very pleasant, the man in the sun-faded suit molested me from a window on the ground floor of the hotel, looking out on the garden. He used the usual B.W.I. Nos. 1 and 2 phrases and did this so annoyingly and ceaselessly, that it was quite impossible to read or reflect. The molestation was having the desired undermining effect.

The effect most aimed at by my persecutors was that of robbing me of my mental balance and general self-assurance, and most of their tactics were calculated to achieve this effect. For instance, one day the proprietor, seeing me approaching the hotel, bawled out from an upstairs window as soon as he saw that he had been observed, "He's right down in the gutter, see! He's a low-down gutter sod. A sod of the gutter, that's what he is, and I don't care who knows it." All said with venom to irritate and cause anger, too.

Undoubtedly these hotel inhabitants all work for the international crooks.

This stay at B.W.I. No. 1 sufficed to show me that the city is a seething cesspool of vice besides which some of the better known are veritable kindergartens.

How such a state of affairs can exist in a prosperous dependency of our Empire is beyond my limited knowledge. Some suitable persons should ponder over the faults of our Colonial administration.

An attempt was made whilst I was waiting for a tram in one of the main streets of B.W.I. No. 1. I had not been waiting more than two minutes, when three natives appeared from nowhere, two of them taking positions at my side, while the third stood directly behind me. Naturally I was about to move a few yards away when I received a violent push, which sent me into the roadway. The force of my fall almost knocked me senseless, but I was conscious of startled cries of horror from different directions, and felt that some large vehicle was bearing down on me. To my horror I realised that a heavily loaded motor lorry was within a few yards of me as I lay helpless. People came rushing, and dazed and terrified I managed to gasp out what had occurred. By this time, of course, the three negroes were nowhere in sight.

Looking ahead I could see that B.W.I. No. 1 was likely to develop into something worse than I could imagine possible, and so I decided to leave everything to chance. I would, I decided, take the next boat on which I could book a passage. I went to the shipping office and received the ominous information that the next boat was for B.W.I. No. 2. Having determined on my course of action I stuck to it and booked a berth to B.W.I. No. 2.

On the day of sailing, I took my baggage on board and, as the boat was not sailing for an hour, I went ashore. On the wharf, a shortish white man of elderly appearance and wearing an English straw hat of the boater variety, shouted after me as I walked along. He resembled the crook that had addressed me in the B.W.I. No. 2 Government Hospital.

"We know where you're going. Get back to England, you sod."

He looked viciously at me. When I returned, he was still standing about on the wharf, and he repeated his little molestation as I went on board, and said viciously, "Get back to England."

---

This boat going to B.W.I. NO. 2 was again a tourist vessel, which visited a good number of islands and places. Consequently, there were many passengers. The concomitants of tourist travel – comfort and amusement – were very welcome distractions and sedatives for my overwrought nerves. The dance band was particularly good – especially when it played melodies, waltzes and soft Spanish music. The food was excellent and I had a cabin to myself. Indeed, there seemed no reason why I should not thoroughly enjoy myself. Unfortunately, however, I had not left my persecution behind me. I seemed to take it with me as part of my equipment, or even as an extra limb. Whenever I sat or walked on any of the numerous decks, I was subject to ceaseless molestations, which followed me everywhere, accompanying even the most private of my actions.

Whenever I walked the decks and passed the men and women sitting in deck chairs, I noticed that every fourth passenger or so would unconcernedly molest me. The ship seemed to be full of crooks. But this I realised was highly improbable, for there were so many passengers. What then was the explanation of the molestations? Some of those who seemed to use words of molestation treated me with courtesy and respect, when they met me in the dining and other saloons of the ship. And many of those who did not seem to molest me one day, seemed to be the worst offenders the next day. There is only one explanation – ventriloquism. Someone was following me as I walked, or perhaps the crooks were scattered here and there along the decks, and used their extraordinary ventriloquial power from their various vantage points.

This may appear far-fetched to some of you, but its truth is incontestable, because one morning I went to the barber's shop, which I found closed. I knocked on the door. As I did someone in the shop cried out, "Oh, don't bother, it's only the dude!" I looked through the window, but, of course, there was no-one inside. I turned round suddenly and saw a figure which I was unable to recognise, scuttle out of sight behind a projection on the deck.

But if the identity of this persecutor was unknown to me, I was soon to be acquainted with others who look little pains to escape my seeing them. Indeed, on the contrary, they seemed to delight in thrusting their unwanted presences upon me.

One day, as I was taking a stroll on one of the decks, a powerfully built, well-proportioned tall man, well-dressed and vicious looking, approached me, and, feigning drunkenness, nearly collapsed upon me. If I had not been on the *qui vive* it would have gone ill with me. As it was I dodged him. He begged my pardon in tones sweet as syrup but at the same time insulting and intimidating. Every time I met him after this episode he turned a murderous eye on me.

I will not recount further episodes of my life on the boat as they were of such a well-known order that they did not considerably alarm me, though I do not wish to underestimate their general importance in the scheme of things as planned by the masterminds of the crooks, whose villainous plan it was to reduce me to the state of a quivering coward. If I had been in any way given to neurasthenia and melancholia, they would have accomplished their desires a long time ago. So far, at least, as far as their main object – robbery – was concerned, they had as yet failed.

CHAPTER XV

# British West Indies No. 2 Again

AT B.W.I. No. 2, I SECURED NEW APARTMENTS, AND THE LANDlord seemed a reliable man, an apparently excellent change after the landlord-monsters it has been my unlucky fate to encounter.

But the neighbors here – as elsewhere – were of the calibre given up to vicious, unholy pursuits; their lives dedicated to crime and sins against the general order of human decency. This degeneracy penetrated even to the altar and the pulpit. Nowhere was there not some speck of rottenness.

Whenever I went to his chapel with my landlord, the shocking performance of molesting rhythmically to hymn chant and sermon was carried out. In fact there were several negroes and negresses who only went to this chapel to persecute me in this way. They would await me outside the chapel and follow me in with meek eyes and countenances of pleasant – black hypocrites! Some of them were the flotsam and jetsam even of this place. They were the toughest of the tough men and women, with awful vice and crime to their account.

In addition to these molesting me the usual B.W.I. No. 2 molestation would come from passing lorry drivers who molested during the service! Strangely (or is it not to be wondered at?), nobody seemed surprised at these shouted blasphemous interruptions of the services (it greatly affected me, as it was meant to).

Again, at the church which I attended regularly for some years, a man in the congregation said molesting sentences at me during every service, using even threats and lewdness, too. Those sitting near me must have heard it; their faces, however, betrayed nothing.

But if you think molestation in the House of God is strange, if not impossible, how much more strange and impossible must you think of the persecution I used to get at a football or cricket match, where I imagined myself unknown and lost in the crowds, whose interest was the game and not myself. Yet, wherever I was, among the crowd at these matches, any outstanding performance on the part of the player – a clever stroke, a brilliant goal, etc., was accompanied by ferocious yells of, "Get out," "Sod him out!"

Sometimes these cries were made by the player himself – when he would gesticulate in my direction, and sometimes by members of the crowd who happened to be near me.

I realise how incredible all this must sound, and unless you have lived as long as I have in the atmosphere of this fiendish viciousness I cannot expect you to believe it, but believe it or not, what I have said is absolutely the truth. These persecutions are exceedingly well-thought out and are calculated to cause you to experience great resentment and irritation, and to disconcert you. The intonation of the voices of all these B.W.I. Nos. 1 and 2 molesters is in the accusative pitch and expresses a vicious real hatred, too. Practically the whole of the populace, you are made to feel, looks upon you as hateful and they all harry you. They vilify you also to hide the fact that they are crooks. Among even such folk as the fishermen I received many shocks. They would hurl insults at me as I sat on the beaches, while they were in the boats near me. Many of these men lived quite near my apartments, and most of them seemed to be whites.

While at B.W.I. No. 2 as I was sitting in the lounge of one of the hotels, I heard voices coming from two occupants of easy chairs behind me. It was impossible for me to see the faces of the speakers, but I knew their voices.

To my astonishment they were making me their conversation matter, and, after other observations about me, I overheard the following:

One of the voices asked, "Why the devil doesn't the old

b—— go back to England? There will be plenty of it to share out then."

The other voice replied, "Oh, he'll go back before long. We'll make it hot enough for him. He can't stay here, and if he wants to leave here we can fix things so as he can't get a visa. If the sod doesn't go back and die there we miss our share."

Though I did not then know their meaning, yet, since having due reflection and consideration I know that these callous scoundrels meant that I would be murdered when I got back to my old quarters in London, where they were endeavouring to drive me to.

I caught sight of these two men as I left the lounge. They were the two tall crooks that I had seen an hour after my arrival on this B.W.I. No. 2 island.

This encompassing my death in East End of London would simplify things for the leading crooks' scheme of robbery.

I left the hotel unobserved by these two fiends, who on this occasion were quite well dressed.

The feeling that I had had on many former occasions, that it was impossible to escape merely by moving about, came upon me strongly one afternoon, just after I had arrived at B.W.I. No. 2. It was as though I was dragging the ghost, not yet a corpse and buried, of my past around with me wherever I went. A man and a woman, who were apparently whites, living close to my quarters, used the words "blast him" and "dude." They were pointing at me all the time that they were using these expressions. Now, as these words had not been used of me until I paid my last visit to B.W.I. No. 1, it seemed reasonable to suppose that they had followed me from B.W.I. No. 1.

Again, the negro doctor whom I had last seen in B.W.I. No. 1 as he drove by me, called out loudly to me, as I was walking along, "Blast you! I'm not going to let a dude like you escape me. You're a proper shit."

He slowed down his car to deliver himself of this pretty speech. I was struck dumb at the brazenness of this affront.

This was not the last time I had to come into contact with this "gentleman." Some months after the above episode I was taking a drive in a motor car, when we were overtaken by the negro doctor, who called out to my driver, "Give it to him, hot and strong. Give it him. Sod him out. Give it to him hard as hell, do you hear?"

My chauffeur, who was a mulatto, gave me one fierce glance and settled down to the vicious utterance of all the usual B.W.I. molesting phrases. He kept it up during the entire journey, using ventriloquism.

"Bum, you're a bum," he chanted, as from the back of the car. "Bum shit. Pooped out of England! Pooped out of America," he said, mixing these phrases with obscenities of the most revolting kinds.

I had not been at B.W.I. No. 2 for more than a few days when I was being molested with ferocious intensity wherever I went.

The mulattoes of the place made an extra dead set on me now, driving to meet me everywhere that I went to, and, as they passed me, stared viciously and murderously from their cars and called out to me, "Get out." "You are pooped out!" "Dude." "Bum shit." "Skunk." "Blast you," etc. My return from B.W.I. No. 1 had apparently greatly upset their felonious intentions. Now I have not the least doubt they had thought I would go to London.

I was truly aghast. Then the apparently white clerk in the shipping agents' office, who had come aboard the ship (on which I had intended sailing for B.W.I. No. 1 – but did not) as I have related – passed me in his car and gave three long piercing blasts on his horn – just like a ship leaving the wharf at the beginning of a voyage. This meant that I was to depart. How annoying he was; he thought to aggravate and that I was afraid of antics like this. Whenever I passed his house, his wife or one of his negro servants molested me, but I held on, defying by my very presence and return, the organisation of this population. How much longer I would be able to hold out was, of course, a moot point.

How far the poison of molestation devilry had penetrated and spread among the population of B.W.I. No. 2 can be gathered from the following.

On warm days, when the sun shone invitingly, I used to spend hours on the beach in an endeavour to keep as fit as possible in as pleasant a way as possible. The beach on these days would be well-frequented. People – mostly young – would spend all day here. I remember the first time I visited the beach, how I was struck with the scene – people glistening healthily in the sun – children frolicsome – an atmosphere of play and gaiety and *joie de vivre*. I soon learned to my cost that this gaiety could turn to organised malignant molesting for the crooks. Mulatto and apparently white girls – well-dressed and well-nourished, the daughters of the middle-class, "respectable" citizens of B.W.I. No. 2 would call out the usual molestations as I approached or as I sat on the beach anywhere. They also shouted out some of the worst obscenities which it is possible to express, and the mulatto girls would utter lewd remarks in most disgusting ways. These performances were always applauded and were the signal for further and greater efforts of molestation. I used to leave the beach, filled with a feeling of shame that such youth and life should be put to such degraded awful crook service. Wherever I sat down some molester – female, or male, or both – would always sit near enough to me to be thoroughly audible and obnoxious, and would say the usual sentences for hours. This torture of the mind, at this period was becoming unbearable and only severe efforts and self-discipline preserved me from complete lack of mental and emotional stability. I was never allowed to read or sit quiet for a minute in any public place. The organisation of this continuing molesting attack was fiendish.

---

Having had a conversation with someone belonging to a prominent merchant's family, some days afterwards I took a book for them to read to the merchant's place of business. I had not mentioned to anyone about my intention of doing so, through I had thought of it for a day or so before I took it. What surprised me at the time was that when I got to this place of business, some of the worst of the coloured riff-raff, blackguards of the town that were always molesting me (though they were never in a "bunch" like this) were standing outside his place of business, looking as though they expected me (all these men were looking up the road at me approaching). His place was not a spot frequented by hangers-about and it was greatly to my surprise when, from a distance, I saw a lot of men gathered there. All the while as I got nearer and approached these evil gaol-birds were staring and when I was able to discern whom they were they all gave me murderous looks. When I was going in the place, the usual sentences were "hurled" at me, and when I came out some vile threats were made by one of these criminals.

This incident greatly puzzled me as I was resting and reflecting that evening. It took me two years to find out "how it was done."

---

To escape this tireless pursuit I would sometimes seek the cool sanctuary of the empty Anglican church in the neighbourhood. Surely, I thought, I would be left alone in an empty church, for any noisy form of molestation would come to the ears of the authorities, I thought, who would be bound to put a stop to the desecration of the House of God. Sometimes, it is true, I would get a half an hour's quietude, during which time my harassed nerves would begin to calm, but suddenly a man's voice would penetrate to me from the outside. This would be followed by a man's head peeping round the door. B.W.I. No. 1 and 2 abuse would flow for hours, or until I left. Even the passing lorry drivers would know that I was in the church, and they would bawl out at the top of their raucous voices, "The British sod is in there. Sod him out! The low-down skunk. Bump him out."

Sometimes passers-by would come and stand in the church porch and whisper sibilantly all the whole time, so that the church seemed full of harsh, clear, molesting threats in a most diabolical fashion. Echoes of, "Who's a sod" "He's a sod!" "We don't want the sod." "Sod him out," "We'll shoot the Jew thief," etc.

To some extent I suppose it was useless to expect decency and civilised behaviour from those who were often used by my persecutors. Most of these mulattoes and negroes (many of them were unto simple brutes, in humaneness – or rather, lack of it) are very vile in their heart of hearts.

One day I was sitting near some negroes in a park, and for some reason or other there was a definite lull in the storm of abuse and molestation. These lulls always presaged violent outbursts, so that I was in no measure deceived by them.

One of the negroes was narrating strange experiences which he had had in Haiti. He was saying, "Jo know, a big bad girl she was sure." (He illustrated her proportions and the character of her "badness" by rolling his eyes and moving his hands). "She warn't no more'n twelve years old. Nope just a kid of a girl, but believe me she had it all."

"Cut the cackle, and get to it," burst in one, more impatient than the rest.

"All right, keep yer 'air on," replied the first negro, "I'm coming to it. This gal's ma was about sick of it all, understan'? She sold her to a doctor, bit like you an' me. What do you think, eh?"

"Say, an' what?" asked one. All the negroes were breathless.

"This 'ere doctor 'e turned 'er slowly into a pig."

"'Ow, tell us 'ow?" asked one with childish eagerness.

"'Ow do I know," retorted the first negro. "All I know is 'e did. 'E did with some smoke thing or other."

This simple story was believed in its entirety by these negroes. I could hardly restrain myself from visible merriment. He also said he had seen the bullets flying in Haiti and he had to roll across a roadway to escape being shot at, which he would sure have been if he had walked.

No sooner had they recovered from the effects of the story than they began to molest me, though I had remained entirely unnoticed while the story-telling was in progress.

I made several business calls upon a gentleman who was from Great Britain. He was a very excellent and worthy man.

Almost every time as I got near to his house a young negro with a bicycle arrived, and on two or three occasions, he was (when I arrived) already outside in the road in front of the gentleman's house, and on one or two occasions he was not there when I went into the house, but when I came out of the gentleman's he was always there.

On each occasion as I was coming away, as soon as the gentleman had shut the door, the gentleman appeared to say (from behind his door) some defamatory phrase about me.

The first four or five visits were a great puzzle to me and worried me a great lot, as the voice was so like the gentleman's voice. Then I thought it was no doubt that these defamatory words were made by this young negro, using ventriloquism.

On one side of the gentleman's house a road ran steeply down to a lower level road. Once I discovered, when visiting the gentleman, that a car containing several of my negro regular molesters was standing quite near to this house, but hidden from view in this sloping road.

On several occasions I had these conversations repeated by my molesters when I got home and I thought this was done by the gentleman's servants eavesdropping.

---

Of a different order of molestation, however, was that of the apparently "white man." Shopkeepers from whom I would buy would call out as soon as I had made a purchase, and was leaving their premises, the usual words of molestation; and just about a week after I had arrived at B.W.I. No. 2, I went into the office of the newspaper which had the largest circulation in the district. Here I ordered (I paid in advance for six months subscription for) this paper. I was treated to my face with civility, but no sooner had I turned my back to leave the office, when a white man, who was the main owner of the paper, called out to me, "Get out! We don't want you! Get back to England, where you belong! You've pooped us out and you're no use here!"

This last statement rather puzzled me for a time, but I took it to mean, after some consideration, that I had so far foiled the thieves, and it looked also likely that I had got to know them too profoundly. Doubtless they thought it time they had their "share."

I now wish to record some further aspects of the way in which Government officials are implicated in the molestation in B.W.I. No. 2.

I had only returned a few weeks to B.W.I. No. 2, when I received a registered letter which had been forced open and roughly re-sealed. In a crayon pencil there was written on it, "Opened at P.O. in error."

I was at once suspicious, and in order to test my suspicions I sent a registered letter to London, and when I received a reply to this I knew that this also had been opened at the B.W.I. No. 2 chief Postal Office.

Later on I sent another letter home – also registered – in which I have a detailed account of a particular molester's method. This man, who had been molesting me in his own way ceaselessly before I wrote my letter, immediately altered his method – and I had only posted the letter some 24 hours!

All this convinced me – as it would convince any reasonable man – that the Post Office staff was largely in the hands of the crooks. There were people in B.W.I. No. 2 who were evidently very nervous about my writing to my friends and others in England and New Zealand *a propos* the workings of the crooks and their ramifications, especially after I had had the second visit to B.W.I. No. 1.

On one occasion, I took several letters to the Post Office to be registered, and the apparently "white" woman clerk asked me to write my name on each envelope.

In addition to this direct affront from the officials of the Post Office, the molestations from both the riff-raff and the well-to-do of B.W.I. No. 2 continued and were increasing every day, even the respectable residential quarters of the town being partakers for the purpose of my persecutors, the crooks. In one locality, which was completely strange to me, where the houses were large and occupied by wealthy people, as I walked along I heard some men calling out – though I could not see them – as I passed the houses, "We won't have you!" "Poop him out!" "Sod him in!" "New Zealand won't have you," etc.

---

On many occasions my business took me to see a professional man in a main street office building. In the rear of this building was the wharf of a ship. Adjoining, and at the side of the door to the building was a gateway, through which access to this wharf was obtained. Every time that I arrived to go into this door (and proceed upstairs to the offices) there was a man standing at his gateway. Usually it was a rather tall negro of about 30 years of age.

As soon as I approached the door, this negro, or he who was standing at the gateway, ran down towards the wharf, and when he got near the wharf, he called out several times very loudly, "Sergeant major."

By so calling out, a man from the vicinity came at once to somewhere underneath and near the waiting room that I was in.

Immediately this called man had arrived, a terribly vile and severe molesting started in a hard metallic voice. He used the most murderous threats and shockingly lewd sentences, besides all the usual B.W.I. Nos. 1 and 2 sentences, until I left the waiting room, perhaps for over an hour. It reached my ears in a subdued, but distinct, voice tone. I frequently tried to stifle the annoyance by stopping or closing my ears with my fingers, and when doing so, I rested my elbows on my knees or put my elbows upon the wooden table. Strange to say, I found that neither of these expedients stopped or banished the sound. I could still plainly hear all the molesting words, though not quite so loudly as when I did not stop my ears, and the sound reached my ears by the air. The sound when I stopped my ears must have travelled through the wood of the floor and of the table and then through my bones to my ears! I could not escape their molesting anyway. How was it done? If these scoundrels are in an hotel or elsewhere they no doubt can send sounds (by means of some instrument) to molest any intended victim who is in the same premises, or even in adjoining premises.

---

These happenings decided me to take the (for me) important step of approaching the Chief Detective. With the intention of gaining an interview with the Chief I entered the Police building. The negro policeman on duty seemed a very decent, well-spoken man, but after a whispered conversation with another negro – who was a clerk or a detective – his whole manner changed, and he looked at me murderously. I have never seen such a quick change in a man. In a minute, from a human being, he became a fiend. After the conversation with the policeman, the negro clerk called out, his features distorted with vile intimidation, "We'll poop him out of every house in the Island. He's got to go back to England."

Eventually I saw the Commander, but he told me to call later, when I would be able to see the Chief. I returned at the stated time and saw the negro policeman emerging from the Police Office. He glanced at me with hatred in his eyes as he hurried away. I discovered that the Chief had come and gone. I was extremely disconcerted and annoyed, but I shrugged my shoulders, thinking that I would see him on another occasion. My discomfiture, however, was uncomfortably increased when I perceived, lounging just near and staring with intolerable eyes at me, the two tall white crooks, in the faded suits, whom I had seen an hour or so after landing for the first time in B.W.I. No. 2, when one of them had said, "We'll know him by his beak," just about two years previously.

They had, written all over their sinister faces, the signs of satisfaction and victory. I shuddered at the way their vicious nurture had distorted nature.

This was a prepared stunt. I had made the appointment, and of course it was known I would be back at the time and crooks rule here very largely and all the coloured police in B.W.I. No. 2 "swim" with the international crooks.

With the two head crooks was a negro chauffeur (dressed in the dark uniform and peak hat affected by chauffeurs) who was a dastardly molester on all occasions.

Night and day, B.W.I. No. 2 played out the tragedy of my existence. With the fiendish cunning and persistency my – shall I call them "evil spirits?" – attempted to reduce my powers of resistance by molestations of my person and my mind. Like a well-constructed drama, the persecutions were working up to a climax – increasing in number and intensity. I felt as if I were being swept, willy-nilly, I knew not where, backwards and forwards, on a wave of crime and viciousness. I was beginning to think that I should not be able to escape my awful fate, which every fresh outrage promised and threatened to bring nearer. I thought, as the great character of another tragedy, that "there was a Destiny which shaped our ends, rough hew them how we may." The night was rent with shouted cries and the "balm of hurt minds" was denied me. With increasing regularity a man, whom I knew by his voice as a neighbor of mine, used to destroy all thoughts I may have had of sleep by regular calling out every five minutes throughout the night until dawn, of phrases which, though by this time quite familiar, still carried stings in their tails. They were spoken from a house quite near. Suffice it to say these experiences were not calculated to strengthen me in sinew or brain. Indeed, as the phrases came to me they were like acid poured into my vitals, eating away my resisting powers. I would literally shudder when whining and wailing phrases kept me from sleep.

"You are drummed out," the voice would say, "drummed out, you bum-shit!" "You thief," "You crook," "You rook," "You English sod!" "You are jewing us, get back to where you belong, or you will be found drowned, found drowned!"

The voice was almost shouting at the end of each such utterance.

---

As I sat or lay under a palm tree in the garden, reading, I once or twice noticed that some little part of my quiet reading was almost simultaneously repeated by a particularly vitriolic and vile molesting neighbor. This neighbor was indoors and about 100 feet away from me, with windows and doors of the house all open.

It was a great and very disconcerting and annoying molest to me at the time. It gave me a puzzling headache worrying, but I did not think anything more about, except its distressing me at the time. It was a pity I did not appreciate its significance.

---

The terrors of the day always seemed a little less terrible after the terrors of the night. The element of the "unknown" and the "unknowable" magnifies the effect of these nocturnal molestings. There were even occasions when I could take, almost without feeling a twinge of uneasiness, the molestations of the day. It was as if my enemies had perceived this, for they piled Pelion upon Ossa, using for their molestation purposes, prominent men of B.W.I. No. 2.

For instance, one day I was taking my customary walk along the seashore, when a gentleman approached me and entered into conversation with me. My suspicions were disarmed by his charming manner. He enquired if I was a stranger in B.W.I. No. 2.

"Not exactly," I replied.

"Oh, indeed, and how long have you been here, may I ask?" he asked.

"You may," I said. "It seems like an age, though actually it is only a matter of a few years."

"I see," he said. "Do you like it here?"

"Not exactly," I replied, smiling bitterly to myself at this naive question.

From this point on we discussed the island and its inhabitants, and their customs. He invited me to an *al fresco* luncheon on the seashore. He had with him a good number of his relations. We talked about many things, but I could see that they were always bringing the conversation back to me – how I lived. Where I lived. What I did. What I thought about. How long did I intend to stay, and so on. I concluded, of course, that all this was just politeness on their part, and after a long conversation I bade them "good day," and proceeded on my walk. I had not gone very far, however, when one of the party – I could not say which one – called out, "Get back to England! You've pooped us! We don't want you!"

I was shocked and surprised at molesting from anyone associated with this gentleman, whom I discovered to be a prominent figure in the newspaper world of B.W.I. No. 2. I was again a little shocked – though all these experiences were pale besides those that disturbed my nights – when, as I was passing this gentleman's house one day shortly after, a voice called out from it (for the house stood alone and there was no one in the road): "Sod, sod! Go back to England!" And on still another occasion this same newspaper man was responsible for annoying me. He had taken me for a ride in his car, though if I knew as much then as I know now I would not have gone. When we were some distance out in the country he said to me, "Get out. We don't want you here." I smiled and got out.

This man, and indeed most of the people of B.W.I. Nos. 1 and 2, simply carry out the orders of the international crooks. They try to emulate one another always. They are promised a share in the proceeds of the robbery or swindling. They are probably afraid to disobey orders, owing to the power of these crooks to inflict damage on their business careers. Possibly the vast and intricate network of threat and counter-threat keeps everyone (all the population) a tool of these crooks in fear of his own career, and makes them on occasions do the most fantastic things, in order, I presume, to outdo their confederates and to have something definite to report at their headquarters. For instance, occasionally someone would let off several "gun" fireworks outside the window of my room where I was sitting. This demonstration of hooliganism would be followed by catcalls and, "I'll get my bull-dog to him," or "We'll shoot him if he doesn't go back. He thinks we won't, but we're only waiting our time."

The hypocrisy of the negroes it was my misfortune to meet was exemplified again and again. The swashbuckling exterior of some of them was astonishing. Even pious negroes, those who professed the Christian faith, were not immune from hypocrisy and viciousness. For instance, a negro builder of the island would, with the punctiliousness of a Spanish Grandee, greet me and speak to me. We would converse together most amiably on topics of "high seriousness," of God and man's place in the Society of Nations; of the peace of the world being only possible by the power of Christ in men's hearts to effect it. These and similar topics were the instruments which made our converse agreeable and edifying in the extreme. But as soon as I had turned my back on this man, and I had walked away a few yards, he would call out in a riling voice, used purposely so that it caused resentment, besides being molestation, "Get out. You'll be drummed out." This negro was a prominent member of his Brethren Chapel.

On another occasion, as I was walking along, this negro happened to be ahead of me. A friend of his, passing, greeted him, and in exchange of greetings my negro "friend" pointed at me unmistakably, and called out to his friend, "We've got his brain pooped."

This brought to light that the molesting was done to "addle" my brain.

This, you will readily admit, I think, was a most disconcerting phrase, too. It showed he was quite aware of all the persecution and its object. Another time the same molestation was embodied in another phrase he used, "We've got his head." This reference to my sanity (or lack of it) was proof that the molesting was calculated to deprive me of my strength of will and balance. It showed confirmatively the villainy intended. No doubt, he meant too, that he was glad that the molest was affecting me seriously. I was exasperated by this subtle form of persecutions and dire purpose.

I was naturally disgusted and disturbed with the new practice of some of the people around me of so placing some putrid fish or human manure, "far gone," that when the wind blew the awful stench would be carried in my direction, whether I was sitting alone, or gardening, or sitting at the open window of my room. This happened not once or twice, when there would have been a possibility of its being an accident, but on many occasions. This crude (or is it subtle?) form of torture only made me fearful of the end of the human race, for it is well known that these "low" human forms breed like rabbits and generally breed their kind.

Sometimes, on the most unlikely occasion, I would come against molestation from perfect strangers. Generally, however, they were informed as to my whereabouts by others of the crooks. Once, when I went with a mulatto, whose relations with me had been perfectly, if not enthusiastically, friendly, to a relation of his far out in the country, I was molested by one of these relations – the son of the house – who came out and stared at me as I sat in the car. I smiled at him, thinking that he was a friendly human who needed politeness and attention to make sociable. I was never more mistaken in my life, for he stared at me fixedly, returning no answer to my "Good afternoon." His stolid look was mingled with contempt and hatred. I had never seen this man before, and he had evidently been sent out of the house by my mulatto "friend" to accomplish this little stunt.

Speaking of mulattoes reminds me of one particularly nasty specimen. He was rather a dwarf, about middle age, who always consorted with the crooks and the ne'er-do-wells of the town. He was the companion of any riff-raff molesters, and I discovered his particular "flair" was that of a super-foxer and watcher, though on odd occasions, when he had nothing to do, he condescended to molest me. Once, when an American ship with tourists from New York docked at B.W.I. No. 2, I saw him narrowly watching the visitors as they disembarked. Suddenly, he was "all eyes." He had seen his man. He slunk quickly away, and without any difficulty I was able to envisage the possible life of this poor unfortunate tourist as long as he stayed at B.W.I. No. 2 – and indeed, probably wherever he happened to stay. I felt I would like to warn this man if I knew him. But thoughts informed me that he would only think I was mad if he had not been subjected to the molestations of the crooks, and he would not need to be warned if he had been so subjected. I simply reflected on it if anything, a little sadder.

Doubtless this hefty dwarf mulatto "fixed" me when I also had the ill-fortune to land at B.W.I. No. 2.

---

I was sitting in my room one afternoon, trying to read, though molesting was going on in a girl's voice (in the voice of a frequent molester). This young woman was using all the usual B.W.I. Nos. 1 and 2 sentences. She was in the house opposite mine.

Suddenly I heard her speak in a very surprised tone of voice to her mother. She said excitedly, "Mother, I can hear every word that the people in ——— Street are saying."

Her mother answered her in a muffled voice.

The street that she mentioned was 400 feet away. She did not mention what enabled her to hear these people talking.

---

The attitude of the police, as well as that of the rest of my molesters, decided my paying a visit to the Colonial Secretary. The coloured police, either coming from or going to their headquarters, lost no opportunity of molesting me. They would stand still when they saw me, and stare evilly at me, saying loudly, "He's pooped. The British shit." Then they proceeded on their way as if nothing had happened. I asked the Colonial Secretary for an interview, so that in half an hour or so I might explain all my position and grievances to him. With a smile he told me that he could not listen to me or grant me the interview.

While I was talking to him in his private room at the Colonial Office, there were men in the road right underneath his window, calling out vociferously, "We don't want him!" "We won't have him!" "Get out, you sod!" "Go back!" "Pooped out!" Do these authorities take heed of this sort of thing?

But this was not the end of this particular experience, for that evening the whole of my conversation with the Colonial Secretary was retailed to me *verbatim* by someone near my house as I was lying in my bed, trying to forget my existence in sleep. How did this subject overhear? This, I am utterly unable to answer. However mysteriously my enemies may have heard, there was nothing mysterious about their aims, for the molesting outside the Colonial Office was doubtless to make me nervous and appear peculiar to the Secretary as I was speaking to him. And the retailing of my conversation was done to disconcert me and weaken any purpose or any resolution in me.

About this time my mind was considerably occupied with the reason of this molestation, and one or two incidents either caused or were consonant with my thoughts. "Why?" I kept asking myself. But let me tell the story in my own way, which is to give incident first and inference after.

Meeting the old grey mulatto Customs officer in the hall on the wharf where the ship passengers' personal baggage was inspected, I dropped into a casual conversation with him. His main concern was the likely date of my return to England.

"When are you going back?" he kept on asking, completely unable to hide his anxiety. He was concerned that I should go back to London. No other place would do for him. I kept on thanking him for his solicitude, but it was completely lost on him. Why did he want me to go away? And why London? Why not New York or Buenos Aires or B.W.I. No. 1? I saw this old grey mulatto only two or three times a year. I had no business with him. Our relationship was casual and conversational in the extreme. We used to talk about the health of B.W.I. No. 2, for sometimes he acted as sanitary inspector, but he was rarely much interested in this topic. It is reasonable to suppose that all this tireless molestation had a purpose. Men – and such men! – do not go to such trouble for nothing. I have come to believe now – though for years I cast about for adequate reasons—that however apparently amicable these people are, they are all after their "share of the swag." They must succeed frequently, else they would be discouraged. They are promised, as I think, by the international crooks, that if their behests are obeyed then they will get their share of the booty. Doubtless, in many cases the victim is ultimately frightened into parting with his money or actually robbed, and eventually murdered, too. Practically all the inhabitants of this place are in the "Crime Swim," so to speak. This may seem unbelievable, but it is my experience that no class or colour is free from suspicion of crookedness. If you knew how money – hard cash – is worshipped out there you would probably be much more willing to believe my sweeping assertion. But take, for example, a typical day and a typical sequence of events. The mornings I sometimes spent in a quiet spot – some park or open space. One morning, as I was walking along, I passed some loitering negroes. They seemed to take little or no notice of me. But after I had proceeded for about five minutes, they rushed by me helter-skelter, shouting and cursing like mad, and as they did this they managed also – to such a pitch have they cultivated this art of molestation – to shout out one after another:

"We'll murder him!"

"We'll bull-dog him!"

"We'll settle him!"

"We'll put him out!"

"The shit!"

"The sod!"

"The skunk!"

"The white dude!"

Proceeding further along, I came almost to the precincts of the police headquarters, and here two negro policemen stared malevolently at me. They came to a standstill when they saw me, and with murderous eyes fixed on me as I moved along, they watched me pass. Then they followed me for a little way, saying, like quick-firing machine guns:

"The bum-shit!" "He's a bum-shit!"

A few hours later, two of the vilest looking negroes I have ever seen – and I have seen some! – stared at me steadily and muttered quite audibly:

"The sod!" "The British skunk!" "We won't have him."

"We've pooped him out!"

In the afternoon I went to a white lawyers office, where I had had occasion to go several times previously. Each time I went I noticed three nicely dressed men – two were mulattoes and one was white. They stood on the footpath right outside the office. One of them I had seen on my last visit to B.W.I. No. 1, where he had employed a considerable portion of his time "foxing" and molesting me in the customary local fashions. Each time, as they saw me coming to the office, their faces would harden and their eyes narrow in their cunning faces, and they drew together. The whole of the time I was in the ante-room of the office, I was molested by the usual sentences. This was when I was waiting in the ante-room. Doubtless this was ventriloquism, of which I have said enough. Enough at least to suggest its prevalence at B.W.I. No. 2. On this particular afternoon just after I had left the office, I passed a mulatto woman with a child at her side. She looked up at me as I passed, and with an ugly leer, she spurted out the word, "Whore." Is not such practically an assault and violence?

It was one of the many atrocious words these people use so freely to madden you. She was "working" with all the rest for the vilest of the earth, the leaders of the underworld.

I had not left this evil creature more then twenty minutes when I passed a working negro, standing in his front garden, quite near my house. He looked at me unkindly. I bade him "Good day," briskly and brightly. Suddenly his face was suffused with passion, a vile look spread over his features, his eyes became murderous, and he said:

"As if I'd talk to him – the rook, the English sod. Go back!"

All along the rest of this street lived negroes, mulattoes and whites, and, as always, I had to run the gauntlet of a perfect fusillade of abuse. One after another they cried out:

"He's got to go!"

"Get out!"

"Go back!"

"Drummed out!"

"He's pooped to England!"

"Sod him out!"

"Sod him!"

As I was walking sometimes, I was as if in some nightmare. The streets seemed too horrible. Perspiration came out all over me. After tea, an apparent white man mentioned before, who to judge from his car and his clothes was fortunately situated as far as the material comforts of this world are concerned, drove by me, loudly sounding the four notes of the "hunting call" on the horn of his motor car. Of course, his aim was to instal terror into me, and also probably to urge those molesting me to greater efforts. He was about 35 to 40 years of age, and he always gazed menacingly at me with murder glinting in his bad, dark eyes.

That evening I went to one of the chapels I occasionally visited. An apparent "white" choir-leader, who was also a leading man in the chapel, about 60 years old, with a large face and body, molested me when he was talking to others, saying to them, "He's pooped," and jerking his thumb at me over his shoulder, he also said, "We'll get some of his cash yet."

So that from this one day alone, it is possible to infer two things, and that these are related. One, that my persecutors were keen on getting me to leave B.W.I. No. 2 and to return to London. Two, that they were after money. So that somehow or other they imagined, or had so fixed it, that on my arriving in London, it would mean the loss of my money to me and the gain of it to them. I must confess that the "how" and "why" of this latter proposition escaped me, neither did I infer as above at the time.

---

One night, after being asleep for some hours, I awoke at about 1.30 A.M. A few minutes after awakening, I opened my eyes, and immediately one of my usual "white" neighbor molesters, whom

I knew well by sight and also by his voice, said loudly, "The sod's opened his eyes."

I had my head laid sideways upon the pillow.

I just closed my eyes and opened them again and I found that I could just "discern" or hear the eyelid that was against the pillow, making as it moved a slight sound, which was in turn heard by my ear that was on the pillow.

The molester was in a house on the opposite side of the road. He was 60 feet away. How did he hear this infinitely small sound?

---

Those of you who have travelled the face of the earth only a little, will know how some races are given to gesticulation, to bodily gestures, to supply their deficiency of expressive language, or, in some cases, to augment the richness of verbal expression which they possess, and those of you who know the part of the world in which these happenings are placed will know that from babyhood the inhabitants of B.W.I. Nos. 1 and 2 are given, by imitation, to many forms of significant gesticulation. It must be confessed that these forms are for the most part lewd and abusive, too, and the concomitants of molestation. Very often I experienced the following, or something akin to it.

Besides filthy gesticulations, negroes and others, many of whom you could swear were white if you did not know better from experience, would, on catching sight of me, do this: – Holding out their arms, with hands and fingers outstretched, they would slowly move them down and raise them rather quickly a little and move them slowly down again, and if I was near enough I could catch the words accompanying these actions, such as:

"He's pooped by everyone here."

"He's in the gutter, where he belongs."

"They've got him."

"Even the Government wants him to go."

These negroes also opened and shut their mouths, as though

they were talking to me, as I approached them. They would do this even when walking singly as they approached. They would give me their effectively cultivated evil looks and their white teeth would lend emphasis to this kind of molestation as they moved their lips. What a great pity they are employed for such base ends!

Again, these inhabitants have cultivated the art of lying until they seem to have left nothing to learn in this branch of knowledge. They can denounce one cleverly and make all sorts of lying accusations, knowing that you are powerless to denounce them to the public authorities. If you report to the police you are made out to be a liar and a fool, or both, or worse.

I was convinced that some powerful organisation gives the natives and all other molesters protection in the event of any complaints of their persecutions.

I was a British citizen from London and got no protection of the law to which I was entitled.

My nerves had been reduced by years of molesting and maltreating by negroes and others.

My molesters were not free-lance scoundrels, or their helpers, but were hand-in-glove with the crooks of London.

From the most unlikely quarters, as I have said before, come some of the worst molestations. Worst because of the unexpectedness. For instance, a nicely dressed white lady came up to me as I left a church service. She asked me to contribute towards some fund. I did. As I left her she said, quite clearly, "He's pooped out to England."

I turned round to look at her. She was standing there with an angelic smile on her well-nourished face, looking as if the proverbial butter would not melt in her mouth. What can you do against this sort of thing?

Or again, on each occasion when I visited a coloured or mulatto lawyer on business, I observed, as I looked through the windows of the office, the two tall crooks in sun-faded suits, whom I had seen an hour after my first arrival at B.W.I. No. 2. One of them used to repeat regularly every time I was in the office there:

"We won't have him here."

"Get him back to England."

To this his companion would nod and smile in a fashion, which has to be seen in order to properly appreciate his villainy.

The typist in the office of this lawyer would also join in the general abuse of my person. As I would be shutting the office door, she would say, as if addressing her typewriter, "We've pooped him out."

Often I passed a mulatto, who was the manager of a large store in the town. He never lost an opportunity of being reprehensible to me, or of employing others – generally ne'er-do-wells of the ruffianly and loafing class of B.W.I. No. 2 – to molest me.

Often, in the street where I happened to be walking or shopping, this man would walk up to one of these ruffians and say to him, "We won't have him long here," "We won't let him be here."

He would be pointing at me and staring during the conversation as only the inhabitants of this place can look – with shocking malice and contempt.

Often they seemed to do this molestation with little or no effort. They had, in fact, become automatically used to being controlled by the underworld organisation. One of my persecutors in particular struck me as carrying out the orders of the crooks with such ease and frequency that she – for she was a negress – seemed never to be thinking about anything else. This did not, of course, make it any less irksome to me. One day I was passing one of the best shops in the town, near which was standing a motor car and three or four well-dressed white people. This negress, who had just been molesting me with some of the usual "pooped out" sentences, came near to these people, and, with a charming smile on her features, she said something which I could not hear, to these white people. One of them, a leading man in the town, said, in a genial tone of voice to her, "Sod him in! Keep at him!"

It was the cheerfulness of the tone of voice which gave to this molest its unexpectedness and sting.

Sometimes the unexpected nature of the molest would only

confirm my already firm belief that most of the inhabitants of the place were in the pockets of the international crooks' organisation behind my persecution, and have no compunction in molesting. For example, one day I was passing near to a building which was having its roof repaired by some men who were entirely, as far as I could see, unknown to me, I heard the foreman call out to his men, "That's the sod I often go up to of a night to worry out. Nice, isn't he? Good for plucking that's all, sod him."

I had one queer experience about this time, which made me feel as if I were at one and the same time a member of the audience and an actor in the play.

As I approached the park, a white man of about 60 years was standing near a car, in which was another white man about 20 years younger; they were both nicely dressed. They both stared hard and viciously at me and appeared to be expecting me. As I got near the older man made a very swaggering gesticulation, which took the form of a very short walk backwards and forwards along by his car. Whilst walking thus, he shouted in a stentorian voice, in a most melodramatic fashion, his arms waving and his eyes "in a fine frenzy rolling," "We must poop, *poop* him, or he'll poop us!"

When he had finished his performance, he got into his car and they drove off quickly. The negroes, who had witnessed this piece of play-acting, were all sitting in their front gardens right opposite. Their faces now registered delight, scorn and malevolence, mixed up in a most queer way, as they stared at me. This, of course was an organised "stunt," and my movements – nay, even my intentions – seem as well known to my enemies as they are to me. When this elderly actor said "poop" he meant that they would not get "their share" unless the crooks' behests were obeyed and I was "pooped" first, that is, forced to go to London. Of course, though known by all the inhabitants, I was not supposed to know this meaning, neither did I then. It is kept a profound secret.

The following outrage is one of the most serious – in all its effects and indications as to the length to which my persecutors were prepared to go.

The lay assistant of doctors at the hospital, who was living near me, lost no opportunity of making my life a hell upon earth, and his devilish machinations culminated one night as I woke up in bed, feeling an indescribable sensation in my head, just a little above my ear. I mostly sleep on my side. My head was therefore sideways on the pillow. After a little white this horrid feeling percolated throughout the whole of my head. It was an extraordinary sensation – pain of a kind I had never before experienced. It was as if I could feel my brain, and as if my brain could feel the hardness of the inside of my skull – a feeling of the separateness of my "brain matter" from the rest of my head. The brain seemed as though it were bursting – as if it were bursting for more room. This lasted for quite a while, and it was only after I had partially recovered – when my brain once again began to function as an organic part of me, that I could bring myself to think of the cause of my misadventure. I came to the conclusion that something, some medical chemical, had been squirted through a gap in the roof shingles above my head. Several times just previously, I had had water squirted at me in this way, and also little stones dropped on my head as I was trying to sleep in my bed at night. But though I knew this to be a serious criminal outrage, I knew, too, that it would be useless to report it to the authorities, and that any report of mine would be denied and countered by a false explanation by my landlord and others. The jeering face of the lay assistant who met me the next morning confirmed my suspicions of the part he played in the outrage. He was the devil in human disguise and capable of any evil, malicious act, and perhaps murder, too. He was a ringleader of the molesters.

Now commenced the last six months of my stay in B.W.I. No. 2, and the persecution was intensified to a degree beyond any human endurance. Its aim was to get me back to London, though how this would benefit my enemies was beyond me. Their actions were also well calculated to make me complain to the authorities so that I should ultimately get into their bad books and be sent back by them with a tarnished character. The authorities, of course, would attribute my accounts of molestations to my imagination – and worse – madness.

I was, therefore, powerless, having to rely on my own ingenuity and powers of resistance to pull me through these ceaseless torments. And this fact had engendered in me a perpetual patience which only irritated my enemies, and spurred them on to still greater heights – or depths – of molestation.

My nights were turned into days. That is, my persecutors followed me even to my bed to perpetrate their devil designs. Every night, as I got into bed, I knew that I was bound for no haven of rest. All the plans of my persecutors were perpetrated to rob me of my composure and balance of mind. They frequently rolled things over the roof for hours, and sometimes loathsome things crawled overhead. I would hear my molesters in a whispered conversation on the roof, discussing the effect of the particular form of molestation in which they had just indulged. This kind of thing would go on until 2.0 or 3.0 in the morning. I could often hear their presence as they pressed on the sand as they stood in the roadway during the molestings in the early hours of the morning. And it was only then that I could think. And then only of what kind of life these, my tormenters, live. If it is the most powerful impulsive in man to seek his own pleasure, what peculiar ideas of pleasure some men must have. This population of molesting fiends, when persecuting, smile to one another with satanic joy. I am sure their pleasure is anticipating a share in robbery.

Sometimes I would be awakened, just after I had managed to fall asleep, by the sound of things being drawn over my bedroom floor, and once or twice I found pieces of broken wire on the floor. Rats which had been doped were also put into my room, and when I put the light on I saw two of three of these "inspiring" animals walking about in a leisurely fashion – their eyes and teeth gleaming from the electric light. They would disappear with a slow deliberate walk, leaving me wondering at the philosophic way they were taking life.

On several occasions I found centipedes in my bed. When I was unlucky enough not to discover them I would be awakened by their crawling over my body. On one occasion I received an unusually nasty bite from one which was seven inches long and which was disporting itself on me. The pain was very acute for about eight hours after I had been stung, and I had to bathe in very hot water before I could lose the pain.

I was not surprised to hear that people who had lived in the place for years had never been troubled in this way. Indeed, this centipede stunt was a new one, for I had never been troubled by them for the years I had been in this part of the world. They had collected them for my "benefit."

Some of the crooks practiced among themselves a peculiar form of rapid talking, so that they could communicate with each other and leave their victim completely in the dark as to their evil plans. Men and women and youths used this rapid talking, as the following incident will exemplify.

I had been sitting on a sea-beach for a little while, when a negro – a near neighbour of mine – arrived in his car with all his family. They got out some distance from me, but so that they could be heard by me. In short rapid sentences they carried on their conversation, which evidently concerned me. This I could see from the glances in my direction. From time to time a voice would emerge clearly from the rapid flow of conversation. Sometimes it was a man's, sometimes a woman's and sometimes a child's voice. These clearly spoken sentences I was quite able to understand, for they were all of the usual blackguardly molesting kind. I walked away amid a perfect torrent of abusive language. Phrases were hurled at my back as I retreated.

"Drummed out!" "Sod him out!"

"Pooped out of New Zealand!"

"America doesn't want sods!"

"Jew thief." "Skunk," etc.

A few days after this I went to see my tailor – a mulatto – who had not indulged in any molestations since I had known him, and I had dealt with him for some years. But this day a change seemed to have come over him, for he said as I left his shop, "How can we let him be here. He will have to go back to England."

All of this, as you will readily admit, is very strange if you don't know their idea. As I left the shop wondering at his strange behaviour, I saw a huge negro, who, as soon as he saw me, put on a menacing look and pointed to the shop behind me. I looked back, but could see no one. Perceiving the bewilderment in my face, this huge creature guffawed most sickeningly. I was soon to discover that the period of intensification of the persecution was upon me, and that the crooks were depending upon "noodling" me – as they would put it – to "get me." That is, I was to have not a moment's rest from molestation. I was to be kept "going." I was not to be allowed to "poop them out." Rather was I to be kept in a mood of perpetual anxiety and unrest. They soon made it clear to me – if it had not been made clear before – that if they did not succeed in worrying me sufficiently to disable me mentally, as it were to "dope" me and get me to London, they would make use of physical violence to force me to leave.

Sometimes I was tormented during the little religious services which were held by travelling preachers within earshot of my rooms. It was during the services that they annoyed me, during the preaching of God's word, by their accompaniments, as it were, of these services. Every time these travelling evangelists came to the lane near the house in which I was staying, I could only hear the usual molesting and lewd sentences of the worst kind being used by some molester who had perfected the art of "chiming in" with the words of the preacher or with the singing of the hymns. This kind of thing had been going on all the time at the church I attended, where every Sunday morning I had always been molested by a man usually, but occasionally by a woman's voice in the congregation using lewdness sometimes and frequent threats of murder and violence. And all this in a church!! And in a church the congregation of which was largely composed of whites! It was enough to make me prejudiced towards all these people. But, happily, I had not sunk as low as that. I felt that they are devils' imps serving evil when they know the good, preferring to be Satan's slaves.

Near my apartment was a "settlement" of "whites," or "apparent" whites. The central force, as it were, of this settlement was a "white" lady. Her family lived in two or three adjacent houses. Her children and her children's children lived around her and formed this little "settlement." They lived in perfect amity and seemed to be well blessed with the goods of this world. Some of the men wore the "official" white suits and pith helmets (though, of course, it is very often the case that whites and negroes and mulattoes who have no official position wear these clothes). The inhabitants of the "settlement" possesses several cars between them, and I believe that some of the men were in Government offices. Their respectability, nay, their "superiority," could not be doubted. But their position in the realms of the underworld, also, remained in little doubt after some time.

The following incident is typical of the behaviour of the inhabitants of the "settlement."

As I worked one day in "my" garden, this lady looked over to me and spoke to one of her daughters and a negress, who were accompanying her as she walked in her garden. She spoke *to* them, but, after the B.W.I. fashion, *at* me. Calling their attention to my presence she said, "He must be the one, don't you think?" She did not say what one.

"It must be him," she added.

She went on, in rather veiled terms, as became her "position" in B.W.I. No. 2 Society, I suppose, to allude to the fact that I was "in the black book." This was the "book" mentioned so often by my molesters on many occasions in B.W.I. No. 2. Of course, if there was such a book, it was doubtless a crooks' register of all intended victims, present and to be. In it, "we" would be described, analysed, docketed and photographed. The population talked of those in the "book" as undesirables. This reference to the "book" by the "white" lady was merely calculated to inculcate an inferiority complex which would drive me away. Sometimes, when they called out I was "informed" that this "book" had names of undesirables. I felt, in all my contacts with the so-called "high-class" residents of B.W.I. No. 2, that this desire to breed in me a sense of decided inferiority was their study and a main concern. These people and their mulatto and negro servants commonly used all the molesting and lewd expressions of the rest of the population. The "white" lady in question was not above a pointed obscenity or two – nor were any of her people. She did not, however, confine her attention to mere words. My fondness for the radio was soon visible to her, for I used to get in the garden to listen to the music and the talks of their loud speaker, but after a time she and any other would not let me listen. If I went into the garden she immediately ordered the radio to be switched off. When the loud speaker had been switched off there was at once the general molest of B.W.I. Nos. 1 and 2 sentences, which lasted until I left the garden. This B.W.I. No. 2 "select" family of "superior" people typified the B.W.I. Nos. 1 and 2 "whites" whom it was my great misfortune to meet. They were not nice people at all. Their association with "people in Society" from Great Britain was hateful in its hypocrisy or criminal and equally hateful, though not so hypocritical. Lots of moneyed visitors came from the U.S.A. and Great Britain during the winter, and I have not the least doubt, from things I saw and heard, that all kinds of trickery and blackmail were schemed in this "select" atmosphere – to say nothing, of course, of other kinds of viciousness. On several occasions, some time before the gas attacks were started, I was in the garden, when this lady told her servant that she could get me killed by a negro for the price of a quart of rum. Of course this was talking at me.

As I was walking in the town I saw the Anglican vicar coming towards me, and as he came nearer, a motor car came along filled with "apparent" whites, all neighbours of mine, who were some of those molesting me year in and year out during my stay in B.W.I. No. 2. One of these called out to the vicar, "We don't want him, he must go." This sort of molest considerably disconcerts one.

This may seem trivial enough, but actually I felt it was a molest with felonious intent. A month later I was going into the town and passing the rum shops frequented by the coloured "tough" population of the place. I went this way because it was my usual procedure. The vicar passed me with his head averted and I noticed his pious features. When I returned later in the day many of the negroes and "toughs" stood along the kerb, all with their heads averted from me and sickly innocence on their vicious faces. It was a truly comic sight, and doubtless they thought they looked like the vicar himself! Of course, I was to take the hint that I was ostracised by all the desirable people!!

I have mentioned before that many of my molesters employed ventriloquism to harass me. This trick was used by many of my molesters, both white and coloured, some of whom were in Government offices. Often as I passed these offices voices would come from the air and I know not where, in a most bewildering fashion. But the most harassing example of this kind of persecution happened to me in the following way.

I went on a motor-boat excursion with a mulatto "friend," who was, of course, in the service of the international crooks; though I was unaware of this at the time. There were three men and three women, all apparent whites. Also there was a little boy. We went first to an uninhabited rocky island, all, apparently, very happy. No doubts crept into my mind concerning their ingenuousness, until I began to hear "voices," not from the boat, but from the sea. This continual molest of all the usual sentences was obviously the product of ventriloquism. In addition it was ceaseless. My companions landed on the rocky refuge, and when they had disappeared from my view – for I stayed behind in the boat – I heard the usual molesting sentences, shouted now in a man's, now a woman's, and now in the piping tones of a child's voice.

Leaving this rocky island, from which my companions took some bird's eggs, we proceeded to several little palm beaches and afterwards to some bigger ones, and ultimately we arrived at the coral strand of a large beach covered in palm trees and entrancing flowers. The air was full of rich perfume and this, combined with the sight and sound of a perfect sky and sea and some singing birds, made everything very wonderful indeed. But wherever I walked or sat about on this gem of Nature's beauty, molesting words came to me ceaselessly. They are bad enough amid the sordid surroundings of the city, but how much more intense they were in contrast to the liveliness of everything around, bathed and gleaming in the sunlight. It was a shocking devil of a travesty in this beauty of palm trees and flowers. It was most revolting to think that these people, who seemed ordinary and decent enough, should do this kind of thing, when they should have been lost in adoration of the sweet beauty. It was a discord in the symphony of God's beauty. They were hyenas and wolves. Everything was lovely bar man; man for whom God made all this beauty.

This ventriloquial power was often used by my tormentors whenever I had occasion to go into the shops of the town. My molester would so "throw" his voice as to suggest that those serving you were doing the molesting. Of course, on some occasions this actually was so. For example, one day I went into a negro jewellers and, after doing my business, during our conversation we talked of many things generally and pleasantly. But even this individual had to molest me, for before I left the establishment he had managed to turn the conversation to "knowing people," and as a parting shot he cried out, "How do I know you are not a scoundrel?"

I smiled at him; he turned very sinister in the face.

Many shopkeepers and prominent business men took part in the vast game of baiting me. If I went in to town by way of a large store kept by "apparent" white people, one of the partners would often be standing outside, talking to another white man, who was nearly always one whose time was given up frequently to molesting me. The partner would say to the other, "We'll get him if only we worry him enough. We must see to it!"

"O.K.," the other would reply…

And worry me they always did. They did everything their lurid imaginations were able to invent to harass and frighten me. One day a negro beggar started walking parallel to me on the road. Suddenly he called out in a tremendous voice of brass, with very intimidating intonation, "I'll tear your throat out if you go see the Commander. I don't care if they kill me for doing it."

Every day and every part of every day I was subjected to

threats of murder and violence. Not even Sunday was sacred, or free from the persecution of my person. Indeed, Sunday, being a day of holiday for most people, provided them with ample time for developing their molesting genius. For instance, one Sunday morning, as I was going to church, a prominent negro professional man and wife passed me in their car. When he saw me, he pulled up and invited me to take a lift to church in his car. This I did and the rest of the journey passed without event. When I got to the Church there were a number of people gossiping in groups before going in. I got out of the car and thanked the negro for his kindness.

"It's nothing," he said, and his wife smiled charmingly.

I walked towards the church, but, before I could enter, this negro called out loudly, "We've pooped you out."

I shrugged my shoulders and went into the church, where the "chiming in" molestations took place through all the service as usual – intimidation and lewdness predominating.

On my way home, I walked along a path in the park, as was my custom at this hour on Sunday. A group of negroes were sitting on a bench on the side of the path. One of these (a very vile ruffian) shouted out, "You are in our book, big sod! You are known all over the world, big sod! You are numbered, photoed and radioed wherever you go and you can't get from us, big sod! See?" and he stuck his huge black face towards me.

This "stunt," of course, had been prepared, and took place often upon a Sunday.

After lunch, I was walking by the church again, when I met a young man, whom I knew very well. He was apparently "white," and occupied himself on Sunday as a Sunday school teacher. He was also employed on week-days as a school teacher when I first got acquainted with him. Later, he became a bank clerk, but this did not alter his molesting propensities. Whenever I passed either the day school or the Sunday school in which he was teaching, I always became the object of his persecutions if he happened to see me, and he would shout out all the "poop" and "sod" sentences. On this particular Sunday, when I met him in the street, he gave me a friendly greeting. I returned it with punctilious courtesy, not deceived by his "friendliness." We discussed pleasantly on many subjects, literary, political and religious. We said "Good day" to each other, but I had hardly turned away when the expected molest came. He said in a harsh, sneering voice, "Pooped out! Get out, yellow skunk!"

I was not very shocked, for apparently cultured persons in B.W.I. No. 2 were capable of the lowest depths of viciousness, were capable, indeed, of using their "culture" as a "blind," so that to accuse them of molestation would sound ridiculous. This young gentleman always used these molesting words when we left each other after talking. The population is really a part of the underworld. I had a friend, an apparent white man, who acted strangely on occasions, and I must tell of him, for the following incident seems important to me, though vague, in its presage of imminent danger. He stayed with me often in the house, and always the outside molestations were pretty fierce. However, he offered no comment, and I did not venture to ask his opinion until the last occasion. This time the persecution did not cease for one minute while he was with me. He made no remark about it, though some of the most obscene and threatening phrases were being hurled at me in his hearing. I could stick it no longer, and I asked him what he thought of it, as these molesting remarks were proceeding from my enemies as "merrily" as a funeral bell. My friend replied briefly, "It has to be."

No other words; just these. A cold feeling gripped me. The inevitability of the ultimate criminal intentions of robbing and violence was thrust upon me by these simple monosyllables, simply uttered. My friend left me soon after this, and I was left in miserable loneliness to ponder on my situation and to realise more appreciably that practically the whole population are "underworld."

Towards the end of 1931, the crooks must have thought they had me completely at their mercy. I got this impression from the arrogance of their tones and actions, and especially from the fact that in the molestations were interwoven facts from my past life – names of my acquaintances when I was a boy at school, names of boys and young men whom I knew as a youth. They mentioned school papers that I had written, and they were fully acquainted with all my school certificates. They boasted that they possessed all my papers. Loudly, they cried out, "We've got all your old junk."

In this way I learned what had become of the papers I had locked up at my business premises. These, I had discovered before I had left London, had all vanished, and now I learnt they had been stolen. The net seemed to be closing in around me, and I felt utterly powerless. Nevertheless, I determined that, whatever the consequences, the world should know something of these crooks, and I began to make notes about some of my molesters and their methods. I made these notes as secretly as I could under the perpetual eavesdropping and surveillance. I carried them always in an inside pocket of my suits, which I had specially made for the purpose. Some time after I had started making these notes, I passed two ruffianly negroes who were standing in my path. As I was circumnavigating them – for they did not budge a centimetre – one of them said, with expression of hatred, "We'll get his notes from him, the great skunk that he is!"

How did they know about these notes?

Some months later, I posted them in a registered envelope containing another sealed envelope with these notes in and marked for my perusal only. This letter was opened by the members of the P.O. staff at B.W.I. No. 2. I knew this by the almost immediate alterations in the methods employed by some of my well-known molesters that they knew the contents of the letter. I realised that I had adequate grounds and proofs. I recollected that when I had given this letter to be registered, the clerk went to another and handed him the letter. The two of them had then whispered something to each other, looking foxily at me.

The white hospital nurse of whom I have spoken saw me at this time, too, and gave me a look of very intense hatred that boded me no good, for she was a determined crook and malicious, a truly characteristic B.W.I. No. 2 woman. This look showed that she was aware of the contents of the registered letter.

About this time I knew, from the scraps of conversation I overheard from time to time, that the purpose of the international crooks was to deprive me of my peace of mind – nay, of my mind. I must be prevented from having any opportunities of consecutive thinking. Their other notion was that it was highly desirable that I should return to London as soon as possible. Many subtle devices were employed to engender this state of affairs, and also to hide the identity of the main international crooks behind all the molestations. For instance, in the course of a man's or a woman's molestations, the molesting party would say, "You are not going to do *me*," or "You are not going to poop *me* out."

This sort of thing is a veritable red herring drawn across the trail, so that I might confuse the instigators of the molestations – the head crooks – with those who were merely the underlings.

The idea of getting me back to London was, as I have shown, also very prevalent, and even my barber (who looked very white), until now apparently a nice, straight-forward man, came out in his true colors. He was, by the way, a leading man in his chapel. But, far from this being a disqualification for the duties of molester, it seemed to be an added qualification in B.W.I. No. 2. I had often heard him preach the Sunday evening sermon in most exalted and uplifting tones. However, one day at this period, when he was attending to me – with usual politeness – he spoke rapidly to one of his white customers, "If we get him back to London, we'll all get our little bit. If not, it's all up with us."

I looked at him, but his features betrayed nothing.

After this, the molesting increased and concentrated upon getting me back quickly to England, and the methods used caused me grave mental and physical discomfort. I was continually hearing threats, such as, "If you don't go back willingly, we will have you pooped out," and "We'll drum the sod out," and "We'll sod his nose."

I took this last as a threat to do me bodily harm, but I had no notion at the time of what was actually meant. This sentence was called out to me for some weeks, before the gas attacks commenced, at first weak, then gradually growing stronger, until at last they became positively unbearable.

I will recount this phase of my molestation with the same lack of exaggeration which I have endeavoured to use in the other parts of this account. In any case it does not need a melodramatic artist to make these gas attacks into nightmares. They were so horrible and ingeniously contrived, that the blunt truth of an inexperienced writer like myself sounds like the veriest fiction. This is only another example of the strangeness of truth.

Many days and night towards the end of 1931, I was utterly unable to get any sleep, and I was rapidly sinking into a state of chronic mental and nervous exhaustion, caused by want of sleep. I would be gassed all night in the following fashion.

I would no sooner get into bed and be getting to sleep than the gas began to become apparent. No noise accompanied its flow, and the gas had no odour and no colour. The whereabouts of the entry of the gas-pipe into the room remained a mystery to me. As the gas was lighter than the air – otherwise it would have affected other occupants of the house below me – it was hardly likely that the gas came through the roof. I suspected, of course, that possibly the lay assistant from the hospital had a good deal to do with this "chemical warfare."

Feeling completely fatigued, I would sink wearily on my pillow. I would be just dozing off, when my breathing would become exceedingly difficult. Some shallow breaths were all that I could take. After a time, I managed, or had to take, a few deeper breaths, and, directly after this, sleep would have entirely deserted me. I would lie starkly awake, my body and mind as tired as they could be. My mind was awake in a sense – horribly awake – yet completely inert! When I was in this state, the flow of gas would be stopped and very gradually its effects would wear off, and my mind and body would once again woo the healing arms of sleep. But the gas would be applied on again just as I began to doze, and again my breathing would be difficult. Then, after a few deep breaths I would be aroused – that is the only word – awake once more. I want to point out that no gas was laid on the premises. In fact there was none to lay on.

Dog-tired, I would stumble through the day and my perpetual inquisition. The molesters now called out that they knew me well and the names of my principal business customers. They also introduced a few new phrases about this time, "We'll Woolwich you." "We'll Thames you!"

This, of course, was intimidation. This "oxygen" awakening, arousing gassing proceeded on and off about every second day for quite a fortnight and made me almost "wrecked." I became quite inert in body and mind.

After this, for several nights, a gas was used with a sickly, sulphurous, objectionable smell. The effect of this was to cause me an intense pain at the base of the skull. Accompanying this pain there were general molesting remarks made by my persecutors, and more particularly one to the following effect: "We'll see you don't remember anything." "We'll get your brain to snap."

The pain must have been written on my features which could be seen in the moonlight nights, for I had not said a word to indicate that the gas had taken effect. The pain was acute and alarming, and I wondered what was due to befall me next. Probably they were aware of its action.

My landlord was so plausible and pleasant during the entire period of these gas attacks, that I did not for one moment suspect him of having anything to do with this gassing, though I can see clearly now that both he and his wife and son must have been aiding and abetting the whole business.

In this way did I spend Christmas, 1931. The molesting was severe, and confirmed my opinion that it does not pay, nor indeed it is possible, for any inhabitant of B.W.I. No. 2 not to follow the orders of the crooks. To obey is practically an unwritten law. The penalties are probably too drastic and summary. Most probably the B.W.I. No. 2 population think a crook-intended victim "lawful" prey and have no compunction or thought of anything but a share of the spoils, and take all orders from crooks as a *sine qua non*.

I made up my mind one day to see the Commander. On my way I met two nicely dressed white girls, about nine years old. They were going to Sunday school. When I drew near to them, I could hear that they were talking of me. Amongst other remarks, I heard one say to the other, "Daddy says you can see what's in his mind. He is trying to 'poop' us out, but Daddy says that we will not let him."

I proceeded on my way, and after some delay, I was allowed to see the Commander. I explained all to him and told him that the gas was still in my system – that I was unable to get rid of it from my lungs (or anyhow some of its effects were not gone yet). I asked him to see about it so that I could have medical inspection at once.

He looked at me, and said tersely, "Come to-morrow."

After a large amount of pleading on my part, he telephoned to the Government hospital. When he had got an answer from the hospital, he came to see me and told me that if I went to the hospital I could see the doctor.

"Why there?" I asked. "Why not here?"

The Commander replied, "Because he's there."

I agreed to go to the hospital, not suspecting anything underhand from the Commander. I was about to take my leave and proceed alone to the hospital, when the Commander told me to wait. He called a negro policeman and gave him some instructions, and then said to me that this policeman would accompany me to the hospital. I walked along with this company and did not for a minute suspect anything of trickery. It is only long since the event that I realise that the Commander had put me in charge of this policeman. Was I not "in charge" at the behest of men more powerful than the Commander – the heads of the international crooks?

Having arrived at the hospital gates, we walked up to the first lot of buildings and asked for the doctor. We learned that he was not there. I was about to make more enquiries, when I espied two of the attendants from the mental department walking towards me. In a window above them I saw the head "white" nurse glaring murderously at me. I knew then that it was all up. I resigned myself to my fate. The two attendants caught hold of me roughly and led me away, forcing me along. They were two of those that had been there when I was there three and a half years previously. One was a mulatto warder and the other was a negro attendant. We had not proceeded far when the negro said to the warder, "I have broken his spectacles."

This fellow must have known where I kept them, for he had pressed his arm upon my chest, where they were, and he had broken them, too.

They took me to a cell and locked me in it. The ravings of the big negro inmate in the cell opposite mine were terrible. His looks through the bars when he saw me were glaring murder, and malignant in the extreme; he had the appearance of a terrible ape. All through the night his ravings deprived me of much-needed sleep and peace of mind. The doctor did not see me for over 48 hours, and even then he said nothing to me about the gas. Indeed, I was so worried about my detention in this awful place, that the thought of the gas did not cross my mind until after I had seen the doctor. But doubtless he had been informed of it by the Commander. His silence, then, was rather strange, was it not?

About the third day, I had to take some dirty clothes to a shed. Just as I was nearing this shed, the raving lunatic whom I have just mentioned above, rushed after me and shouted out, "I'll brain you, you big sod."

This lunatic was so dangerous that practically always he was locked in his cell. He must have been let out on purpose to pursue me. I only narrowly escaped from him.

Some days after, I was given a bedroom upstairs. This was an end room. There was a flight of outside steps right outside my room which led to the ground below. Inside the building was a corridor, to which my door opened.

After I had gone to bed of a night, and sometimes in the early morning before I got up, some of the attendants would stand on the stand on top of the landing to these steps and, being right outside my bedroom, every word that they said was audible to me.

They would stand there for some minutes on each occasion and use some of the usual molesting sentences and make some hair-raising and flesh-creeping threats of what was to happen to me. This outrageous infliction was done about eight times. These officials are a branch of the underworld. Government servants too!

Some man came to pay me a friendly visit. As I was talking to him in the grounds near the gate, one of the more dangerous negro lunatics, a man with a very evil, ruffianly face stood by us all the time we were speaking. Generally, this man was never allowed to be without an attendant, but on this occasion, he was assuredly employed merely to molest and frighten me.

One day, I was sitting in the grounds outside the building, quite near to another inmate (a negro), who was mumbling to himself on various topics. After a time, he cast his reflective eyes upon me for some time, and, a little while afterwards, he said to himself in very thoughtful, slow style, "It's a funny thing to me, there must be a reason, I am sure: all the English that come into this place are always sent home again to England."

On another occasion, an inmate (apparently a white man), suffering from delirium tremens, came up to me and stared right "into my soul," as it were, for quite a minute, and then held out his hand for me to shake and gave my hand an awful "grip of iron" for a minute or so.

One of the negro inmates had an ankle chain, to which was attached an iron, weighing about 150 pounds. Whenever he wanted to walk, he had to carry this weight with him in his hands. This fact always caused great merriment to the reflective negro mentioned above.

Some days later (after I had been "in" about a fortnight), I was given my clothes and told to go. Of course, I felt greatly relieved in every way.

Like a fool I returned to my old rooms. My suspicions were not upon my landlord at all; but, of course, on reflection now, I can clearly see that he was connected very deeply with all the molestations.

As I walked up the lane to the house, I met two white women

in a good motor car; both of them were about 35 to 40 years of age and both of their faces were almost as white as a sheet of paper and each was wearing dark spectacles.

One of them said loudly to the other, when they were quite near to me, "He looks as though we'll have to give him some more. He looks much too well."

I slept in this place one night only, for it was quite evident that some scoundrelism of the worst order was part of the atmosphere of all in the neighbourhood. My absence and change made it more obvious.

I found fresh apartments, and now I was quite safe from the crook inhabitants of this beautiful land where only man is vile. The landlord was an honest man from Britain and his ways were straight as God wants all to be. Devious ways are natural to the inhabitants of B.W.I. Nos. 1 and 2; they are brought up so from childhood. They are nurtured for crooks, or for the crooks' large family, the underworld. International crooks are real gentry to them. They look up to and respect them greatly. I expect they aspire to emulate them.

Do not imagine that my molesters ceased torturing, or even flagged. They did not. I was still molested in church and this was just as previously, by a "voice," using all the usual "infliction;" molesting also occurred in the streets as before, and when I went into the Public Library, a big well-dressed, black suited negro, of about 45, followed me in each time, and during my endeavours to read, he was (ventriloquially) pouring out the obscene phrases incessantly, as long as I remained there (perhaps for two hours). Of course the white lady attendant and librarian must have heard this!

This is the end of the true account of what I have experienced in London and since I left England and resided in New Zealand and in the British West Indies, in what I call Nos. 1 and 2.

These tormentors have acted like devils' fiends. The international crooks are devils, to whom murder is a mere nothing so long as they attain their nefarious ends.

There is a sinister intention in their every action. The repetition of the phrases is no light affliction, but it is an everlasting torment. It is really continual outrage, violence and criminal assault. I have been living in a veritable Hell upon Earth. I write this to bring to the light of day their demon methods.

I trust sincerely that any who have suffered like myself in any way, or who have been victims of any of the crooks and the underworld's whiles and stratagems, will also bring these fiends' tactics and inveigling artifices to light; that they will expose the ramifications of their work and the extent of their influence, to the public and to the police. It is only by publishing their artful devices and nefarious deeds and making them known world-wide, that their activities can be checked, and, let us hope, exterminated.

I trust any will write to New Scotland Yard, London.

CHAPTER XVI

# B.W.I. Notes

An authority, residing in Florida, said that if you grow beans and similar plants round and about your house, the mosquito bites are harmless.

The paw-paw is a very nice fruit, and it must be nutritious, as there was an English high official in one of the B.W.I. that could eat nothing else in a serious illness, and he lived on paw-paws for a year. Shaddocks are a beautiful citrous fruit. The natives use the leaves of the castor-oil plant on the head for headache. They put them in hot water for a minute or so first.

In the tropics the tides very little, and they appear to be only two or three feet high (from low water). Water sprouts are often observable, hanging from the clouds.

In the B.W.I. there are some small birds that sing sweetly. The B.W.I. blackbird is black, with a long tail like a woodpecker, but the blackbird doesn't sing, he only has a "call" of about three notes.

Of a night in the almost full moon, you sometimes see a moon-light rainbow. It has a "fairy"-like appearance. Of a night, fireflies are beautiful, too. The best thing you can drink in the tropics is iced water (water that has been boiled, for safety). Don't drink spirits. Canadian dry ginger water is splendid, the best temperance drink obtainable.

Toasted bread is a fine thing to eat in the tropics if you get any stomach weakness. A bottle of chlorodyne is indispensable in event of diarrhoea, a few drops curing it. Of an evening, towards sunset, the long rays of the sun often give an appearance of two sunsets, and I have before now been puzzled which was the real one, the one in front of me or that to the rear! In both directions it has looked like a sunset, the sun's rays going to a focus both at the sun as they go right to the rear, and right to a point.

Many of the coloured people nail up the doors and windows of their houses every night to keep out evil spirits. This is unlike Mongolians, who leave their tent doors open all night, and the wife sleeps on a mat on the ground in the tent nearest the door; their dogs often stealing eatables while everyone sleeps.

I met a Scotsman who lived many years in the B.W.I. He was a fine gentleman. I remarked on his Scottish accent being strong, and he said that he greatly prized it and was proud of it.

I met an Englishman and asked him why he was crying, and he told me that his dog had just been run over and killed.

I am sure there has been a lot of unrecorded and undiscovered crime in the B.W.I., as I learnt that some of the islands have no extradition laws and possibly no registration of deaths, which means that no certificate of death is required.

The experiences of a severe hurricane are that you live in a house until it is over, with all the doors and windows nailed up, and perhaps you are unable to leave or get out for two or three days, so that if you have not any store of food in the house you are badly placed. At first the wind comes whistling on one side of the house, while the rain hits the house like shot pouring on it. After perhaps nearly a day the wind has got round to the next side of the house, the rain still driving, and in turn it generally gives each side of the house a good long spell of pressure, so that anything moveable (perhaps the house) is blown away, or over. Generally, there is a tidal wave during the hurricane, and this affects all houses near the waterside and often washes them away, or destroys them. All water craft are liable to be taken to some funny places, such as well inshore. Amidst the roar and rushing and whistling sounds, you hear little buildings tumbling and boards crashing. When you get outside you find the ground bare of any crops.

CHAPTER XVII

# Return to Britain

IT WAS IN THE ENGLISH CHANNEL, ON A FROSTY MORNING IN March, 1932, when this large ship that had some travellers and a large number of tourists on board, was near the end of a West Indian and African voyage. It was the coldest weather I had experienced during my travels. The sea was as quiet as a lake, and the sun was shining as we caught the first view of the land that is so much in the thoughts of those who leave it, and a land that counts for such a great deal in the world's progress to better and higher things.

During my absence I had spent three years in New Zealand (that hopeful and beautiful land), where the Auckland winter is like unto Britain's in April, and I had resided four years in the British West Indies (islands of splendid tropical growths and of beautiful scenery), where it is much hotter in the winter than it is in Britain's hottest summer. I had also been travelling for three months upon the ever-changing and inspiring oceans, and had observed some of those wonder-arousing flying fish, and whales and other large denizens of the sea, also birds flying hundreds of miles from any land; also uninhabited islands and rocks, and beautiful palm islands with coral strands gleaming in the sun; and, too, some grandly rugged mountain scenery on the coast of Central America, Haiti and Cuba. I had felt the overcoming heat of the tropics. I had felt the joy of the sea when the weather is fine, and the sea and the mind are more or less at rest; then one experiences something really free and joyous in one's very soul, and realises the spirit of the wondrous works of God for man,

man whose love God wants. The wonder of the world's stars stirs one's imagination on seeing those "fresh" ones that are only observable well down South.

During my time abroad I had experienced good weather practically all the time, except for about a week's storm whilst on the ship in the Pacific, and the "rushing" experience of a few hurricanes in the B.W.I. (one of which lasted several days and was the worst experienced for a good many years). A severe hurricane means (if your house is on a small base, it will blow over and lay on the ground) you are a prisoner in your house until the besieging rain and wind abate. If you went out you would have to proceed upon your hands and knees and would most probably faint or fall ill. Hurricanes are the cause of much work, which is sometimes a blessing to the population.

When in the Pacific, a ship about 300 miles in front of ours wirelessed that she was in a very bad storm. The captain of our ship therefore did not proceed any distance for about 24 hours, the result being that we escaped the worst part of the storm.

---

After the Customs inspection, I got into the boat train, and great was my pleasure in viewing the nice country and beautiful satisfying appearance of the 90 miles of well-cultivated, well-husbanded land, passed on the way to London. Together with the picture effects of villages and towns with their churches, it was lovely to behold. It was the longest "stretch" of cultivation that I had seen since I had left Britain some years before. Its "note" seemed to be of peace, if I had to say what I felt at this time. It made me hope that the British will always be endeavouring to live more arightly and seek to obey God more faithfully. I know that all these things are related, not only in our private lives, but rationally, too. Righteousness gives peace and God protects those who obey Him.

During the whole of this train journey to London, though I was sitting in a compartment containing reliable people who had travelled in the ship with me, and whom I knew quite well – good companions of the voyage – yet the just audible voice of a woman molested me every few minutes (with a B.W.I. Nos. 1 and 2 molesting sentence, or a threat) all the way to Waterloo. It came to me in a very quiet, but very distinct tone.

This was here in Britain!

You will note that I had practically never been "word" or voice molested in Britain before (neither in New Zealand).

I had thought it would be impossible that the crooks could molest so in Britain. Yet I was to be molested so night and day for a year in 1932 in this "free" Britain. It was not free to me anyhow, this molesting making me virtually at the mercy of, and in the chains of, the crooks. How many victims are experiencing this?

When I arrived at Waterloo, I took a taxi to Paddington G.W.R. Station. During the whole of this taxi drive through the London streets (the busiest streets that I had seen since I had left London) and through Hyde Park, the B.W.I. Nos. 1 and 2 molesting sentences reached my ears continuously, with hardly a minute's interval, and they were quite loudly spoken and did not cease, though my taxi drove along and dodged in and out of the traffic all the way.

There were two cars (each of which contained three men) that aroused my suspicions, as these cars apparently endeavoured to keep near to the taxi all the journey; they "simply" stuck to it, following it and keeping as close, either in front or at the rear, as they possibly could through every move in the traffic; they were practically never out of my sight.

The men in both of these cars were all clean-shaven and wearing leather brown felt hats. Each of these men glanced foxily at me all the journey. Doubtless another man was sitting on the floor of the car, using a megaphone, or possibly speaking through a "broadcaster," to molest me.

These men were between 30 and 45 years of age. Probably they were some of those that foxed me when I got to Paddington railway station.

Having seen my luggage into the cloak room at Paddington,

I proceeded to the booking office, where I observed that I was being "foxed," having seen one leather-brown hatted man at the cloak room and another standing quite near to me at the booking office. I then noticed that wherever I went in the station one of these men followed me, looking overtly and sitting near me, or standing about near to where I was. They were hearing anything that I said and keeping me under close observation; there seemed about six or seven of them; all of them wore clerical grey (somewhat worn) suits and no overcoats, though it was a frost.

Having purchased my ticket, I spoke to a gentleman for a little white. I told him that I had some while to wait for my train, and he mentioned a "picture house" which was quite near by.

After a little while, I proceeded on a little walk outside the station. As I proceeded along, one of these leather-brown hatted men ran out of the railway station like a deer, glancing threateningly as he passed along. He ran out of sight...

Shortly after, I returned into the station, and observed several of these men standing separately about the station, but each of them viewing me narrowly when I was in their proximity. One of them followed me everywhere, even when I went into the lavatory. One sat near to me in the refreshment room and I was so accompanied and foxed until I got into the train. They were all unpleasant, evil-looking men.

About half an hour before my train started, I got into a compartment and sat there until I arrived at Carmarthen, where I had to get into another train. As soon as I had taken my seat in this train at Paddington, I heard the usual B.W.I. Nos. 1 and 2 molesting sentences, spoken in a man's voice, and it was in a fairly loud, distinct tone, too, almost continuously spoken. The voice seemed to come from the platform, somewhere near the booking office, but it might have been from a man in a car in the road, just outside the railway station, perhaps using a broadcasting machine.

This incessant molesting continued until the train started on its journey. Again, when the train had left Paddington station, the molesting soon restarted and kept on the whole of the about seven hours' journey to Carmarthen.

The voice was now much more subdued that it had been in the railway station (but it was very distinct), and the usual B.W.I. Nos. 1 and 2 sentences were largely used, such as, "Pooped out," "Get back," but a lot of intimidating sentences also came, threats of doing away with me and such-like were "hurled" every now and then. This journey, being the first unaccompanied one that I had had in England for ten years, I felt that I should let a friend know of my whereabouts, so I wrote a card to one and got a gentleman in the train carriage to post it as he got out at his home town. Of course, I recalled that in the B.W.I. Nos. 1 and 2, the molesters and others had all so much insisted on my going "back to England." I now thought that there was possibly something "in the wind," so to say. I thought that perhaps there were some desperate criminals on the train, following me about. Of course, possibly sending this card saved me from having a tragic experience of some kind. I fancied the molester or molesters were probably in a compartment quite near to mine and that they would hear me ask the kind passenger to post for me.

After the train left Newport, I was alone in my compartment all the way to Carmarthen. There was a nicely dressed man in the next compartment; he was a heavily built man with a very evil cast of countenance, and was about 50 years of age. A little while after we left Newport, this man put the lights out in his compartment. The molesting voice seemed now to come from someone quite near to me, and some frightful threats were said, too. At Carmarthen, when I changed into the Aberystwyth train, I did not see anyone on the platform, except the guard of the Carmarthen train, and apparently no one got out of my train (from London). At the time it rather puzzled me, on account of the molesting that had kept on right to Carmarthen. Several men got into this train before it started from Carmarthen for Aberystwyth. Yet the molesting started again directly the train left Carmarthen and kept on until I got out at Aberystwyth.

On this part of the train journey, the sun soon began to show itself and the sky was clear and blue and the hills (together with the blue sky) and the sheep reminded me of glorious New Zealand.

Arrived at Aberystwyth, I was glad to get out of the train and walk, after sitting down eleven hours. I walked down several roads and then proceeded up Penglais Road, as far as the gateway to the Welsh National Library; and as I proceeded up this road I was molested all the while by the B.W.I. Nos. 1 and 2 sentences, which reached me at short intervals fairly loudly. Both going up this hill road, and as I walked down, too, the sound of the voice seemed to come from my rear, and I looked dubiously at several men as they overtook me and passed along ahead.

I wonder whether the molester was in the hedge which runs along one side of this road, or was the molester in a motor car that kept a good way off? I did not observe any slowly driven motor car.

Eventually I found the gentleman whom I was seeking.

I found digs in Trefor Road (up towards the top of the road), Aberystwyth, and on the second day there, the molestings commenced that kept on continuously until the middle of January, 1933; that is, that lasted for ten months.

I was persecuted in the house by a man's or a woman's voice (several people took it in turns to molest). All the B.W.I. Nos. 1 and 2 molesting sentences and adjectives were used. They were "hidden" molestings, being spoken usually so quietly that they were only a little more than just audible, though they were always very distinct.

It must have been from some broadcast machine which they must be able to use "ventriloquially," as at times the voice sounded as though it was "in" my house. Sometimes it sounded as from somewhere in front of the house. When I went upstairs and entered my bedroom at any time, day or night, the molesting started immediately; the phrases came in a continuous flow, the usual "pooped" sentences, and threats and filth, too.

Whenever I was in the lounge, even though others were in the room, the B.W.I. Nos. 1 and 2 sentences came occasionally to my ears, coming as quiet whispers.

If I was in the house all by myself, the molesting words came quite loudly, just as through someone in the house was talking ordinarily, but rather quietly.

I could never satisfactorily determine where the molesting voice derived from: either from an adjoining house or from a house on the opposite side of the road, or elsewhere.

When I had been in Trefor Road about three weeks, I was having tea one afternoon with the other boarders in the front parlour. One of the gentlemen was speaking to me, when the words, "Bum ——," were said by one of my molesters. These words came as loudly as we were talking, and it was said in a man's voice and seemed as from someone in the room. Of course, I knew that it was a molester, but the company did not have any inkling of this being the fact; their "common" sense told them that it was someone in the room that had said the blackguardly words. How could I remark upon it in any way? If I had not known I would also have thought that it was said by someone present in the room.

This ventriloquial molesting, whilst I have been in company, has been inflicted upon me innumerable times since.

How was it done?

VITAL CLIMAX

# Your Thoughts Heard by Someone Unseen and Unknown to You

If the following fact is unknown to the authorities then this will explain a matter of the utmost vital importance to everyone. It is undoubtedly the most important item in my experiences. Your thinking can be heard by a listener using an apparatus, and this person is probably someone very vile, an evil person, surely an enemy, a criminal with felonious intent, a crook anyhow, and perhaps of violence and possibly a murderer, unseen and unknown to you.

Just a few days after the incident of the molesting in the parlour, I was sitting in the same room, and was reading a letter that I had only just received. I was reading the letter quietly and to myself, and of course my mouth was not moving, my lips were quite still. I had already read most of the letter, when I suddenly had an extraordinary instantaneous realisation come to me. I became abruptly aware that what I had just read two seconds before, was being spoken to me by someone who had overheard my reading! That is, to put it plainly, the very words that I had only just before *read*, had been heard by some molester and he had repeated these words as he heard them. So that I heard (just after reading them) these very words *spoken* by him. The repeating of words that I had read came quietly audible, but distinctly, in a man's voice.

Where was he? Who was he? How was it done, or rather, how is it done? How did he hear the unspoken, the not even lip read (by him) words, words that had not been even whispered words?

I was in the room all by myself and the door and the windows of the room were all shut.

All of a sudden, again, another thing came to my comprehension and to my knowledge. Thinking must be the same as silent reading. I was reading in the same fashion as we think. It struck me that it must be the same process. We do not move our mouths when we think. I felt similarly to when I had heard the old crook speak in the hospital at B.W.I. No. 2. I perceived that this instrument explained many extraordinary happenings that had occurred and befallen me.

At last it came home to me, and I realised that these crook molesters were using an apparatus or instrument, or what not, which enables a listener (by means of using it), by its means, to hear you thinking, to hear your last breath; a whisper of yours must "appear" quite loud to the listener using this apparatus, providing perhaps that he is within 150 yards of you!

Thinking is the same as silent reading, for, since the above "came" to me, I have found that molesters using the apparatus repeat and comment upon both my thoughts and my reading, and also my writing (that is, what I am silently writing or reading). It is done simply as a molest to distract and distress you and it is a severe persecution.

Here are some items: –

The listening apparatus is accompanied by a broadcasting apparatus when they molest you. When I was being molested, the listener used both together (of course, when the party listens and molests you, you are then unaware of their presence) that is, he or she sometimes repeated my thoughts, my silent readings or writings, answered them or commented upon them.

Of course, it follows that the instrument enables the listener to hear any of your conversation from quite a distance. I have experienced comments or repeatings, or both, of or upon my conversations, sometimes days afterwards.

Often the molester fell back on the old B.W.I. Nos. 1 and 2 jargon.

On many occasions, whilst I was in the road just outside

my house, I have had my thoughts repeated, just after I had thought!

How was, or how is, it done?

I was not able to ascertain where the molesters were, but I know that they must have been in some house near to mine. They might have been next door either way, or a few doors away, or on the opposite side of the road, though when I was at the back of the house in the bathroom, it seemed to come from the house next door.

Shortly after discovering this apparatus which enables a listener to hear your thoughts, I became vividly aware of its presence and use. The molesting fiends were listening to me continuously every day and all day and all night, without any interval.

Any time, and all the time that I was indoors, I was under this persecution. Now I was not only persecuted by the usual B.W.I. Nos. 1 and 2 sentences, but, in addition, I had the awful infliction of my mind being racked by fire, a worse experience by far. The molester now made comments on my thoughts. This distresses and distracts sorely and maddeningly. It was real, actual violence of the worst kind inflicted upon me. The constant "companionship" of some unseen, unknown enemy, perhaps a murderer, listening to all my thoughts, to all I read and wrote, and to all my conversation. The very knowledge of this fact terrorises and distracts you.

I was under almost unbearable agony of terrible torture in my digs in Trefor Road, Aberystwyth. It was really "hell on earth" until the middle of January, 1933, when I left.

It was a very intensified, excruciating molesting to the mind. The very constancy was maddening. Almost directly I awoke came sentences of filthy suggestion, or of dire threats, or my waking first thoughts commented upon or answered.

This attack on one just waking is extraordinarily trying torture. You never get used to it. You generally think when you awake, and to have thoughts that you would never utter, actually spoken by a molester is very riling, and of course awakens you. It is likely to banish sleep for some time.

Whilst I was reading or writing or thinking, simultaneously I would hear whole sentences repeated; sometimes it would be perhaps only names that the listener molested me by repeating. The listener was at this molesting all the time and, as the words came in different tones, I am certain that there were several men and women that took it in turns to be on this continual "watching."

It is very disconcerting when you know that your privacy has gone, that your every thought even is heard and known, that you are perpetually under observation to an undreamed of extent, let alone being molested besides, and all this by evil people of the worst description, who have felonious intentions towards you.

These crooks get to know you really; they get to know all your mind; they also get to know a lot of your business.

Surely, after a time of this "watching," the crooks possess you more or less, when you have to endure their molesting besides; anyhow, you "seem" to feel that you are not free. Are you free?

No doubt they have "played" with (in many cases) business transactions before now by means of listening at "both ends," so that they know all of a business matter previously to any business being done by the parties concerned.

When you become aware of them hearing your thoughts (you only know this by hearing them repeat or comment upon or answer your thoughts or repeating your quiet reading or writing) it makes you perhaps afraid to think of some matter of your business, perhaps of something very important. You may have even heard them repeating your thoughts upon this especial matter.

In this case you have a great inclination not to think about this more or less important matter, as you are aware that they are listening in their "watch" upon you. You get afraid to think, but you must not give way to this inclination; you must think ordinarily and you must think duly and properly about all your affairs, or you are coming under their criminal and baleful influence, which is the very intention of all this molesting. One thing that they endeavour to inculcate is fear, to cripple your brain, to make you irrational, and so to affect your actions. Don't let their words be more potent to you than your thoughts of your true interests and affairs. Don't be disturbed. Your thoughts are repeated to madden, disconcert, distress and try you.

Having had some weeks of this terrible persecution, I commenced to write particulars of these molestings, and about the third week in June, 1932, I spoke to a friend one morning as we met on a deserted part of the sea front with no one to overhear. We both agreed upon a visit to London. I then walked straight home, and directly I had got indoors the conversation that I had had with my friend was practically repeated *verbatim* by the molester.

How did he (the molester) "get" it?

On the trip to London, when my friend and I got into the train at Aberystwyth, the B.W.I. Nos. 1 and 2 molesting sentences immediately commenced coming at short intervals, and this persecution continued the whole of the journey to Paddington. It came to my ears in a just audible, but distinct, whisper of a voice. Of course it was distressing. Arrived at Paddington G.W.R., we sat some few hours in the waiting room there, and during this time the molesting came continuously until we left. It sounded as though this ceaseless flow of sentences came from outside of the room, from the station approach road outside, and I presume that it was from a standing motor car in the road. We proceeded to a cafe near by and had our breakfasts. During the time that we were partaking the meal, the molesting sentences still "followed," and kept on until we left the cafe, and it sounded as from someone in the room. Having breakfasted, we took a train on the Underground railway to the Temple. After a short time, molesting sentences came to my ears (intermittently) until we got out at the Temple; it sounded as from a man in the next compartment of the train. Possibly a ventriloquist was at the cafe and on this train. Walking along the Embankment from the Temple station to Scotland Yard, just about two minutes after starting walking, the molesting started again, and consisted of some very intimidatory threats, and came fairly loudly, too, and very distinctly. I presume that it came from a following motor car. Possibly it was from a ventriloquist walking along.

At Scotland Yard I was shown into a waiting room, and very shortly a detective arrived. He asked me my business and I asked him to read the brief account of the molestings. After reading some of it, he said it was very improbable that they would pursue me all those years, and he said, "Who is to pay them?" He also said, "How is the instrument worked? It's impossible. There is no such instrument."

Then he dismissed me.

So I left him and of course I was very dissatisfied and distressed that such living facts should go unheeded.

On the return journey to Aberystwyth, I was molested precisely the same as on the journey to Scotland Yard during the whole of the journey.

After this visit to Scotland Yard the molestings were increased. Some of the names called out now I had clean forgotten (if you can say so when it is only by the mention of another or other names that the "forgotten" one is, with difficulty, recalled). These molestings now altered in method, the terror of it was intense and it was in a louder voice, too.

Every night as I was getting to bed, and until I got to sleep, and directly as I awoke at any time during the night, recalling names were said perhaps of someone known to me 40 years or more previously, and of whom I had had no acquaintance since (raked up names), were called out, or a shockingly awful threat came to my ears just as the listening molester hears you are getting to sleep again; or another recalling name is mentioned, perhaps preventing any more sleep that night.

This mentioning of recalling names keeps your mind distracted; you seem quite unable to keep your mind from activity. It will work and tries to recall the name; perhaps there is a faint remembrance of it at first (when these long-ago-forgotten names are mentioned).

It is their being so long forgotten that taxes the mind, the remote ones try you most. Such names, even if you have just awakened, almost wakes you right up: it strains the mind and it is this straining that does it.

Undoubtedly deliberately done to madden and to destroy the brain.

Some crook mental doctors, asylum attendants, some parties well and intimately acquainted with the workings of the mind, or long practice by crooks, or all these together, must have acquainted them with the efficacy of this diabolical mind torture.

Of course books on mental study and on the brain must be studied by them. They study to keep your mind working continually. All of this incessant molesting is done to keep your mind on the stretch all the time.

An all time stretch that strains continually, slowly cripples and injures, and must eventually utterly exhaust the brain and mind energy.

These recalling names showed espionage as a fine art. It clearly showed that the head or leading crooks had used infinite pains and astounding and extraordinary care and patience to get at all relations, friends and acquaintances, to make sure of getting me. These recalling names could only have been obtained by exhaustive enquiries from my childhood relationships – from members of my family and from other relations, and from friends and acquaintances; of the "recalled," some had been dead years ago, and some of them I had not seen or thought of for perhaps 50 years.

Some of the names mentioned must have been obtained by seeking and "pumping" relations and friends who, at the time of these names being "called" to molest me, were dead, and who must have been "pumped" ten years previously to these molesters so using the names. Otherwise, some of these names would not have been obtainable. This shows their diabolical scheming.

The names that they called out included more than any one of my relations, friends or acquaintances ever knew.

A proper systematic search, enquiries and watching, and making notes of every item, probably for some years, and probably in a major part of it by a "friend" of some of my family; and also a similar search must have been made upon my known friends and acquaintances of my boyhood and youth to find out all the details of my friends' names and things appertaining to me. Every thing that it was possible to think of these head crooks had "looked up." It is quite impossible that these names could have been obtainable in any other way. Names which were mentioned, I had not recalled or heard of for 40 years, let alone ever mentioning them.

At about the time of the commencement of this persecution of me in London, in 1922, there were a lot of the heads of the international crooks visiting a lawyer near me locality, who was acting in relation to stolen bonds. No doubt these "heads" then learnt of me as a likely victim. I have not the least doubt these "heads" directed all this searching and molesting, and held the "cards" of my case. This business of the stolen bonds came to light in the courts a few years later.

Without doubt my abduction had been intended, and that is why they had used all this care in obtaining all this information. Probably some similar looking man, one of their tools, would have been my substitute. No doubt I would have been murdered eventually, after being abducted, anyhow if I had been abducted in London or New Zealand.

I had only narrowly escaped abduction, both in London and New Zealand, by always (as near as practicable) being accompanied by an escort.

You may rest assured that it was a well-planned plot, very cunningly arranged and designed and executed in the latest twentieth century fashion!

They have continuously watched and considered all "points."

Anyone in Britain can be freely molested and persecuted to death in 1935.

The molesting negress that lived opposite to my first apartments at B.W.I. No. 2 had often called out that I would be taken away in a motor boat to some sandbank, where I would be given just enough food to live upon and a hut to live in.

When I got to Aberystwyth, the crooks thought that by continual molesting that they would drive me (by foul means) to London; that is, by making it "hot" for me in Aberystwyth.

No doubt it must have come as a "brain-wave" to one of their leaders that, as I was not sufficiently in their clutches, all this information that they had taken so much trouble to obtain could now be used effectively to harry me, to make life at Aberystwyth quite unbearable; it became a handy and great resource to be profitably used after all by these thoughtful, murderous crooks.

The study of the brain. All these molestings are a red herring, too. The continual unceasing molesting employs your mind all the time, so that you are unable to think (anyhow, unable to think truly rationally), for whilst you are troubled thinking of their molesting and your thoughts are put on them and you are distracted by their persecution, you are not thinking sufficiently, not giving enough consideration, or even any at all, on what you should, your main things, your business, and your everyday affairs.

The crooks are holding you (somewhat) already. They are beginning to possess you by preventing you thinking. The continuity of the persecution employs your mind all the time, so you get no time for quiet thinking; you are unable to think of anything except the molesting.

In July, 1932, the word molestings at night were always spoken fairly loudly; quite audible to anyone, I thought.

One night in this month I had awakened at about 12.30 and the molesting had started at once (as it always unfailingly did immediately, at any time, I awoke). Molesting sentences of the B.W.I. Nos. 1 and 2 usually, and filth and threats were proceeding all the time for half an hour, when just about 1 A.M., I heard a man's voice say quite loudly, "Shut up."

The molesting at once stopped for a little while, when these words had been spoken. Then the molesters continued in a much subdued, lower tone of voice (subdued to the just audible), just "discernible," but very distinct tone that all molestings now were at, until January, 1933.

I was greatly cheered directly I heard that "Shut up."

I had often wondered how it was that no-one ever said anything, or complained about the continual flow of molesting persecution. At times it was very lewd and often consisted, too, of murderous threats. Of course I could not explain this.

Now I thought Scotland Yard would listen to me considering that I had this "Shut up" to report, in that someone else had heard the molesting.

I thought this listening instrument to be of extreme importance to Scotland Yard, and I thought they could get hold of this listening apparatus by seeking to find where the molesting came from; that they would find the precious listening apparatus there.

So I made notes of the whole of the incident and proceeded again to London and to Scotland Yard. The molesting on this journey was a replica of the previous journey to Scotland Yard. The molestings on all the railway journeys there and back and in Padding G.W.R. railway station waiting room, and in the cafe outside, were just as before.

Arrived at Scotland Yard, the officer or detective that saw me would not listen to me or read the notes that explained all my purpose in calling again. He referred to my previous visit. He said that they were too busy and could not be bothered by me.

I returned very disappointed to Aberystwyth and had to endure the same molestings (of course) as it seemed as though the crooks and the underworld were the most potent force in "free" Britain.

Britain is not free as long as this listening apparatus is allowed to be in the hands of the underworld.

The whole of the time that I was staying in Aberystwyth, every time that I had been to the bank to do business, the molesting voice always "told" me (as soon as I got home in Trefor Road) all the particulars of the transactions that I had dealt with, and mentioned the exact amount and details of any money business that I had conducted at the bank. Mind you, this was always done as soon as I got home, and often there was only myself (except the staff) in the bank at the time of the visit.

How, may I ask, is this done?

The crooks have made a real art in imitating the intonation of others' voices so as to blend theirs practically exactly with the sound and tone of other people's voices. Whenever anyone came to the door of my house or of the next door, I could, when upstairs, hear the voices of the people of the house and the caller, if they held any conversation. On almost every occasion when anyone called, the milkman and everybody that spoke at all, were made to say (that is, the molester chimed in so marvelously intoning with the talkers that the only words that I heard were those of my molesters) persecuting sentences of B.W.I. Nos. 1 and 2.

Every time I could suppose that it was those at the door downstairs saying, "Yes, he's got to go." "We won't have him." "We don't want him." "He's pooped." "He's pooped out." "He's got to go back." "Yes, he was pooped out of New Zealand." "We won't have him here," etc.

It was only because all these sentences were known to me that I knew who was using these phrases!

A week after my arrival in Aberystwyth, I went for a walk with a farmer to the top of Pen Dinas. As we were just coming down this hill, we sat for a little while. As we were so resting, I took a piece of printed paper out of my pocket to read. At once a molester's voice said, in a just audible tone, "I hear rustling paper. It's no good thinking you can trick us."

A few other sentences of a like nature were also said in the same quiet tone.

Looking from where we sat there was not a soul in sight I could see clearly around in all directions for quite a hundred yards from our position.

How did he or she hear such a slight sound as that made by the rustling of such a small piece of paper?

Shortly after, as we were nearing the foot of the hill, I noticed a man of about 40 years of age, with a woman of about 24, coming down the hill on another pathway, and I observed that this woman carried a rather small suit case. Both of them were respectably dressed and were about five feet five inches in height.

As on subsequent journeys to London, I saw the same couple (or else some couple just like them) and the women carrying a similar suit case. I presume that this suit case contained a listening apparatus, together (perhaps) with a loud speaker.

No doubt, besides listening to hear all that I spoke about to my friend, this molesting couple had spoken these words to intimidate and disconcert me, and also to make me aware I was unable to escape their vigilance anywhere.

Is the following experience one that others have been subjected to? Is it really personal assault carried on without let or hindrance?

From the first few days after my arrival in Trefor Road, in March, 1932, until mid-January, 1933 (when I left Aberystwyth), I was always persecuted by B.W.I. Nos. 1 and 2 molesting sentences, and also some other phrases as I walked either up or down Trefor Road; in this road the voice generally sounded as coming from the higher part of the road. Also, as I walked in Lovden Road, either up or down, I was always molested too, with the same sentences (also when in the lavatory in this road); the voice seemed to derive from near the corner house in Queen's Road; the sentences were sometimes quite loudly spoken and were often very obscene, filthy, and also frequently very intimidatory. Also in North Road these words always came to me, as I walked from Trefor Road to the Queen's Hotel; in this North Road the words seemed as though from up the hill on the right, and occasionally it sounded as coming from somewhere near the tennis court refreshment room on the left (of course, it then was possibly from a house in Queen's Road); sometimes the molesting voice was rather loud.

I was always similarly molested in Queen's Road, as I walked from the shelter to Bath Street or Bath Street to the shelter, and the voice seemed to emanate from a house opposite the shelter in Queen's Road.

Crooks, or their employees, unfailingly always molested me at the following places whenever I was in the vicinity, the whole time up to January, 1933: –

At the Clock Tower, at the Castle and in the neighbourhood of the railway station, these molesting sentences never failed to be "hurled" at me. Also, at the junction of Terrace Road and North Parade, and on the Marine Parade at Terrance Road, and also on the Marine Parade at Pier Street.

Whilst sitting on the Marine Parade, men standing at Pier Street and Terrace Road sometimes called threats, as "Get out, or I'll murder you," etc., even though I was sometimes 100 yards away. I was also always molested at the wooden jetty at the harbour's entrance.

The molestings that I got at these places were spoken rather loudly at times and might have been heard by anyone, and no doubt they were sometimes heard and noticed by those in the vicinity at the time.

All the above roads and points of rendezvous were places that I was molested at unfailingly from the date of my arrival in Aberystwyth in March, 1932, until January, 1933, when I left Aberystwyth. Occasionally, the remarks "hurled" at me at these places were not the usual B.W.I. Nos. 1 and 2 molestings, but were sundry personal insults or threats.

On the average I walked down to the wooden jetty at least three mornings every week and sat down there for an hour or two each time.

Whenever I sat on this wooden jetty at the harbour's entrance, I was always molested the whole time and I quite believe this was often from a man who got near and right under me, underneath the deck of the jetty, getting as near as possible to where I sat. I feel quite sure this was how the molesting was frequently done. I think it is the only satisfactory explanation, as often there was not a soul in sight and I was perhaps alone (or with a friend), and yet the molesting words seemed to come from quite near to me. It was sometimes weirdly near. The B.W.I. Nos. 1 and 2 usual molesting would be inflicted upon me as from someone quite near, and came intermittently, perhaps for two hours. If I was with anyone it was in a very subdued tone.

Sometimes, whilst I was at this jetty, the molesting came from a car up the road, and on some occasions from a car in the lower roadway of the harbour side. At this jetty I was sometimes molested from someone on the opposite side of the harbour, using the usual B.W.I. Nos. 1 and 2 or other sentences.

Whenever I say on this jetty from March, 1932, until January,

1933, I was unfailingly foxed there and molested (perhaps intermittently), without once being free from this persecution if I was at this rendezvous.

As I walked past the Castle to this jetty, molesting words always "followed" me *all* the way to the jetty and seemed to come from the Castle.

How was this done? I could never find out.

On the first Sunday in March, 1932, that I was at Aberystwyth, I attended St. Michael's services. Liking the preaching, I attended this church all the time that I stayed at Aberystwyth, from March, 1932, until January, 1933. I always sat towards the front and quite near to the west wall. I attended the 11 A.M. and the 6.30 p.m. services until October or November, and after that I only attended the 11 A.M. service each Sunday. I practically always entered and left by the west side door of the Church.

On the first attendance at this church I was molested by occasional stereotyped threats that I had been persecuted by in B.W.I. No. 2. This was the voice of a molester who frequently molested me afterwards when I was at home, and no doubt he was in church and it was ventriloquial. Afterwards, every time that I attended a service in this church, I was severely molested in a very quiet voice, generally in a man's voice, but sometimes in a woman's voice. Usually it was B.W.I. Nos. 1 and 2 sentences that were used; a large proportion were lewd and threats of violence. The lewd ones could not have been of a viler expression (this in church, in Britain!). Very often sentences of abuse were also said.

It is most important that witnesses to this desecration of worship should notify the authorities. I feel almost certain that some person in the congregation must have heard some of these sentences which "came" to me intermittently during the whole service, including prayers. It was always most distinct and occurred every service that I attended for ten months, from March, 1932, to January, 1933.

Practically every time as I was leaving after the service and going out of the door on the gravel path outside, someone would call out quite loudly one of these sentences: "The beast." "Look at him." "To think of it." "The blackguard." "Look at the beast," or such molesting phrase.

This was a typical B.W.I. No. 2 style of persecution and a very upsetting and disconcerting "inferiority complex" stunt. A diabolical "monkey trick" of fiendish torture as all this calculated molesting was. There were generally about a dozen people near the doorway. A "brow beating" stunt.

When Communion was taken after the 11 A.M. Sunday morning service, during the months when the visitors were staying in large numbers in Aberystwyth, I always left the church at the end of the service before the Communion Sacrament, and of course I would pass those staying on to take the Communion. Every such time I was molested by about five men who were from about 25 to 35 years of age and all of whom had light brown hair. They sat all in a row in a pew somewhere near the west door, and as I approached (on my way out) these men, one of them would always make a relative remark as all the five stared at me malevolently, "He's angry." "He's lost his temper," or some such words. These men had a suggestion about them of being "toughs" or "roughs." Sometimes this church molesting was very distinct, but so quiet that it was a whisper's "ghost" and difficult to trace its source.

Is this church molesting often done in Britain, or was this the first time of its introduction into Britain?

Whenever I listened to the band playing on the Marine Parade bandstand of an evening, I was molested usually by a man's voice. All the B.W.I. Nos. 1 and 2 sentences were used during the time that the music was being played. Often, if I sat right near the road, a good motor car with two well-dressed young men of about 25 years of age in it would come quite near and stop, perhaps all the two hours. These two men, or perhaps one sitting on the floor of the car, would molest with B.W.I. Nos. 1 and 2 persecution, or filth or threats all the time that the band was playing, and be silent between the items.

Often, when I sat on the seats near the passing cars on the Marine Parade, every passing car "said" some molesting sentence. That is, a ventriloquist said one of these sentences: "Get out."

"Go back." "You're not wanted." "Pooped out," etc., as each car passed. No doubt the ventriloquist sat quite near me.

During Aberystwyth's visitors' season, July, August and September, 1932, very often, as I walked along the crowded Marine Parade, I would be followed by molesters, men usually, but sometimes by these men accompanied by young women. I believe their molesting was ventriloquial. One of them would keep up a continual flow of the usual persecuting sentences. Usually, the voice came from someone apparently at my rear and they would follow me right along the sea front doing this stunt. There was a large gang of young men that wore the usual light grey flannel trousers and light brown jackets, and all were clean-shaven and wore no hats and were from 24 to 36 or so in age. These followed me everywhere and continuously molested, and often (perhaps mostly) used ventriloquism. There were also some young women attached to them.

Every time that I went into the public library I was molested. The sentences were often intimidatory, but generally B.W.I. Nos. 1 and 2 usual sentences, mostly in a man's voice, and were spoken very quietly, but fairly continuously.

Every time that I was walking past the lifeboat slipway on the Marine Parade, if there were a good many of the boatmen round the flag-mast, I was unfailingly molested by apparently one of these men, who used in a loud voice a few of the B.W.I. Nos. 1 and 2 molesting phrases.

I was also molested in the English Wesley Church in Bath Street, where in November and December I attended the 6 P.M. service on Sundays. In addition to someone in the congregation molesting with the usual sentences during the whole of each service, there was a young woman, who was a crooks' decoy, that always endeavoured to get into the pew with me and sit at my side. Some services she varied this performance by sitting right in front of me in the next pew. She stared at me incessantly during the whole of each service. I have a recollection of her being with a man with dark brown eyes and eyebrows (thick) and clean-shaven and of about 30 years of age and about five feet eight inches tall.

I always entered this church by the eastern door in Bath Street and sat as near the back of the church as I could get and against the eastern wall. One night, as I was leaving this church, there was a tall clean-shaven man standing in the road outside the church; he had dark eyebrows and wore dark clothes and was about 40 years of age and strongly built. Directly he saw me, he said loudly, "Pooped out." Of course this was a molest for me and typical of B.W.I. Nos. 1 and 2.

He said this though I was talking to a friend.

I experienced some gas attacks (outrages) during December, 1932, in my Aberystwyth digs. The gas was odourless and colourless and I was only aware of its presence in my room by its effect upon me.

On these gassing assaults I could not sleep for nearly the whole night through.

On several occasions this gassing was administered on a Saturday night and the next day I felt "done" and was rendered almost unfit for even attending church services.

The gas came into my bedroom when I had got into bed. I always had the window open both top and bottom, but how the gas came, or from whence, I cannot say.

I would get into bed quite tired and sleepy, but as soon as I was getting to sleep the gas would affect me as at B.W.I. No. 2, and I was awakened and quite unable to sleep. The molesting sentences then came intermittently, and so by the gas and the persecution, I had a very trying experience of crook terrorism and a great trouble in seeking to be even restful.

This gas attack was administered on a Friday or Saturday night. I presume that the gas was from the premises where the molesters were with the listening and broadcasting apparatus, and I imagine that they could hear how I was affected by listening to my breathing, and they so heard when to and how to, regulate the gas. Their listening apparatus enabling them to hear the very slightest breaths and also enables them to hear the least change or alteration in one's breathing. That is how they know when one awakes.

On one or two of these gas attacks the gas must have been of a different nature, and it affected me differently. It gave me a sort of transfixed feeling to the brain; a sort of paralysing; seeming to keep my face muscles somewhat distorted; it also rendered me unable to be placid and collected.

The worst attack that I experienced in Trefor Road was during the three nights before Christmas, 1932 (Thursday, Friday and Saturday). I was gassed the whole of these nights and was unable to get any sleep on either of these nights. I could get no sleep, for as soon as I was getting drowsy the gas came to me again and aroused me afresh. Added to this, the devils' fiends combined terrible threats and other molesting phrases of B.W.I. Nos. 1 and 2 with this gassing.

On Christmas Day I was a wreck in body and mind. The gassing affected me very badly, rendering me quite inert in body and mind; every nerve and brain cell, every fibre and muscle was dead tired and "dead beat." I felt that I had no power for anything. Listening to music was excruciating agony, and I was quite unable to read or exert my brain at all. I was quite listless and "dead."

Was this climax to the general molesting done to intimidate me? Or was it done to drive me away, to move me on to some place where they might chance to get a better hold on me?

Or was it done to make me complain to the police, or to mention it to friends and acquaintances so that I should be considered under delusions or mad? I am quite sure neither the police not anyone would have believed that I was speaking of what had actually happened if I had told them!!

Dangerous criminals in China and Mongolia are often put in stand-up cages (usually in the market places), where they are unable to sit down, having to stand all the time until they die. No food is allowed and death gradually comes to them, starting at their feet.

So the crooks, by continually molesting and gassing, can kill by inches, the brain being unable to rest and deprived of all sleep and the body slowly dying.

This gassing was a real nocturnal terrorising outrage. They do this in "free" Britain without let or hindrance! The victim is absolutely under the crooks' terror and quite unprotected by the police!

On or about the second day after Christmas Day, I was passing by the corner of Queen's Road and Albert Place, opposite the Queen's Hotel corner, when a big clean-shaven man, of about 42 years of age and wearing dark blue overalls "appeared" to say, "We've been gassing him."

This man was repairing the gutter or roof of the corner house, or of the house adjoining it. There was a long ladder up to the roof.

The whole of the time that I was living in Aberystwyth, every time I was in the vicinity of this corner, I had been molested by a man's voice. He used abuse or intimidatory sentences usually. Probably this usual molester said ventriloquially on this occasion, "We've been gassing him."

I had not mentioned about the gassing to anyone.

Evidently these blackmailing crooks and forgers wanted me to mention it, relying upon it that if I did complain to the police or anyone else, I would be thought imagining or under delusions or mad.

Perhaps I might have even been sent to a mental asylum! All at the crooks' behest!!! For that is what it would amount to.

---

Yet I feel that I have not been defeated. Now in Britain, near the impersonal contacts of the sea, I can look back on those dark days and assuage (in some part) my soul by putting this account before my fellow men…

I trust that some will understand and feel the horrible tragedy of my life through the written word.

Those years have been almost entirely of continuous trying experiences and anxiety, with no relaxation whatever; and those years of crook molesting have also undoubtedly wrought harm to me in all ways.

I give my story also in order to make known the irony of fate shown by my history. When this continuous molesting started in July, 1922, and until I left London in December, 1924, there was practically no word molesting; also during the three years that I stayed in New Zealand there was no word molesting.

The whole of the four years that I spent in B.W.I. Nos. 1 and 2, the word molesting as a rule was quite loud and often shouted; it did not matter wherever I was, even being frequently loudly spoken at services in churches or chapels that I attended. This even though some of the most awful obscenities were said.

I had thought that Communists were mixed up in all this persecution until in 1928 I heard the old crook speak "at" me in the Government hospital in B.W.I. No. 2.

When I heard the B.W.I. Nos. 1 and 2 molesters call out, "Get out," "Go back," etc., I for some years did not understand the sense or object of these remarks.

By the molestations in December, 1931, calling out the names of my business clients, etc., and also by their mention of a particular paper that had strangely disappeared from my office in August, 1924, I first became aware of their having frequently entered my office of a night and of their learning all my affairs by perusing my correspondence, etc. This missing paper had been abstracted by the crooks, and they told me, during molestations in December, 1931, of what they had been doing so many years previously. They certainly must have thought they "had" me in 1931.

It has only been by God's grace that I have been able to endure and survive this terrible ordeal, so I must quote the words of a famous learned man:

"I know of no safeguard for character, no stronghold that can preserve against the temptations and seductions of life, except faith and life unto Jesus Christ our Lord."

# Addendum

Truth is better than romance; it serves the times and it is a responsibility. These things happened under the British Flag and in the second quarter of the 20th century.

It is nearly 1937, but I do not think there is yet a member of any C.I.D. in Great Britain who really appreciates the frightful effectiveness of the gangsters listening to and repeating one's thoughts (ventriloquially usually), continual ventriloquial molesting and staring with dreadful expression to intimidate.

In 1934 I described the use of this listening apparatus to one of the most well-known (but then lately retired) detectives of New Scotland Yard. Only a few years previously he had been one of the most eminent of the C.I.D. men. He merely made fun of the idea of it and scorned it as mad imagination, yet I had had evidence of its use early in 1928 at Colon (Panama) and at B.W.I. No. 1. One asks: Does New Scotland Yard know of it in 1936?

To know of its use by criminals is of vital importance to all, but a public London scientist wrote me in July, 1935, that such an apparatus does not exist!

The detective mentioned above explained what at the time was to me a conundrum, as due to a prison dodge of speaking out of the side of the mouth. It is plain to me now that the detective was mistaken. It was a case of accomplished ventriloquists.

Are the police aware of the use the crooks make of ventriloquism? The first time that I called at New Scotland Yard (June 1932) the official said that the instrument was an impossibility. I insisted that it was being used. He greatly resented my assertion, said that he had over twenty years' experience and that he would put me under lock and key. I ceased to argue, as I appreciated officialism.

For the Police to be ignorant of gangster methods is a public menace. These methods have certainly been used for years. The Police may (in their ignorance) instead of helping the victims render them a more easy prey to the gangsters by sending them to despair.

VICTIM.